# BUILD

# BUILD

## THE POWER OF HIP HOP DIPLOMACY
## IN A DIVIDED WORLD

MARK KATZ

OXFORD
UNIVERSITY PRESS

Oxford University Press is a department of the University of Oxford. It furthers
the University's objective of excellence in research, scholarship, and education
by publishing worldwide. Oxford is a registered trade mark of Oxford University
Press in the UK and certain other countries.

Published in the United States of America by Oxford University Press
198 Madison Avenue, New York, NY 10016, United States of America.

CIP data is on file at the Library of Congress
ISBN 978–0–19–005611–7

1 3 5 7 9 8 6 4 2

Printed by Sheridan Books, Inc., United States of America

*To Beth and Anna and all the artists*

# CONTENTS

# ACKNOWLEDGMENTS

ارکش, çox sağ ol, ধন্যবাদ, ကျေးဇူးတင်, hvala, merci, na gode, धन्यवाद, terima kasih, maltiox, សូមអរគុណ, weebale, misaotra anao, obrigado, waita hako, gracias, asante, ขอบคุณ, teşekkür ederim rahmat, jёrejёf! In other words: thank you!

These are just some of the languages spoken by those who have advised, assisted, supported, and taught me in the five years during which I researched and wrote this book. Six continents and more than two dozen countries are represented here. The global nature of hip hop never fails to awe and humble me.

My gratitude extends globally but starts at home: with my wife and daughter, Beth Jakub and Anna Katz. Simply put, I could not directed the Next Level hip hop diplomacy program, traveled to dozens of countries, and written this book, all while maintaining a demanding full-time university position, without their love, support, and sacrifice. In Chapter 3 I quote Junious Brickhouse, who laments that he feels like an asshole for leaving the communities he had just started to bond with during his Next Level residencies. Junious was no asshole, but I've come to realize that I was. Too many times, I left Beth with housework, child-rearing, and cat-wrangling, and I was away from these amazing people more than any of us wanted. For that, I am sorry. Beth and Anna deserved more of me and more from me, because I owe them everything.

Drawing by Anna Katz, June 2015. Collection of the author.

It has been an honor to know and to work with the U. hip hop artists who participated in Next Level. As I finish writing this book, there have been 111 of them, and they are ADUM⁷, Melanie Aguirre, Victor "Kid Glyde" Alicea, Shirlette Ammons, Suzi Analogue, Eric "Mr. Trixter" Angelini, Serouj "Midus" Aprahamian, Andre Barden, aka DJ A-Minor, Marc "Mista B." Bayangos, Dahlak Brathwaite, Chazmere, Christopher Behm-Meyer, aka DJ B*Money, Gabriel "Asheru" Benn, Toni Blackman, Junious L. Brickhouse, aka House, Buckwild, Charles Burchell, Wandee "WandeePop" Candelario, Justice Cadet, aka J-Live, Geoffrey "Toyz aRe Us" Chang, Dan "Dirty Digits" Chaves, CHINO BYI, Jaci Caprice Clark, Kyle "JustSole" Clark, Deena "SnapShot" Clemente, Maddy "MADlines" Clifford, Tara "Big Tara" Crichlow, Derick "D-Cross" Cross, Trinise "AtLas'" Crowder, Vincent "Gyrefunk" Czekus, Jessie Davis, aka DJ Nebraska, Tarik Davis, aka Konshens the MC, Lino "Leanski" Delgado, Diamond D, DiViNCi, Zephyr Ann Doles, Brian "Raydar" Ellis, Ami "Tsunami" Ferreira, Karla "Karlita Waakafella" Flores, Leigh "Breeze-Lee" Foaad, Ken Fury, Elliot "Phillipdrummond" Gann, Juan Gomez, aka DJ Juan G., Laleyna "Amore Querida" Gomez, Kareem "Bboy Kareem" Gwinn, Lauren Harkrader, aka DJ Chela, LaShondra Hemphill, aka RyNea Soul, iLLspokinn, Baba Israel, Cobaine Ivory,

Lance Johnson, Ansley "Jukeboxx" Jones, Mahogany Jones, DJ 2-Tone Jones, Kuttin Kandi, Ami Kim, Shasta "Klevah" Knox, Daniel Kogita, aka King Khazm, Ahmad Ali Lewis, Nick Low-Beer, aka Nick Neutronz, Jacob "Kujo" Lyons, Edson "Bboy House" Magana, Macca "Bgirl Macca" Malik, Brandon Marshall, Danielle Mastrion, Medusa the Gangsta Goddess, Christopher Mike-Bidtah, aka Def-i, Chane "Big Piph" Morrow, Benumerata "Benu Da Soothsayah" Muhammad, Desi Mundo, Azad "Azad Right" Naficy, Akim "Funk Buddha" Ndlovu, Dumisani "Dumi Right" Ndlovu, Sheikia "Purple Haze" Norris, Margie "Kaotic Blaze" Nuñez, One Be Lo, Jorge "Popmaster Fabel" Pabon, Erica "Amerriica" Parpan, Jeremy Pena, aka B-boy Jeremy, Angelique "Giddy" Perez, Frankie Perez, aka B-boy Frankie, Nicholas "Decap" Piantedosi, Raymond Pirtle, Jr., aka DJ Raedawn, DJ Princess Cut, DJ Quest, Rizqi Rachmat, Haleem "Stringz" Rasul, Tierney Reed, aka T.R.U.T.H, DJ Kevie Kev Rockwell, Danny "Dan Tres Omi" Rodriguez, Joshua "Rowdy" Rowsey, Divinity Roxx, Amirah Sackett, Sanoizm, Sam Sellers, aka Rabbi Darkside, Kane Smego, Deidre "D.S.Sense" Smith, Russell Sticklor, aka DJ Plain View, Supreme La Rock, Teao "Teao Sense" Thompson, Miki Vale, Marisol Veléz, aka Pinqy Ring, Ryan "Future" Webb, Chris Williams, aka DJ Trife, Korin "Knxout" Wong-Horichi, Toki Wright, YAKO 440, G Yamazawa, Kerwin Young, Nancy Yu, aka Asia One, and Daniel Zarazua.

Four of the artists I just mentioned are so nice I need to name them twice. I am thrilled and thankful beyond words that my colleagues and friends Junious Brickhouse, Jaci Caprice Clark, Mahogany Jones, and Kane Smego assumed the leadership and management of Next Level in 2019, when I stepped back. I take great pleasure and comfort in knowing that Next Level is in their capable hands.

I want to mention another type of artist who has served Next Level: our photographers and filmmakers Jen Cohen, Juan Gomez, Anshul Gupta, Petna Ndaliko Katondolo, Frankie Perez, Saleem Reshamwala, and Lisa Russell. The images and stories they have documented and shared will long remain a testament to the power of hip hop art and culture.

I'm also grateful to journalist Harry Allen, hip hop artists Julian Caldwell, aka JSWISS, Javier Garcia, Omar Offendum, Will Power, and Rocc Williams, American Voices Executive Director John Ferguson, and "Hip Hop Connection" host Rod Murray for their insights into hip hop and diplomacy.

In the course of researching this book, I have met people from around the world who have opened their arms to me and opened my eyes for me. These artists, educators, interpreters, organizers, promoters, and locally employed staff at US diplomatic posts (who are much more than the acronym LES suggests), continue to inspire me. By country, they are: Algeria—Mohammed "Djemi" Djamaa, Yacine "Poppin' Pasta" Gouasmia, Fatma Zohra Souidi; Australia—Mirrah Fay Parker, Amos Sale Setu; Azerbaijan—Farqani Aliyev, Aziz Azizov, Kamran Memedov, Husniyye Nemet; Bangladesh—Mohammed "ABD" Abdullah, Jonathan Gomes, Asif Ifteza, aka Bigg Spade, Sabreen Rahman, Asiful Islam Sohan, aka Black Zang; Belgium—Fatima Elamji, Fares Forsan, aka Fforsan; Bosnia and Herzegovina—Zlatko "Zljay" Durakovic, Lejla Pasovic, Sabina Šabić; Brazil—Karla Carneiro, Rafaela Romualdo Belo Guse, Samuel Henrique da Silviera Lima, aka B-boy Samuka, Alan Jhone Moreira, aka B-boy Papel, Roberta Pope, Bruno Rafael, Bruno Timorato, Zulu DJ TR, Yas Werneck; Cambodia—Chanmoy Nem, aka Mora; Colombia—Luis Carrascal, Lilibeth Rodriguez Diaz, aka Mariposa, Johel Rojas; Croatia—Iva Hađina, Filip Ivelja, aka Phat Phillie, Mirta Lluj, Nikolina Paic; Dominican Republic—Dionis Rivera Rincón, aka Don Music; Egypt—Amr Ali, Adel Dekinesh, Ahmed El Hareedy, El Khayal, Ahmed Mohammed, aka Afroto, Sarah Shalaby, Ahmed Yassin; El Salvador—Carlos Alfredo Godínez Garcia, aka Cue Bass, Alejandra Mangandi, aka Bgirl Mangandi, Ivan Monroy, aka Lebanji, Luis Balthalzar Rodriguez, aka Blaze Uno (RIP), Edson David Rochac Ventura, aka Stimpy; Guatemala—Yefry "MChe" Ardón, Fredy Alberto Chávez Escobar, aka D'Lak, Xavier Rolando Rukikel Ik Ortega, aka Xaman Roots; Honduras—Ainara Calix Montesinos, Mc Ko-co, Gustavo Moreno (RIP), Rapaz, Carmen Urcuyo; India—Sayak Barua, Sanjay Bhattacherjee, Malabika Brahma, Saadia Dayal;

Indonesia—Lufthi Abdurrahman, Supriya "Iya" Budiman, Mohammad Indra Gandhi, aka Dom Dom, Ginandjar Koesmayadi (RIP), Citra Resmi, aka Mystique, Wanda; Madagascar—Tsiry "Panda" Kely, Tantely Rasoanaivo, "TongueNat" Ralambomamy; Mexico—Rafael Enrique Garcia Alanis, aka Kicke; Morocco—Yoùsrà Aftati, Abdenbi El Fakir, aka El Meknassi, Amine Wakrim, Atallah "Double M" Mohamed, Soultana; Myanmar—Cherry Khaing, aka Ya Ya; Nigeria— Ernest Ibe, Mima Angulu; Turkey—Hazal Kaya; Senegal—Amadou Aw, aka Maxi Krezy, Pape Mamadou Camara, Poppa Aly Gueye, Ina Makosi, Aminata Samb, Toussa Senerap; Serbia—Marija Bjelopetrovic, Marko Milic, Andjelko "Angelo" Pavlovic; Tanzania—Rodgers Cidosa, Lusajo Kajula-Maonga, Deus Kajuna, Noel Kilonzo, Gema Lambert, Amani Msangi, aka Kiche Legend, Nash MC, Chedi Ngulu, Masero Nyriabu; Thailand—Thirabhand Chandracharoen, Manop Horpet, Kanchalee "Kelly" Jitgang, Boonyachana "Joseph" Tissakul; Tunisia—Rami Mhazres, aka DJ Supaflava; Uganda—Daniel Gilbert Bwette, Kifuko Moureen Drichiru, aka B-girl Key, Mark Kaweesi, Nbaggala Lillian Maximilian, Aineomugisha Alimansi Wanzu, aka Spyda; Uzbekistan—Khilola Kim, aka DJ Loreen, Muhlisa Rasulova; Zimbabwe—Luckie Aaroni, Nyari Mazango, aka FTR, Plot Mhako, Samm Farai Monro, aka Comrade Fatso, Thando Sibanda, Truthness Sibanda, Ngoni Tapiwa, aka Upmost, Adrian Zenasi, aka Professor.

Next Level is a complex initiative that could not operate without a dedicated team. Before Next Level existed, or had a name, Pierce Freelon encouraged me to apply for the grant to create the program and worked long days and nights with me to prepare the application. One of the first people I hired was the indefatigable Paul "Mama Hen" Rockower, who did much more than manage the first dozen residencies—he helped create Next Level. Michael Cohen oversaw Next Level's operations in its early years, and I appreciated his warm, positive presence. George Huntley and Susan Williams were crucial to the running of the program while it was housed at the University of North Carolina at Chapel Hill's Department of Music, where I teach. When the grant moved to UNC's Institute for the Arts and Humanities during my term as Director, my wonderful colleagues, especially Allison Burnett Smith and Tommie Watson, helped me juggle my IAH and Next Level directorships. Business manager Rebecca Williams was instrumental in managing the complex finances of the grant, with much-appreciated assistance from Betty Morgan, Elise Richards, and Heather Yousef. June Guralnick, Ashley Mattheis, and Rita O'Sullivan offered excellent work in the area of evaluations and logistics. I'm also appreciative of the generous support, financial and otherwise, from Department of Music Chairs Louise Toppin and Allen Anderson, Innovate Carolina Director Michelle Bolas, Senior Associate Dean Terry Rhodes, Dean Kevin Guskiewicz, Dean Barbara Rimer, Vice Provost Ron Strauss, Vice Chancellors Judith Cone, Barbara Entwisle, and Terry Magnuson, and Chancellor Carol Folt.

UNC's Institute for the Arts and Humanities has been a home to me for the past dozen years. The warm, collaborative atmosphere, the convivial interdisciplinary conversations, and, yes, the superb food, have empowered me to do my best work. I have learned so much from the brilliant scholars and artists I have encountered through the Institute. Many of them helped me think more broadly or critically about my subject, cheered me on as I wrote the book, or read some or all of the manuscript, so a hearty thanks to Cemil Aydin, Michele Berger, Emily Burrill, Mark Crescenzi, Jennifer Ho, Emil Keme, Charlie Kurzman, and Chérie Rivers Ndaliko.

Meridian International Center became Next Level's administrative partner starting in 2016, and it has been a great pleasure working with their Cultural Programs staff, including Lindsay Amini, Cole Fiala, Terry Harvey, Athena Hsieh, Madlyn Kaufman, and Kara Zelasko. They have done much more than just manage—they have helped make Next Level a more creative, effective, and robust program.

It's simply a fact to say that Next Level would not exist without the State Department, which funds the program. I am particularly indebted to two program officers, Jill Staggs and Michele Peregrin, both of whom unfailingly supported Next Level's mission and operations. Our work abroad was facilitated in innumerable ways by dozens of US Foreign

Service Officers over the years, with Calvin Hayes, Kelly McCaleb, and Sunshine Ison among the standouts. And a special thanks to Michael A. Jakub, former Director of Technical Programs in the Office of the Coordinator for Counterterrorism, and my father-in-law, for his insights and advice.

"I know how busy you are, but . . . ." This phrase typically prefaces any favor asked of a fellow academic. We truly are busy, so it is a testament to the generosity of my academic colleagues that so many took the time to speak or correspond with me about my work. So thanks very much to Emily Abrams Ansari, Will Cheng, Alex Crooke, Daniel Banks, Omar El-Khairy, Danielle Fosler-Lussier, Adam Haupt, Loren Kajikawa, Moira Killoran, Tim Sterner Miller, Felicia Miyakawa, Rebekah Moore, Ali Colleen Neff, Chris Nickell, Sean Peterson, Griff Rollefson, Arthur Romano, Kendra Salois, Joe Schloss, and David VanderHamm. (And to Will, Loren, Joe, and Kendra: thank you *so* much for providing such vital feedback on the whole manuscript.)

At UNC I taught two courses, one undergraduate and one graduate, both called Hip Hop Diplomacy, in which students read draft chapters from this book. I cannot overstate how valuable it was to hear their perspectives, ideas, and critiques. I offer my profound thanks to every one of these students: in MUSC 390H, Chiazo Agina (with extra special thanks for building *Build*'s website), Alex Anton, Shauntel Baker, Kathryn Brown, Andrea Brucculeri, Eugenie Chen, Shaylyn Clancy, Pedro Duarte, John Cho Edmonds, Eliza Harrison, Martin Hill, Adams Hobart, Summer Lanier, Isaac Malave, Will Metcalf, Mattias Miller, Cooper Nester, Katie Olson, Josh Payne, Marigrace Seaton, Bevan Therien, Christian Towner, Stuart Williamson, and Anne Worth; and in MUSC 950, Claire Bunschoten, Tyler Bunzey, Erica Fedor, Ben Gates, Aldwyn Hogg Jr. (who also lent valuable assistance as an indexer and proofreader), Meli Kimathi, Grace Kweon, Stella Li, Sinclair Palmer, and Erin Pratt.

This is my second book with the redoubtable Oxford University Press. First and foremost, I give thanks to my editor Suzanne Ryan for her good-humored, incisive feedback, her unstinting support, and her friendship. Assistant Editor Victoria (Vika) Dixon was a helpful and friendly presence throughout the process. Much appreciation, too, goes to Project Manager Damian Penfold and copy editor Tim-Rutherford Johnson. I wish I knew all the people working in design, marketing, and publicity at OUP to help build *Build*; my gratitude goes out to all of them. A final thank you to OUP for hiring the world's best hip hop publicist (as well as a trusted advisor and friend), Christie Z-Pabon, to spread the good word about *Build*.

I want to close by thanking and honoring the extended Katz family, especially my parents, Evelyn and Warren. It's my mother who instilled in me a love of music, art, and culture. She taught me to appreciate Mozart and Schubert and Gaugin and Pollock. Now I get to teach her to appreciate hip hop, and I'm grateful for her eagerness to learn. In writing this book I came to realize that, in a way, I am finally following in my father's footsteps. He was a builder, and for decades his construction company made homes for hundreds of families. He is happy that I have a career that I love; still, I know he would have been pleased had I found success in his profession. But as he knows, building isn't so much about constructing houses, it's about creating spaces where people can live and thrive, it's about fostering community. And that's what this book, aptly titled *Build*, and the work that stands behind it, is all about. It's just that instead of bricks and mortar, it's beats and rhymes that create these spaces and communities. See, Dad, I'm a builder after all!

Carrboro, North Carolina, June 2019

# ABOUT THE COMPANION WEBSITE

*Build*'s companion website www.oup.com/us/build provides a wide variety of materials related to this book. A chapter-by-chapter companion offers photos, maps, text, and videos related to subjects and issues discussed throughout the book. Other supplemental materials include interview transcripts with artists, educators, State Department personnel and others as well as links to additional resources. The website will be updated regularly.

# INTRODUCTION

Queens Community House, New York, July 2016. Frankie Perez brought his friend Mark Kaweesi to dance practice. "They were so welcoming," Mark fondly says of his time with Frankie's crew, Supreme Beingz. As Frankie remembers, "We were practicing together, not really saying much because we were focused on our training. It was beautiful."[1] The two breakdancers, or b-boys, both in their mid-twenties, were doing more than just honing their moves that hot summer day. They were learning from each other and about each other. In hip hop terms they were *building* together.

A decade earlier Mark Kaweesi was an orphan living on the streets of Kampala, Uganda. He was ambitious. "I always wanted to focus on something bigger, on something greater," he explains. "I never wanted to accept that I was a failure." For a while, soccer seemed like a way out, but he couldn't afford the bribes necessary to secure a place on a traveling team. International aid organizations offered assistance, but Mark only felt exploited. "They take these photos of you when you're standing in garbage in the street. Then they buy you a plate of food from the thousands of dollars they get from donations instead of implementing programs that would help." At the time, Mark was making no more than 50 cents a day fetching water and hauling trash.

He then learned about Breakdance Project Uganda (BPU), founded by another Kampala orphan, Tekya "Abramz" Abraham.[2] Mark had always loved hip hop dance, and was thrilled to take the free classes. BPU wanted something in return, however. "They told me, 'In this organization, the only thing we expect you to do is to teach others for free.'" So whenever he learned a new move he would teach it to someone. It didn't matter that Mark was a beginner, and it didn't matter whom he taught. His only instructions were, "Whoever wants to learn something, please do teach them."

It was 2008, and Mark, now 18 years old, had a profound realization. "Guess what, I'm a teacher now," he recalls with wonder. And with this revelation came a sense of purpose. "I found a place of belonging. I found a place where I was being appreciated." An excellent instructor, he started getting paid gigs—a workshop here and there at a local school or prison. He took a course on creative facilitation and developed a distinctive pedagogy for teaching children. Some of the prominent international schools in Uganda—which he could never have afforded to attend—started hiring him to teach dance classes. Mark was no longer homeless, and was supporting himself through the two things he loved most: dancing and teaching.

Seven thousand miles to the west in New York, Frankie Perez was also finding salvation in hip hop dance, or as he refers to it, breaking. "Breaking really helped get me out of trouble during those teenage years," he attests. "A lot of the friends I had were in gangs. Even in eighth grade I had friends who were selling drugs. That could've easily been my path, too. But the hip hop community helped me stay out of it." He joined a dance crew and started to win competitions, or battles. Through battling he built his reputation, refined his craft, and launched a career that would take him around the world.

One of his travels led him to Uganda—and to Mark Kaweesi. Their paths first crossed in June 2015, when Frankie led a dance workshop for two weeks in Kampala hosted by Breakdance Project Uganda. The two men hit it off, quickly earning each other's respect. "The connection can be a deep one," Frankie says, "because we're relating over something that we spent so much time and energy doing. That's the connection that I can have with somebody coming from a place like Uganda, while I grew up in New York City."

Their connection lasted beyond those two weeks in Kampala. A year later, Mark left Africa for the first time. The recipient of a prestigious Mandela Washington Fellowship, he spent six weeks in an intensive professional development program at Wagner College, just twenty miles from the community center where Frankie's crew practiced.[3] Their reunion, Frankie explained, "wasn't a one-off thing. When we met in Uganda it was the start of a relationship and when we met in New York, it just showed that we're going to continue working together."

This relationship—a friendship born out of hip hop—was made possible by the United States Department of State.

Frankie's visit to Uganda was sponsored by a State Department–sponsored initiative called Next Level, a program I directed from 2013 to 2018.[4] Next Level is an international exchange program that sends teams of US hip hop artists to work with youth in underserved communities around the world, and subsequently brings representatives from each country it visits to the United States for artistic and professional training. It is a form of people-to-people diplomacy, where private citizens of different nations come together to seek common ground and forge mutual understanding. More specifically, it is a form of cultural diplomacy, where a state's arts, cuisine, literature, and the like provide the platform for people-to-people interactions. Richard T. Arndt, a veteran of US cultural diplomacy programs, described the purpose of this work:

> Quietly, invisibly, indirectly, my cultural colleagues and I spent our lives representing American education and intellect, art and thought, setting foreign ideas about America into deeper contexts, helping others understand the workings of the peculiar US version of democracy, combatting anti-Americanism at its taproots, linking Americans and foreign counterparts, helping the best American and foreign students study somewhere else—in short, projecting America, warts and all.[5]

Here, the culture in question is hip hop, thus the term *hip hop di-plomacy*. Hip hop diplomacy dates only to the early years of the 21st century, but it is part of the US government's decades-long deployment of the arts in international relations, a descendent of the famous jazz tours that sent the likes of Louis Armstrong and Duke Ellington around the world in the 1950s and 1960s.[6] The jazz tours of the twentieth century and the hip hop workshops of the twenty-first—as well as other exchanges like the Fulbright Program—are products of the State Department's Bureau of Educational and Cultural Affairs, or ECA. Its mission: "to increase mutual understanding between the people of the United States and the people of other countries by means of educational and cultural exchange that assist in the development of peaceful relations."[7]

The partnership between hip hop and the US government is an unlikely one. The dissonance is obvious. Hip hop is celebrated for its oppositional stance, especially against the US government, which has marginalized and

Hip hop mural in Dakar, Senegal, January 15, 2015. It features a well-known statement by Léopold Sédar Senghor, poet and first president of Senegal (1960–80), which translates as "Culture is at the beginning and end of everything." (The original quotation ends with the word, "développement," or development.) Photograph by Mark Katz.

oppressed the communities who created this art and culture. Look no further than Public Enemy's iconic song "Fight the Power," its anti-authority position explicit in its lyrics and in the group's name. And *diplomatic* is hardly the first word associated with hip hop. Countless hip hop songs celebrate or spotlight crime, misogyny, and violence, none of them consistent with the image and messaging the State Department seeks to project abroad. To supporters *and* critics of the music and culture, the very idea of hip hop diplomacy can be deeply troubling, even an oxymoron.

The risks inherent in hip hop diplomacy arise from the inescapable fact that diplomacy is ultimately intended to serve state interests. For some critics, hip hop poorly represents the United States; for others, cultural diplomacy exploits hip hop. Taking the former perspective, political scientist Michael Curtis has questioned the State Department's use of rappers in its diplomatic efforts, arguing that "their lyrics do not posit a peaceful or democratic future, and are unlikely to help change perceptions of the US . . . Their performers are not the standard bearers of nonviolent behavior or of tolerance. Nor are they useful in illustrating the diversity of American life."[8] Anthropologist Su'Ad Abdul Khabeer has criticized hip hop diplomacy from a very different perspective, identifying it as part of the US government's "management of an imperial relationship with the 'Muslim world'" in the post 9/11 era. "As an effect of power," she asserts, "the low-impact cultural diplomacy strategy must be seen in aggregate. Multiple low-impact events, small inputs, and each tidbit of information are pooled to spin a particular narrative of American exceptionalism in order to justify US empire."[9]

Both perspectives must be taken seriously—misrepresentation and co-optation are ever-present risks of state-sponsored people-to-people exchanges. But we must also beware of false equivalencies. Hip hop is more than the collection of words and images associated with certain popular artists; diplomacy cannot be reduced to a tool whose sole function is to advance state power and expand empire. There is no singular US government agenda, or State Department agenda, or even ECA agenda. The bureaucracies that execute US foreign policy are never wholly unified. They are complex and opaque, guided by ever-evolving and sometimes contradictory pressures, peopled by Foreign Service Officers, civil servants, and contractors who, on a daily basis, work to transform chaos into some semblance of order.

Just as any fair assessment of hip hop diplomacy must take a skeptical stance, it must also account for the agency and creativity of the US artists who have embraced this work, among them well-respected activists and educators, underground legends, pioneers, and Grammy-winners, as well as the thousands of artists and fans that hip hop diplomacy touches around the world. Agency, of course, must be understood in the context of broader economic, political, and social structures. In this book, I toggle between structure and agency, examining the broad forces that shape individual action as well as the individuals who shape the world around them. But let me be clear about my focus—and my sympathies and biases. More than anything, *Build* is about those who seek self-expression and community through hip hop. Their work reveals an unresolvable tension, one that animates this book: that just as hip hop—and hip hop diplomacy—can bridge cultural divides, facilitate understanding, and build community, it can also be misused, exploited, and hurt those it is meant to help. To explore this tension is to probe the multifaceted power of art, and thus to gain insight into its significance in international relations and human affairs.

## WHY HIP HOP?

For Mark Kaweesi and Frankie Perez, hip hop was a lifesaver. "Hip hop saved my life" is a phrase uttered in dozens of languages across the world. It's often said quite literally—that hip hop offered an alternative to addiction, crime, poverty, or despair. As a teenager in the Rio de Janeiro favela known as Cidade de Deus (City of God), Rafaela Romualdo left home to escape an abusive stepfather, but soon fell into the drug trade. She doubts she would have survived much longer had she not found hip hop, which gave her life direction and meaning. When I walked with Rafaela, now a well-regarded rapper, through the streets of the City of God, we passed a young man spray-painting "O HIP-HOP ME EDUÇAO"—"Hip-Hop Educated [or Raised] Me" on an empty wall next to a church. The graffito captured her truth as well as his. She later wrote to me, "Hip-Hop is the guiding thread of a light that rescues young people from crime and makes them think that through culture there is a way out."[10] Hip hop was also a way out for Detroit rapper D.S.Sense—a way to escape the discrimination and hardship she endured because of her bisexuality. "I've been ostracized by friends, family alike. I faced homelessness. And even in that period of home-lessness, that dark season, what kept me optimistic was the art form of rhyming and hip hop, the genre itself. I won't say that I saw the light at the end of the tunnel. But I knew that at least I'd shovel my way to it, until I could see it. And that's what hip hop has given me—tenacity."[11]

To many, hip hop is not just a lifesaver, it *is* their life. Konshens the MC, a rapper from Washington, DC, put it this way:

> To me, hip hop isn't just b-boying and DJing and rapping and doing graffiti. Hip hop is truly a culture, it's truly a way of life. Hip hop is what raised me, outside of my mom's house.

"O Hip-Hop Me Eduçou" ["Hip-Hop Educated (or Raised) Me"], Cidade de Deus (City of God), Rio de Janeiro, Brazil, March 18, 2017. Photograph by Mark Katz.

> When I walk to the corner store to get a pack of Backwoods
> [cigars], that's hip hop. The way I dress is hip hop. The way
> I greet my homeboys up the street is hip hop. The stories that
> we tell each other, the way we tell them, that's hip hop.[12]

And when Konshens speaks of hip hop raising him, of it being at the center of his culture, his fashion, and his stories, he's invoking hip hop's power to build community. And part of the power of hip hop diplomacy—perhaps its most important power—is the possibility of fostering global community.

Hip hop is perhaps the most listened-to musical genre on earth.[13] What is it about hip hop that draws and connects people like Mark Kaweesi and Frankie Perez? Or that raises, educates, and saves the lives of Rafaela Romualdo, D.S.Sense, and Konshens? Broadly speaking, three factors help explain its massive, global popularity: its flexibility, its accessibility, and its mythology.

By flexibility, I mean its expressive flexibility, its ability to create, incorporate, and generate sound and sense in infinite variety. Typically, hip hop fans are most immediately drawn to the music's beats and rhymes. The interplay between percussion and poetry can serve as a vehicle for fierce braggadocio, tender expressions of love, and everything in between. The beats (typically created by DJs or beatmakers, also known as producers) and the rhymes (created by rappers, also known as MCs) are only part of hip hop's appeal. Beatboxing, a form of vocal percussion that draws on DJing and beatmaking for its sonic vocabulary, is popular the world over. But hip hop is not just about sound. It has the visual element of graffiti art, or writing, as many of its practitioners call it, with an array of styles and a distinctive history. And then there is the element of dance. Hip hop originated out of the relationship between DJs and dancers, as DJs discovered that repeating, or looping, short percussion solos known as breaks helped foster a new dance style that came to be known popularly as breakdancing (though many practitioners refer to it as *breaking* or *b-boying* or *b-girling*).

These elements have been remixed by artistic communities around the world. I've heard MCs spit rhymes in Arabic, Burmese, and Croatian as well as Swahili, Thai, and Uzbek, and this is just a fraction of the world's languages that have (w)rapped their tongues around hip hop. From the beginning, hip hop drew not just from funk and soul for its beats, but from a variety of world traditions, from Afrobeat to salsa. And as hip hop spread beyond the United States, it adapted itself to local music and dance styles and indigenous instruments. Just in my own experience, I've encountered Bengali baul, Colombian cumbia, Nubian funk, Serbian turbofolk, and more mix beautifully with hip hop beats and bars. This expressive flexibility helps account for hip hop's global spread.

Another aspect of hip hop's appeal is its accessibility. Only a body and a voice are needed to rap, beatbox, or dance. Graffiti art requires materials but artists can make do with whatever is at hand. Even DJing and beatmaking, which typically demand laptops, software, drum machines or other gear, have become more accessible since the turn of the millennium as equipment has become cheaper, more portable, and more robust. Hip hop can also be accessible to disabled people, who accommodate hip hop to their bodies and needs. For Brazilian B-boy Samuka, who lost a leg to cancer as a child, excelling as a dancer allowed him to feel "normal" as a teenager, "equal" to his peers.[14] Samuka met legendary US b-boy Kujo during a Next Level residency in 2017; Kujo, who is deaf, brought Samuka into his renowned international dance crew, ILL-ABILITIES. According to its website, "The 'ill' in ILL-ABILITIES does not refer to 'sick' or 'unwell' but rather to incredible, amazing, intricate, talent. Rather than seeing the negative limitations of 'disability,' this crew focuses on their positive, or 'ill,' abilities."[15] Soon Samuka, who had never traveled outside of Brazil, was performing in the United States, France, and Singapore, often sporting a t-shirt with the crew's motto, "No Excuses, No Limits." For him, hip hop was both salvation and passport.

Hip hop is also accessible in that it's easy to find, especially in mediatized form. Recordings and radio have been spreading the music

Ajahn Thepsin, master of Nang Talung (Thai shadow puppet theater) and rapper Dumi Right collaborate, interpreter in foreground, Surat Thani, Thailand, February 18, 2016. Photograph by Mark Katz.

for decades, but the culture has been disseminated most powerfully via Hollywood, through movies like *Wild Style* (1983), *Breakin'* (1984), *Beat Street* (1984), *House Party* (1990), and *Juice* (1992). Brothers Akim and Dumisani Ndlovu (aka Akim Funk Buddha and Dumi Right) fondly remember the impact of seeing *Beat Street* as teenagers when it was first screened in Harare, Zimbabwe. As Dumi explains:

> We were so amped in fact that we paid to see it multiple times in the theater and after each showing we'd hang around and then start a dance cypher [improvised performance] as patrons exited, often to resounding applause. Initially the theater owners tried to chase us out as troublemakers. Upon seeing the crowds react though they ended up inviting us

back and giving us free movie tickets to come perform offi-
cially at future screenings.[16]

The videocassette then opened up the possibility of *studying* hip
hop outside the United States. Many international hip hop artists
recall how, as youth in the 1980s and 1990s and into the 2000s,
they watched tapes of these films over and again, often in groups
of friends around the one VCR available in their community. For
countless artists, these films were their hip hop primers. Others
encountered hip hop for the first time though music videos, whether
on TV or tape. In the film *Slingshot Hip Hop*, Palestinian MC Suhell
Nafar of the group DAM recounts the impact of seeing the 1993
video of Tupac Shakur's "Holler If Ya Hear Me." "It looked like
he filmed it in our hometown, Lod. Even though we didn't know
English and didn't get the lyrics, we made the connection. Tamer
[Suhell's older brother and a member of DAM] got all the Tupac
tracks he could find and learned English by sitting at the back of the
class, translating the lyrics into Arabic, and sharing them with me."[17]
   Then came the digital revolution of the 2000s, allowing hip hop to
become truly global. Filesharing networks like Napster allowed music
to circulate outside corporate control and gave unprecedented access to hip hop fans and creators.[18] In just a few years the media land-
scape changed again with the rise of Facebook (2004), YouTube (2005),
SoundCloud (2007), Spotify (2008), WhatsApp (2009), and Instagram
(2010)—platforms that gave fans and practitioners new ways to see and
hear hip hop and to connect with likeminded souls, whether locally or
across vast distances.
   A third reason for hip hop's global appeal is its powerful mythos.
Hip hop has a potent origin story: in the 1970s, talented, industrious
African American and Latinx teenagers in the Bronx, New York developed a new art form and culture, one that went on to become a globally influential industry and way of life.[19] GrandWizzard Theodore,
the pioneering Bronx DJ who introduced the world to scratching, put
it this way: "Hip hop came from nothing. The people that created hip

hop had nothing. And what they did was, they created something from nothing."[20] To hip hop artists around the world, "The Bronx" is a name uttered with reverence, and the concept of creating something from nothing resonates profoundly. When I asked a 20-year-old white Croatian dancer named Iva what appealed to her about hip hop, she immediately invoked the Bronx and the pioneering dance group, Rock Steady Crew:

> [Hip hop] began in the Bronx. Zagreb is the farthest from the Bronx. But right now, OK, with the economy and our situation politically we feel the same they felt in the early '80s and '70s. It's really hard to find a job. It's really hard to live as an artist. You really have to bleed for that status. Rock Steady didn't have money. They didn't have studios. They just had their own imaginations that got them through dark times. And that's how we feel here.[21]

A rapper, entrepreneur, and hip hop activist known as ABD once suggested his own hip hop myth:

> I think of hip hop as this superhero. Well, he got no capes and stuff. He's just one of those boombox-on-his-shoulder-flying-across-the-world superheroes. "Oh, there's struggle over there. I'ma go there. I'm gonna spread myself out to the people and uplift them and show them how to come together through positivity and love." That's how I think of hip hop.[22]

A rapper from the United States could well have told this story. But I spoke with ABD in his hometown of Dhaka, Bangladesh, and our conversation took place within a distinctive soundscape of quarreling car horns, clanging rickshaw bells, and the Muslim call to prayer. It didn't matter that he was born 7,800 miles from the birthplace of hip hop. "There's a reason hip hop has spread so fast so far," he explained. "Hip hop, to me, is directly related to struggle. It would have not been born if there was no struggle. We have so much poverty over here. Hip hop is just a form of self-expression that is relevant to the Bangla youth." ABD's "government name" is Mohammed Abdullah. In the twenty-first century there is nothing strange about a Bangladeshi Muslim named Mohammed who is familiar with African American Vernacular English and hip hop style. With 150 million people sharing his name (and its variants), there are almost certainly more rappers named Mohammed than Mike.[23]

Look at the list of 195 countries recognized by the United Nations and try to find a country where hip hop *doesn't* have a presence. It's in Afghanistan, where MCs have made news rapping about the Taliban and forced marriage, and it's in Zimbabwe, where an initiative called Step Up 2 HIV uses hip hop dance to educate young people in the hopes of achieving "an AIDS-free generation."[24] It's in Venezuela, where rappers Apache and Canserbero took on police corruption in their rhymes, and it's in the archipelagic South Pacific nation of Vanuatu, where a DJ and producer known as Local Remedy has used his music to address poverty and hunger among the islands' villages.[25]

Local Remedy is an apt name. Hip hop is widely and rightly recognized as a product of black culture. It arose in response to the particular lived experience of black youth in New York in the 1970s and 1980s. Yet from the beginning, hip hop has exerted a powerful pull on people who are not black and whose histories and traditions are very different from those of hip hop's pioneers. The worldwide spread of hip hop serves as a fascinating example of globalization. Originating from an economic and cultural superpower, hip hop has clearly become a commodity, generating billions of dollars. And yet it is not the homogenizing force that one might expect, one that necessarily deemphasizes the local or encourages conformity to a US model. ABD, for example, says that hip hop can be as Bangladeshi as it is American. Referring to a massive hip hop concert in Dhaka on November 17, 2014, he wrote in a Facebook post, "What happened on the 17th was more than fusion. It was embracing Hip Hop into Bangladesh. Hip hop music thrives on samples of historic blues, soul, funk, and jazz artists. We as

Bangladeshis sampled our [poets] Najrul [Kazi Nazrul Islam] and Lalon and more to create Hip Hop with their blessings and energy. This was Hip Hop adapting to Bangladeshi culture."[26]

Su'Ad Abdul Khabeer perceptively captures the complexity of hip hop as a global cultural product when she describes it as "a traded commodity and an oppositional culture *at the same time*."[27] Hip hop diplomacy embodies this tension, where practitioners may fight the power and serve it simultaneously.

## THE POWER OF HIP HOP DIPLOMACY

It's not hard to understand why the US State Department would take an interest in hip hop. Here is an art form that is readily identified as American but at the same time has been embraced by communities around the world. Hip hop is thus well suited to connect citizens of the United States with the citizens of other countries, acting as a goodwill ambassador without carrying the taint of US imperialism. Moreover, hip hop resonates deeply with youth, the fastest growing segment of the global population, and a demographic any state ignores at its peril.[28]

Still, it might not be obvious what foreign policy objectives hip hop diplomacy serves. I would point to two: enhancing the image of the United States and promoting US interests abroad. People-to-people diplomacy—including hip hop diplomacy—is a form of public relations conducted largely in private and on a small scale. The State Department sees great value in getting US citizens on the ground, interacting with their counterparts around the world.

The story of Mark Kaweesi and Frankie Perez reveals people-to-people diplomacy at work. Their friendship made them question the caricatures and stereotypes that represent their countries to the outside world. Mark's experience challenged the view of Americans as "proud and arrogant," one he says is common in Uganda. "America is not one person," he realized. "It's different people that have different mentalities, that have different ambitions, that have different opinions." And because young people all over the world embrace the music and culture, hip hop diplomacy in particular has the potential not just to challenge assumptions but to generate positive associations with the country of its birth. When I asked Tsiry "Panda" Kely, a Malagasy beatboxer, MC, and producer, to describe his image of the United States, he answered without hesitation: "The country of hip hop, the country of liberty, the country where you can realize your dreams. This is my image of US."[29]

Public relations can also be an explicit form of damage control. When Next Level visited Belgrade in 2014, the US-led NATO bombing of Serbia in 1999 was still a raw wound. I witnessed this in my first minutes in the country when a taxi driver learned that I was from the United States, looked at me in the rear-view mirror, and said with disgust, "I don't like Bill Clinton." Marija Bjelopetrovic, the Cultural Affairs Assistant at the US Embassy in Belgrade, explained that having US hip hop artists lead workshops for Serbian youth helped address this festering resentment.

> Serbia still has negative feelings towards the United States because of the bombing during NATO time. It's impor-tant that kids and the general population can actually be in contact with the Americans to see that, you know, they're normal people. That they're not these fanatics. That they're not cops that are running the entire world and so on, that they're just general, everyday people who laugh and have fun and enjoy life and so on. A lot of Serbians have never communicated with an American before, so to us, that really helps the Embassy build a better image.[30]

Just a year earlier, the Serbian public approval rating of the United States was only 9 percent. At the time we spoke, it had more than doubled to 20 percent, an outcome that Bjelopetrovic attributed to intensive engagement. The State Department has likewise turned to hip hop as a means to improve the country's image abroad with Muslim populations, where approval ratings for the United States often range from poor to abysmal. This kind of attention to image is hardly superficial, for when it comes to international relations, a nation's reputation can make the difference between cooperation and conflict with other states.[31]

Cultural diplomacy can also help advance particular interests of the United States abroad. Every US diplomatic post in the world works to promote certain priorities in its country. The Embassy in Brazil has six—education; social inclusion; trade and investment; democracy and human rights; peace and security; and science, technology, and innovation—and every post activity is meant to support one or more of them.[32] When Next Level visited Brasilia and Rio de Janeiro in 2017, the embassy and consulate were eager to promote social inclusion by working with youth in communities that have been underserved, sometimes quite literally marginalized.[33] Social inclusion also meant offering opportunities to young Brazilians with disabilities, and although it wasn't planned this way, the US team included beatmaker King Khazm, who uses a wheelchair, and b-boy Kujo, who is deaf. The example of Samuka, the dancer Kujo met in Brasilia and later invited into his crew, ILL-ABILITIES, offered a perfect example of how the program could, as the Embassy's website articulates, "empower marginalized people to take advantage of burgeoning global opportunities" and "enjoy equal access to markets, services and political, social and physical spaces."[34] Social inclusion was also a priority for the US Embassy in the small Balkan country of Montenegro, where we worked with the historically marginalized Roma population, and particularly with Roma women, a doubly oppressed population. Cultural Affairs Officer Sunshine Ison cited the presence of three American women (MC Mahogany Jones and dancers Deena Clemente and Wandee Candelario) as essential to our work. "Having these amazing, strong hip hop artists who are women," she told me, "show that it's okay to practice your art, that it's okay to be a woman and be strong, that you have a right to choose your destiny, and that you have a right to talk about the issues that are important to you."[35]

Fostering conflict resolution is also a common priority among US diplomatic posts. When in 2013 the State Department's Cultural Programs Division put out the call to non-profit organizations to create what would become Next Level, conflict resolution was a central theme. The purpose of the program would be "to develop and administer an international exchange program in hip hop and urban arts that incorporates artistic collaboration, professional development and outreach to youth *to explore and address conflict resolution strategies*."[36] For countless young people, hip hop has served as a means to find alternatives to the conflicts that swirl around them and to transform the conflict that churns inside them. Hip hop diplomacy, then, offers the possibility of transforming conflict through cross-cultural performance and collaboration.

## BUILDING

In hip hop culture, to build is to elevate, to add positivity to the world. To build *with* someone is to collaborate, to work towards something that can be achieved collectively, but not individually. This notion of building can be traced to the teachings of the Five Percent Nation, a cultural and spiritual movement that emerged in New York City and has shaped hip hop since its beginnings. Today, the English word "build" and its hip hop definition are known all over the world; in fact, this book's title was inspired by an artist I met in Zimbabwe during one of the first Next Level residencies. Ngoni Tapiwa, better known as Upmost, told me that he was worried when he learned that a group from the United States was coming to Harare. "I hope these guys don't think they're coming to teach us hip hop," he recalled thinking. "I hope they're going to learn as well and *build* with the hip hop that exists here. So my fear was that it was going to be, 'We made hip hop so let us teach you.'"[37] To build with someone is different from teaching someone, or, to use a hip hop term that suggests domination, *schooling* them. Building, then, offers a constructive, mutually beneficial model of engagement. To carry the metaphor further, hip hop diplomacy can build bridges, connecting people who would have little reason to interact otherwise. Having hip hop in common does not eliminate difference, but it provides a starting point for finding common cause and celebrating difference. As Rami Mhazres, a Tunisian DJ known as Supaflava—and a Muslim—said, "Hip hop has no boundaries. When I can sit with you and I know that you're Christian, atheist, Jewish I have no problem with that. We can communicate, we can *build* something, we can work together. Why should I fight you? We are brothers."[38]

Building can be collaborative, but it can also be divisive, destructive. As Donald Trump's anti-immigrant campaign cry, "Build that wall!" revealed, what we construct can inspire connection or it can sow misunderstanding, generate suspicion, and destroy relationships. Even well-meaning attempts to build can do harm. The history of US diplomacy is replete with examples of diplomats schooling others in condescending, demeaning ways. And this can happen in hip hop diplomacy. Upmost's desire to build with the Next Level artists was informed by a negative experience with a US hip hop group a few years earlier. The "ugly American"—arrogant, boorish, ethnocentric, and ignorant—may be a caricature, but it is based in reality, and too many US citizens traveling abroad, diplomats among them, have damaged international relations even when their intentions were good.

Inevitably, hip hop diplomacy is rife with unresolvable ambiguities and freighted with the potential to do harm. Consider Next Level's 2016 residency in Honduras, where the US Embassy tasked the program with using hip hop to promote home-grown artistic entrepreneurship and encourage alternatives to violence. The dozens of young people who participated in our workshops constantly expressed their appreciation for the opportunity to connect with the US team (MC Azad, B-boy Jeremy Pena, DJ Kaotic Blaze, and beatmaker DiViNCi). Prominent Honduran rapper, MC Ko-co, head of the hip hop organization El Arte de las Calles (Art in the Streets), said that local business and non-profit organizations rarely supported his anti-violence work. "The private sector doesn't believe in this idea, they don't believe in hip hop. They see it as a bad thing. It's hard too with the other local embassies because they don't have these programs. The only one [that helps] is the US Embassy."[39]

And yet, at the same time we were building with the hip hop community in Tegucigalpa, we were also aiding US efforts to stem the exodus from a country terrorized by gangs that originated in the United States and by the US-supported Honduran military, known for its human rights violations and extrajudicial killings. Hondurans who seek asylum in the United States are subject to deportation, even when they face specific threats of horrific violence. Many deportees have been murdered upon their arrival at home. "We're helping to deport kids to die," *New York Times* columnist Nicholas Kristof wrote a few months after we returned.[40] How should we feel about a program intended, at least in part, to encourage young Hondurans to stay in a country plagued by problems created or exacerbated by the US government? And what are the consequences of deploying US hip hop artists to do this work on behalf of the State Department? Are they being exploited, treated as pawns? Are they selling out when they sign up for programs like Next Level? Do they become complicit with the bad acts of the United States government?

The possibility that hip hop diplomacy can do harm haunts me. This possibility impels me to be more aware: aware of asymmetrical power relations, aware of my country's troubled history with so many of the places I visit, aware of how my own actions affect others. I am also aware of the ambiguities, even paradoxes of hip hop diplomacy. As self-described "anti-government" DJ, activist, and Next Level artist Kuttin Kandi, put it: "Hip hop has its own contradictions. We live within the contradictions."[41] Awareness of these asymmetries, ambiguities, and contradictions leads me to approach this work with a care, respect, and humility that promotes, though never guarantees, understanding, collaboration, and community—in a word, building.

## WHO AM I AND WHAT AM I DOING HERE?

I don't look hip hop. I've been told this by colleagues, students, friends, relatives, and strangers—just about everyone except for hip hop artists, who have fewer preconceived notions of what hip hop looks like. I know why I don't look hip hop. It's because I'm white. And not just white: I'm a middle-aged professor, I dress in a clean-cut style, and I speak with what linguists call a "General American" accent, which is usually heard as white. That I have spent twenty years researching and writing about hip hop, that

Rappers practicing their rhymes at a Next Level workshop, Tegucigalpa, Honduras, January 22, 2016. Photograph by Mark Katz.

I have traveled to more than thirty countries for this research, that I have interviewed hundreds of hip hop artists, that I have studied turntablism and can execute a decent transformer scratch—all of this is at odds with what many people assume when they first meet me.

In hip hop, being white is, as MC and DJ Rabbi Darkside told me, "never a non-issue." Rabbi is keenly aware of his own whiteness: "I wouldn't disrespect the people that I'm collaborating with by thinking that it would be a non-issue, so I'm always ready to engage in conversation around it. I'm always trying to be aware of the ways that intrinsic white privilege plays out in everything from conversation to planning to the way I'm hearing and listening to people. I'm totally attuned to the possible microaggressions just based on that dynamic."[42] And what scholar Elijah Wald says about whites who play black music is equally true for those who study it: "I think white people living in a racist society—like me—need to understand that the choice to play the music of black Americans either includes showing deep respect for the people who created this music, or is deeply problematic. There is history there, and ignoring it is a political statement, just like acknowledging it is a political statement."[43]

Because I study an art form that is rooted in black culture, my whiteness is an issue. Treating race as a non-issue is a privilege only accorded to those whose skin color does not mark them for different—and often disrespectful, unfair, and violent—treatment. When I'm moving within hip hop communities I'm well aware of my whiteness. In the places I've visited with Next Level there are names for people who look like me: *bule* (Indonesia), *farang* (Thailand), *gringo* (Colombia, El Salvador, Guatemala, Honduras), *khawaga* (Egypt), *mzungu* (Congo, Tanzania). But the way I am singled out for my whiteness is very different from the treatment people of color receive. My whiteness has yet to put me in danger, and most of the time I accrue unearned benefits—safety, access, the benefit of the doubt—because of it. Still, I have long been disabused of the idea that racial colorblindness is possible and that my own whiteness need not be a subject of self-reflection.

If my whiteness has marked me as an outsider in my hip hop work, it has marked me as an insider with the mostly white civil servants and Foreign Service Officers who support Next Level. My identity as a well-traveled, upper middle-class white person who holds degrees from reputable, predominantly white institutions and speaks with a General American accent makes me familiar to them. This familiarity allows me to be an effective translator when I speak on behalf of or advocate for the artists I work with, whether in the United States or abroad. This has been true in academia as well. I have been able to secure funding, gain access to those in positions of power, and have my voice heard in influential forums, and to do this in service to hip hop practitioners.

During my time as Director of Next Level, a vital part of my long-term strategy was to leverage the advantages of my identity in order to share power with the hip hop community. The plan was simple, though it took years to execute: build Next Level and then leave it in the hands of those it serves. The first step was to bring Next Level artists back to the program to manage residencies. (The original manager, the excellent Paul Rockower, was not a hip hop artist, and left Next Level in 2016 in order to sever ties with the United States government after Donald Trump was elected president.) Kane Smego was the first artist-manager, followed by Junious Brickhouse, Jaci Caprice, and Mahogany Jones. The next step was to bring artists into leadership positions. Brickhouse became Associate Director in 2017. He and I became co-directors and Smego was named Associate Director in 2018. In 2019 Brickhouse became the sole Director of Next Level, and I stepped away. With this, the leadership of Next Level was solely in the hands of hip hop artists.[44]

In 2009, five years before my first Next Level residency, I shared a late-night meal with Jorge Pabon, a pioneering hip hop dancer better known as Popmaster Fabel. While we picked at our food, I asked Fabel, a frequent guest on college campuses, about his experiences in the world of academia. Over the next several minutes he related, with growing intensity and ire, the various indignities he had endured at the hands of academics. On more than a few occasions, he had felt slighted and exploited, and complained that many of those who interviewed him or asked him to speak or dance offered him nothing for his time and expertise. One remark particularly stuck in my mind. "You [academics] get tenure because of us, but we need to feed our babies, too."[45] A few months earlier I was talking with another hip hop pioneer, DJ Cash Money, an influential figure in the 1980s hip hop scene in Philadelphia. I was interviewing him for my book *Groove Music: The Art and Culture of the Hip-Hop DJ*, and as we wrapped up our conversation, he left me with an exhortation that resonates with me still. When I thanked him for giving me so much of his time, he responded simply: "We need you to get this right."[46]

Scholars like to complicate and to problematize. We do it for good reason: matters are often not as straightforward as they seem, and we have the expertise and responsibility to probe, to ask difficult questions, to resist the lure of oversimplification. And I certainly make clear that state-sponsored cultural exchange is a difficult, often fraught enterprise. However, in the end—or rather, from the start—I want to argue for the value of hip hop diplomacy. I believe in the life-changing, community-building power of hip hop. I believe in the positive potential of hip hop as a form of diplomacy. I believe that hip hop can reveal the best side of modern international relations, in which posturing and propaganda can give way to understanding, appreciation, and empathy. I believe all this because I have seen evidence of all this, across time and continents and cultures.

## CHAPTER 1

# HISTORY: FROM JAZZ AMBASSADORS TO HIP HOP DIPLOMATS

Nairobi, Kenya, 1973. "I think of you as my people," jazz trumpeter Dizzy Gillespie proclaimed to the crowd in Swahili just before he and his band played.[1] The occasion was the tenth anniversary of Kenya's independence from Britain, and the US Department of State had sent Gillespie to help them celebrate. The legendary American artist would seem to be an ideal musical envoy, and had been the first jazz musician to tour on behalf of the State Department back in 1956. But it was now 1973, and Gillespie was not the locals' first choice. The Kenyans wanted the Jackson 5. Or at least another prominent American soul group that could give the youth "music suitable for dancing."[2] In a cable after the concert, Ralph Lindstrom, the second in command at the US Embassy in Nairobi wrote, "THOUGH CROWDS LARGE, REACTION TO GILLESPIE MUSIC ON PART OF MOST KENYANS PRESENT MILD AND POLITE."[3] Jazz was no longer the favored US musical export among global youth.

Bronx, New York, 1973. Seventy-three hundred miles from Nairobi, the youth were clamoring for the same thing as their Kenyan counterparts: soul music suitable for dancing. And that is exactly what many New York DJs were putting on their platters at parties that hot summer. Most of these DJs and most of the parties have long been forgotten, but one gathering is still remembered today, consecrated by some as the birth of hip hop. The party was held on August 11, 1973 in the recreation room of the high-rise apartment building on 1520 Sedgwick Avenue in the Bronx; the DJ was an 18-year-old known as Kool Herc.[4] This was not hip hop as we now know it—it hadn't even been named yet—but Herc and a number of other young, mostly African American DJs started a musical practice that became a genre that then became a worldwide youth culture and multibillion-dollar industry. It also became, 28 years later, a State Department–funded form of cultural diplomacy.

The year 1973 offers a snapshot of US musical diplomacy in transition. Gillespie played Kenya; Duke Ellington and his orchestra visited Ethiopia and Zambia; blues guitarist B.B. King jammed with Nigerian legend Fela Kuti in Lagos; the 5th Dimension toasted Eastern Europe with its "champagne soul"; and the Philadelphia Orchestra played Beethoven to Madame Mao in Beijing.[5] We see one form of cultural diplomacy fading in its appeal—jazz was no longer, as the *New York Times* declared in 1955, the country's most potent "sonic weapon"— as the State Department searched for vibrant new forms of musical exchanges.[6] It was not until 2001 that the United States took its first tentative steps into hip hop diplomacy, and then another dozen years before it committed to a program dedicated to the art form. To understand the complicated and ambivalent relationship between the State Department and hip hop we need to look back to the 1930s to witness the unlikely origin story of US cultural diplomacy and then to the 1950s to explore the potent mixture of race, music, and politics that marked the era of the jazz ambassadors.

## FASCISM AND THE ORIGINS OF US CULTURAL DIPLOMACY

National security threats have long been the animating force behind US cultural diplomacy. First, the threat was fascism. Later, it was communism, and then terrorism.

One way to understand the origins of cultural diplomacy in the United States is as an effort to enlist the arts in the fight against fascism. As early as the mid-1930s, anxious US diplomats in Latin America were reporting an increasing prevalence of Nazi propaganda. With the beginning of World War II, these fears only heightened. Rumors told of Nazi airstrips in Colombia and paramilitary units hidden among Latin America's German expatriate communities. Secretary of State Cordell Hull called Argentina a "bad neighbor" that harbored "a seething mass of German intrigue and plotting within its borders."[7] Many of these rumors were unfounded or exaggerated, but concern among officials in Washington was strong enough to warrant action.[8]

Enter Franklin D. Roosevelt's Good Neighbor Policy. Established in 1933, it was intended to ease tensions between the United States and Latin America by articulating a non-interventionist stance and by engaging in mutually beneficial trade agreements and exchanges. The neighbors met regularly, and out of one such meeting—the 1936 Inter-American Conference for the Maintenance of Peace—came a recommendation from the US to formalize north-south exchanges. An ambitious plan arose to establish a permanent office within the State Department that would promote cultural exchange, not solely within the Americas, but globally. The Nazi threat was cited repeatedly to create a sense of urgency, and it worked. On July 27, 1938— just slightly over two months after the idea was proposed within the State Department—a new Division of Cultural Relations was in business.[9]

And then things slowed down. A year passed before the Division even started talking in earnest about the arts. The initial gathering was held with great fanfare at the Library of Congress in October 1939, with representatives from government, academia, philanthropy, and the entertainment industry in attendance. Although it began auspiciously, two warning signs portended a rough road ahead. One was the State Department's reluctance to devote much financial support to the Division. The group that had been formed to oversee the division's musical initiatives later aired its frustration: "the Committee has had no funds with which to undertake numerous measures which are urgently needed . . . Competent advice and concrete assistance have been lacking, up to the present; there have not therefore been solid foundations on which to build."[10]

A second warning sign was the disagreement about the type of music that the Division of Cultural Relations should support. Many felt the United States would show its best face with classical music. But the prominent musicologist Charles Seeger offered a dissonant counterpoint to the discussion, advocating for less rarefied forms of musical exchange. "But let us also live true to our democratic principles and encourage primarily the communication of that which is *common* between the common men of all countries. This, in music, must now, and for some time to come, be done in folk and in popular idioms."[11] (Charles's 20-year-old son, Pete Seeger, already an active performer, went on to become a famous folk singer.) *Washington Post* critic Ray C.B. Brown publicly disagreed: "I would take issue with Mr. Seeger on the advisability of placing primary emphasis on folk and popular music," he wrote.[12] Most of those involved sided with Brown, and it would be another 17 years before the US government would send a popular music group on tour.

While the Division of Cultural Relations deliberated, a competing government initiative sprang up in August 1940. The Office of Inter-American Affairs (OIAA) was more powerful, better funded, and more agile.[13] To head the Office, President Roosevelt appointed the wealthy, well-connected Nelson Rockefeller, who quickly established a committee to oversee musical exchanges in the Americas. The OIAA started sending performing arts groups south in 1941, among them the Yale Glee Club, the League of Composers Wind Quintet, and the American Ballet Caravan.[14]

The first cultural diplomacy tours—and those for the next several decades—largely consisted of public performances, typically in concert halls and auditoriums; it was only much later that the focus shifted to workshops, masterclasses, and more interactive encounters. Still, there was a clear understanding from the beginning of US cultural diplomacy, one that persists to this day, that visiting artists were also expected to connect with locals as part of their duties. As an early government handbook noted, "off-stage appearances are considered to be almost as important, if not fully as important, as artistic performance, and therefore vital to the overall impact and success of each tour."[15] The young men from the Yale Glee Club, for example, were singled out in one communication for being on their best behavior: "Conduct of the boys was exemplary. They were quiet, refrained from getting stinko in public, and were the best ad the US has had down here in a long time."[16]

So it was that two years passed between the establishment of the Division of Cultural Relations and the first good neighborly tours in 1941— organized not under the auspices of the Division but the OIAA. In many ways, these two years characterize the history of US people-to-people cultural diplomacy: we see a program undercut by poor funding, burdened by bureaucratic redundancy, and slowed by cumbersome processes, but one that, despite all obstacles, managed to connect citizens of different nations through the arts. And although not without their critics, these exchanges were largely received enthusiastically abroad.[17]

## THE COLD WAR AND THE RISE OF THE JAZZ AMBASSADORS

With the end of World War II, the goals for cultural diplomacy changed. No longer was it necessary to beat back the Nazis. But a new threat emerged—communism—and a new international conflict arose: the Cold War. The arts emerged as a tool in this conflict with the Soviet Union, and in 1954 the State Department launched its Cultural Presentations Program and its first regular cultural diplomacy programming.[18]

Although cultural diplomacy during the Cold War is most closely associated with jazz, popular music hardly dominated the State Department's cultural programming. In fact, from 1954 to 1963 fully 83 percent of the artists approved for State Department tours were classical musicians.[19] The presentation of renowned US classical musicians, government officials believed, would make a powerful statement to the nations of the world, both adversaries and allies. By countering the perception that the United States was the land of the uncouth and the uncultured, these State Department programs helped demonstrate that the Soviet Union had no monopoly on prestige. As Assistant Secretary of State for Public Affairs Andrew Berding exhorted in 1958, "We have to show through our actions that the United States is a highly-cultured nation with real achievements in the arts, education, literature, etc. and make that manifest to other peoples."[20]

Despite the predominance of classical music, jazz came to play an outsized role in Cold War diplomacy, both for the intense media attention it attracted and because it addressed, often head on, the country's legacy of racial inequality. The Soviet propaganda machine made much of US hypocrisy as a democracy built on slavery and one that continued to oppress a segment of its citizenry through legalized apartheid. Although there was no denying these charges, jazz—an art form created by African Americans—was a potent symbol of progress during the Civil Rights era. As a critic enthused in a 1955 *New York Times* piece, "American jazz has now become a universal language. It knows no international boundaries, but everyone knows where it comes from and where to look for more."[21] But it could only be a symbol of progress if jazz musicians, especially black artists, could conspicuously demonstrate the vaunted freedoms granted to them by their country's Constitution.

Likely in response to the recent urging of African American congressman Adam Clayton Powell Jr., the State Department started including jazz in its overseas programming. In late 1955, the Department's Music Advisory Panel considered three famous bandleaders: Louis Armstrong, Duke Ellington, and Dizzy Gillespie. They settled on Gillespie, offering this backhanded recommendation: "Gillespie is an intelligent comedian, cultivated, with novelty acts, and his musical material is interesting. A tour is therefore recommended for him."[22] What later came to be unofficially known as the Jazz Ambassadors program was born.[23]

At the time jazz was already known to much of the world. US jazz musicians had been touring internationally for decades. The music was also circulating globally on millions of records and through countless hours of radio programming. Especially influential was the Voice of America's "Jazz Hour" show, which first aired in 1955 and gained, by some estimates, 100 million listeners worldwide at its peak. Its longtime host, Willis Conover, perhaps did as much to spread the love of jazz throughout the world as any single performer.[24]

It is in this context that Gillespie set off in 1956. He and his band blew through Iran, Bangladesh, Pakistan, Lebanon, Syria, Turkey, Serbia, Greece, Ecuador, Argentina, Uruguay, and Brazil—103 performances over two grueling tours. State Department officials were vocal in their praise. As the US Ambassador to Yugoslavia remarked, "Gillespie's band has made our job much easier."[25] For more than two decades following Gillespie's first foray, the State Department sponsored tours by some of the best-known jazz artists and groups in the world. Louis Armstrong was next, visiting Ghana in 1956, and returning to Africa in 1960 and 1961; Dave Brubeck made waves throughout Eastern Europe in 1958; in 1962, Benny Goodman became the first jazz artist to tour the Soviet Union; Duke Ellington offered scores of concerts for the State Department between 1963 and 1973; the likes of Count Basie, Stan Getz, Woody Herman, and Randy Weston traveled under the government's support as well. In 1958, the State Department started a partnership with the famed Newport Jazz Festival in 1958, which supported international tours into the 1970s.[26]

The relationship between the State Department and the jazz musicians who performed on its behalf is fascinatingly ambivalent. This ambivalence reveals some of the inescapable tensions that define US cultural diplomacy and pervade it to this day. Composer and pianist Dave Brubeck voiced a central conflict when he declared his music "an instrument for peace, rather than a Cold War weapon."[27] In 1961, he collaborated with Iola Brubeck, his wife, and Louis Armstrong to create *The Real Ambassadors*, a satirical album and musical that drew upon their State Department tours. The first song gets right to the point: "No commodity is quite so strange/As this thing called cultural exchange."[28]

Consider just two events that made national headlines in the months before Dizzy Gillespie got the call to serve his country as a jazz musician. In August 1955, Emmett Till, a 14-year-old black boy, was lynched in Mississippi for speaking to a white woman; the confessed murderers were never convicted. In December 1955 Rosa Parks was arrested in

Alabama for refusing to move to the back of a public bus. Gillespie and his band, as well as the foreign press, were well aware of these events as these tours unfolded. And yet Gillespie, and the African American artists who followed in his footsteps, were enlisted precisely to help counter the image that their country's racist policies had fostered. In *Satchmo Blows Up the World*, Penny Von Eschen captures "the glaring contradiction" at the heart of the State Department's strategy:

> [T]hat US officials would simultaneously insist on the universal, race-transcending quality of jazz while depending on the blackness of musicians to legitimize America's global agendas was an abiding paradox of the tours. Intended to promote a vision of colorblind American democracy, the tours foregrounded the importance of African American culture during the Cold War, with blackness and race operating culturally to project an image of American nationhood that was more inclusive than the reality.[29]

This paradox, however, did not seem to undermine the effectiveness of the program: the potent symbolism of African American artists moving and speaking freely around the world helped project an image of a robust democracy to the Soviet Union, and the world.

What was the impact of more than twenty years of jazz diplomacy? Occasionally, specific performances were said to have allayed tensions and turned anti-American sentiment as, for example, when Gillespie's performances in Athens in 1956 were said to quell student riots (at least according to some reports).[30] More broadly, these tours enhanced the image of the United States in many parts of the world and encouraged a more nuanced understanding of the country. The good will they engendered among citizens and governments in some cases strengthened relations with allies and would-be allies. And the symbolic value of sending diverse groups of talented musicians who were free to express themselves, whether through speech or music, sharpened the distinctions between the United States and the Soviet Union, between democracy and communism. But jazz was both balm and weapon, and herein lies the inescapable ambiguity of cultural diplomacy, and what makes it impossible to characterize in any simple way.

## SEEKING NEW WAYS TO ENGAGE: THE BIRTH OF HIP HOP DIPLOMACY

In September 2000, Toni Blackman got a call about an unusual gig. Her brother picked up the phone: "It's the State Department," he called out to his surprised sister. The gig was an African tour under the American Cultural Specialist program, which sends actors, dancers, musicians, poets, and the like to conduct workshops for foreign audiences at the request of overseas diplomatic posts. Blackman would be the first hip hop American Cultural Specialist. In her early 30s, Blackman was extravagantly talented. She was a rapper (or MC, a term many practitioners prefer) and a spoken-word artist, an actor, writer, and teacher, and a community activist with a master's degree from Howard University. She had just moved from Washington, DC to New York in search of a wider range of professional activities, but it was DC that changed the course of her career. As it turned out, Blackman changed the course of US cultural diplomacy.

As Blackman tells it, staff in the Bureau of Educational and Cultural Affairs (ECA), the home of the Department's cultural diplomacy programs, had been flipping through the pages of *The Source*, a popular hip hop music and culture magazine, hoping to find an artist who could represent the country in international tours. "They couldn't find anyone there. They were looking for someone who had travelled internationally, who was an educator, who was actively performing as an artist, who had experience in Africa and maybe Southeast Asia. That was me."[31] Blackman had been active in the DC arts scene on multiple fronts, and it was through these connections that she came to the attention of State Department program officer Evangeline (E.J.) Montgomery, who had experience mounting international art exhibitions, first for the United States Information Agency (USIA) and then for State Department. A champion of African American art, Montgomery was an acclaimed artist herself.[32] Just a few years from retirement, Montgomery hadn't been a particular fan of hip hop. But learning more about Blackman's work changed her mind. "Well, you know I never knew I liked rap," Montgomery told her. "Looks like I do like rap."[33]

At the time, US cultural diplomacy was in a state of disarray. In 1999 the USIA, which since 1953 had been a key part of the government's public diplomacy machine, was dissolved, many of its functions folded into the State Department. Funding for cultural programs dwindled. The State Department's own Advisory Committee on Cultural Diplomacy was unsparing in its criticism, writing that the dispersal of USIA personnel "destroyed the institutional memory necessary for the maintenance of cultural ties."[34] Former US Ambassador to the Netherlands Cynthia Schneider echoed this grim assessment: "The integration of all public diplomacy activities into the State Department in 1999 dealt cultural diplomacy a near death-blow. By 2000 the total budget for all public and cultural diplomacy activities amounted to less than 8% of the State Department budget, or approximately one third of one percent of the Pentagon budget."[35]

By 2000, hip hop was a global cultural phenomenon, but there was good reason for the State Department to approach it with caution. Hip hop may have been popular, but public perception at the time was often negative. The same month that E.J. Montgomery called Toni Blackman, a *Newsweek* poll asked, "Do you think rap or hip hop contains too much violence or is it generally not a problem?" In total, 68 percent of respondents said that it was in fact a problem; even much of the 18–29-year-old demographic agreed, with 44 percent granting that hip hop was too violent. In response to the question, "Do you think hip hop music has a bad attitude toward women?" from the same poll, 58 percent said yes.[36] When, in 2001, the National Urban League asked 800 African Americans across the country, "Do you think that most hip hop and rap artists are good models for black children and teenagers, or don't you think so?" Seventy-six percent didn't think so.[37] The Department's cultural programs staff would have to contend with the negative public reaction that a government-supported hip hop initiative might provoke, and they lived in fear of antagonizing lawmakers. The "nightmare scenario," one program officer told me, was a *Washington Post* story with an incendiary headline about taxpayer dollars supporting violent music. In this scenario, a legislator with an uncharitable opinion about hip hop spots the headline in the morning and by the end of the day has demanded the defunding of all State Department cultural programming.

If the State Department was going to touch hip hop it had to proceed *very* carefully. It needed exactly the right person to be the face and voice of government-supported hip hop. And that was Toni Blackman. E.J. Montgomery could not have invented a better candidate. Not only was Blackman a talented artist, an experienced teacher, and a world traveler, she contradicted all the negative stereotypes of rappers. In high school she was a cheerleader and the chair of her school's Spirit Committee, stereotypically wholesome pursuits. A member of the debate team in college, she was "articulate," that backhanded compliment white people often bestow on black people who exceed their low expectations. And not only did she graduate from college, she had a master's degree. Blackman recalls much being made of that fact, and how much it reassured people of her qualifications. "I was the safest of the options," she told me with a laugh.[38] To top it off, the *Washington Post* had already given its stamp of approval. "Toni Blackman," one piece noted, "is making all the right moves these days and has placed herself squarely upon a crucial nexus in the evolving theater arts scene"; another notice called her one of "Washington's finest hip hop poets."[39]

Gender also played a role. Being a woman has rarely been a professional advantage within hip hop, but in this case the stereotypes of women as gentler, more caring, and less aggressive than men served her well, reassuring doubters that she wouldn't embarrass the Department or her country.[40] Women, in fact, were at the center of the birth and development of hip hop diplomacy. Blackman, Montgomery, and Montgomery's colleague, Sandra Rouse started it all. In 2013, as we'll see, another team of State Department women conceived of the first cultural diplomacy program devoted solely to hip hop.

Although Blackman may have had unimpeachable credentials, it was no simple matter to move the idea of a hip hop cultural specialist through the bureaucracy of the State Department. The Department's organizational structure is complex and hierarchical. The Bureau of Educational and Cultural Affairs is just one of more than two dozen bureaus, each overseen by an Assistant Secretary of State who reports to one of six Undersecretaries of State, who report to one of two Deputy Secretaries of State, who in turn report to the Secretary of State. And each bureau has its own nested structure. The Cultural Programs Division, which sponsors arts exchanges, is one of four divisions within the Office of Citizen Exchanges, itself one of eight offices in ECA. E.J. Montgomery and Sandra Rouse were just two program officers trying to make a difference within a vast bureaucracy.[41] "God bless them," Blackman says of Montgomery and Rouse, who had to "fight for the little money they get." "I say God bless them," she explains, "because they do meaningful work that is necessary, and then often do it even when their own personal or political interests aren't represented, and it takes a certain kind of special person to be able to do that."[42]

As Blackman suggests, State Department staff are supposed to work apolitically, and hip hop diplomacy has enjoyed support under both parties. It was born during republican George W. Bush's administration. Next Level, the first State Department cultural diplomacy program dedicated to hip hop, was created under Barack Obama, but it continued into Donald Trump's presidency, and its funding was even increased in 2017. The civil servants and Foreign Service Officers who launched and have supported hip hop diplomacy have done so regardless of which political party is in power.

In February 2001, Blackman, the State Department's first American Cultural Specialist in hip hop, departed for a three-week tour of Dakar, Senegal and Accra, Ghana. The State Department had already had a long history of sending musicians to these West African cities. And it's no accident that so many of the State Department–supported performers who went to those countries—both of which played a significant role in the trans-Atlantic slave trade—were African American. In fact, as

Blackman recalls, "there were people who apologized to me for slavery." She believes that part of the reason she connected so strongly in Senegal and Ghana "is that I could be from either one of those countries, in terms of my physicality. And I know it made a difference. Depending on how my hair is braided or styled and what I have on, I can be from either one of those countries. And then the men in my family look like men from Senegal and then most of the women look like women from Ghana."

Blackman's first stop was in Dakar. At the Maison de la Culture Douta Seck, a government-owned cultural center, a crowd of about 2,000 squeezed into an outdoor space dominated by an ancient, massive baobab to see Blackman's performance. It was "hip hop heaven," she says—"the energy was so intense . . . they were so serious about their hip hop." As gratifying as it was to perform for such appreciative crowds, she felt uneasy to discover that she represented not just herself, but also her art, her country, her gender, and her race. At a national press conference, journalists peppered her with questions she had rarely encountered: "What is your generation going to do to make sure that hip hop continues to grow and elevate and expand? What is your responsibility as a woman of African descent to the continent of Africa? What are you going to do about the negative message Snoop Dogg is sending out?"[43] This was when she realized what it meant to be performing on behalf of her government. "It was almost insulting that they put all that responsibility on me. And it was very difficult for me not to turn into that little black girl from the Bay Area and roll my neck and say, 'Look, I'm a poet. I spin rhymes, I write rap, why are you asking me this?'" But she came to understand that, as a cultural diplomat, "you represent something much larger than yourself." And on a personal level, she saw an opportunity for growth and an opportunity to make a difference. "It put in perspective for me," she explains, "how I could be most effective in my lifetime."[44]

Blackman's first diplomatic trip, and especially her time in Senegal, had a lasting impact, both on her and the artists with whom she collaborated. Between 2001 and 2018 she visited Dakar more than

Toni Blackman, Île de Gorée, Dakar, Senegal, January 7, 2015. Photograph by Ina Makosi.

a dozen times. She witnessed the growth of the hip hop scene there, and also contributed to it, particularly as a mentor to women artists. Blackman was not only the first hip hop artist to work on behalf of the State Department, but she became one of its most traveled performers, working in dozens of countries on five continents. In the first part of the new century she, more than anyone else, was the face and voice of hip hop diplomacy.

Just six months after Blackman's return from Africa, two skyscrapers collapsed a few miles from her home in Brooklyn. Following the terrorist attacks of September 11, 2001, the Department of State increased its cultural programming, particularly in response to international disapproval—notably but not solely among Muslim-majority nations—of America's military actions in Afghanistan and Iraq. Cultural diplomacy had come to take on a significance and urgency not known since the days of the Cold War.

One of the first post-9/11 forms of hip hop diplomacy actually came from outside the State Department, in the form of the Voice of America's "Hip Hop Connection" radio show. Launched in 2002 as a 30-minute feature within the Voices of Africa program, it grew into a self-contained hour-long show broadcast first to Africa, and then to the rest of the world. It featured hip hop music and news, and interviews with prominent artists—among them Ludacris, Method Man, and TI—who stopped by the studio in Southwest Washington, DC to chat with the hosts. "Hip Hop Connection" also took on an active role in the fight against AIDS in Africa and included educational programming and even visits by the show's hosts to Malawi and Zambia. According to longtime host Rod Murray, the show was established to engage younger audiences, and to get these listeners interested in other Voice of America (VOA) programs.[45] Like the VOA's "Jazz Hour," hugely popular during the Cold War, "Hip Hop Connection" worked alongside the State Department's people-to-people exchanges to promote better relations through contemporary youth culture.

In the post-9/11 era, cultural diplomacy came to be seen as an exemplary form of *soft power*, a term that political scientist Joseph Nye coined to describe the influence that a state can exert through appeal and persuasion rather than through directly coercive action. As he explained, "A country may obtain the outcomes it wants in world politics because other countries—admiring its values, emulating its example, aspiring to its level of prosperity and openness—want to follow it."[46] But in the wake of unpopular invasions and human rights violations, international admiration of the United States was at a low point. Once again, cultural diplomacy was called on to play a remediating role, acting as a salve to be applied to America's self-inflicted wounds.

Starting in 2004, the State Department's engagement of hip hop artists expanded and intensified. Many of these tours and residencies took place in Muslim-majority nations, but America's reputation needed repair everywhere, and the itineraries reflect a broad-based approach. After Toni Blackman, one of the State Department's first hip hop envoys was Houston's Havikoro Dance Crew. The organizer of their first trip—to Azerbaijan in April 2004—was John Ferguson. A classically trained pianist and executive director of the non-profit arts organization, American Voices, he had for years been arranging cultural diplomacy programs for US embassies around the world; this would be his first foray into hip hop. Hip hop was not particularly well known in Azerbaijan, and some locals objected to Havikoro's presence at a jazz festival in the capital, Baku. "Can someone explain to me how this new-fangled breakdance is jazz?" asked one writer.[47] According to Ferguson, the dancers were the first US hip hop artists to perform in Azerbaijan, and were wildly popular: "Everywhere that Havikoro went there would be a huge turnout from young people, especially in the 12 to 25 age range."[48]

One year later, Havikoro was in Vietnam to kick off the tenth anniversary of the normalization of relations between the United States and Vietnam. This tour, also arranged by American Voices, was a formidable undertaking, with shows before more than 4000 people in both Hanoi and Ho Chi Minh City; many more saw the television broadcasts. A report from the US Embassy reveals that the choice of hip hop was intended to offer "a vivid example of how we can reach younger and broader audiences by looking to unconventional sources within America's diverse music culture."[49] It was a risky move that nearly failed. Communist Party officials, apprehensive about the effect of hip hop on Vietnamese youth, were reluctant to issue the permits for the events. Only intense lobbying averted disaster. In the end, at least according to the embassy, this "cultural exchange extravaganza" was a "public relations triumph" that accomplished its main objective: it heightened the positive image of American culture and helped improve US-Vietnam relations.[50]

As the b-boys of Houston took Vietnam by storm, ECA's civil servants were retooling their musical diplomacy programming back in DC. In 2005, a jazz-focused program became Rhythm Road: American Music Abroad, and later simply American Music Abroad. The new name signaled a change in scope, which now included contemporary popular music. In that first 2005–2006 season, three hip hop acts embarked on month-long tours: Toni Blackman, the Washington, DC trio Opus Akoben, and the Atlanta group AFAR. Blackman visited southeast Asia; Opus Akoben traveled to the Middle East; and AFAR toured southern Africa and South America.[51]

Also in 2005, Karen Hughes, formerly a close advisor to President George W. Bush, became Undersecretary of State for Public Diplomacy. One of the highest ranking officials in the Department, she was a vocal proponent of cultural diplomacy during her two-year tenure. In a 2007 article she noted how the United States had tripled its funding for cultural diplomacy since 2001 and was expanding its reach in innovative ways; she mentioned hip hop favorably as part of the State Department's expanded portfolio.[52] Hughes specifically lauded the Los Angeles–based band Ozomatli as a fine example of cultural diplomacy at work, citing their visit to Nepal to help promote a voter registration drive.

Ozomatli became one of the most frequently deployed and perhaps least likely exponents of hip hop diplomacy. The group had a long history of promoting social justice activism through politically-informed songs that combined rapped vocals, funk grooves, and influences from a variety of Latin styles. They were, sonically and visually, a perfect symbol of the multicultural United States—performing in Spanish as well as English, melding musical traditions from around the world, and representing a variety of immigrant groups. Yet they were also well-known for their anti-government stance. In their 1998 song, "Coming War," for example, they protest

> Uncle Sam is robbing you blind and putting shackles 'pon
> The minds of your children for real, son
> Beware this system and go to war with this institution[53]

Ozomatli's record of speaking out against the government communicated a potent message during a time when their country's reputation around the world could hardly have degraded further. Their 2007 performances in North Africa and the Middle East offered an example of democracy in action, suggesting to Muslim youth that the United States truly valued difference and dissent—at least enough to send a band that had railed against its own government. Ironically, the United States was so hated that perhaps the only way to gain the trust of its detractors was to send Americans who agreed with their criticisms.

In 2012, ECA added two more exchange programs to its stable, in the process bringing more hip hop into the mix. CenterStage and OneBeat were designed as inbound programs—facilitating cultural exchange by inviting artists from around the world to perform in the United States. In CenterStage's inaugural year, the Indonesian group Jogja Hip Hop Foundation toured six cities on the east and west coasts; one photo from CenterStage's website showed pioneer hip hop DJ GrandWizzard Theodore posing with the group.[54] OneBeat took a different approach, forming ad hoc ensembles of domestic and international musicians to tour the United States, among them several rappers.[55] By 2013, dozens of US hip hop artists had toured scores of countries, whether as one-off events at the invitation of embassies or through programs such as American Music Abroad.

Soon hip hop was to have its own program, and become a focal point of US cultural diplomacy.

## TAKING HIP HOP DIPLOMACY TO THE NEXT LEVEL

It was 2013, and three program officers in the Cultural Programs Division—Julia Gómez-Nelson, Michele Peregrin, and Jill Staggs—got together over coffee to discuss an unusual problem: they had money, and needed to figure out what to do with it.[56] Funding had become available to create a new cultural diplomacy program on the scale of American Music Abroad and OneBeat, and the challenge was to devise something that would serve the State Department's priorities, meet the approval of the higher-ups, and suit the needs of overseas diplomatic posts.

The Mutual Education and Cultural Exchange Act of 1961 is best known for launching the Fulbright Program, the State Department's flagship international exchange program. More broadly, it led to the founding of the Bureau of Educational and Cultural Affairs, home of the Cultural Programs Division. The program officers dreaming up the new initiative had to keep in mind ECA's core mission, which, as the preamble of the Act declares, is to "increase mutual understanding between the people of the United States and the people other countries by means of educational and cultural exchange," which in turn would "assist in the development of friendly, sympathetic, and peaceful relations."[57] How that understanding is to be achieved, and how such exchange would take shape, necessarily changes over time. At least since the incendiary protests of 1968, both in the United States and throughout the world, this has meant appealing to youth. And according to the steady flow of reports and requests from overseas diplomatic posts, the youth wanted hip hop.

These program officers did not need to be convinced that the next ECA cultural diplomacy program should focus on hip hop. But as in 2000, when Toni Blackman was first engaged as an American Cultural Specialist, they were worried about the optics of government-supported hip hop. In fact, just as the program officers were brainstorming over coffee, something like the "nightmare scenario" that had worried colleagues back in 2000 actually occurred. In early 2013 the neoconservative opinion magazine *The*

*Weekly Standard* cited a State Department press release announcing that "San Francisco-based hip hop group Audiopharmacy will tour Southeast Asia and the Pacific as part of the American Music Abroad program."[58] It was red meat for critics of the State Department, the Obama administration, and hip hop. "The US State Department is going hip hop," declared the *Washington Times*, noting that "the size of the tab Uncle Sam will stick to taxpayers is unclear."[59] Conservative bloggers quickly followed suit, heaping derision on what was presented as a self-evident waste of federal funds.

Although the episode generated no serious fallout, State Department officials were alarmed, ever warier of "going hip hop." Or as Paul Rockower, at the time director of communications for American Music Abroad, put it, "State freaked out."[60] This episode did not dissuade ECA's program officers from pursuing a hip hop program, but they would have to offer a compelling case to their superiors. They did this in part by offering an innovative approach. First, the program would be interdisciplinary. Traditionally, visual arts programs did not include the performing arts, and vice versa, and among the performing arts programs dance and music were usually kept separate. As the document describing the program makes clear, a successful proposal would have to include three of the following: "music, dance, MC/spoken word, film, and visual arts."[61]

Second, the program would have concrete objectives beyond simply "fostering mutual understanding," a typical phrase used to describe other cultural diplomacy programs. In particular, the program was explicitly intended to promote entrepreneurship and conflict resolution strategies among youth, two priorities within the State Department meant to address serious real-world problems. This was clearly a strategy to demonstrate the relevance and potential effectiveness of the program and to convince doubters to take hip hop seriously.

A third distinctive feature of the program was the two-way nature of the exchange. Many ECA programs are either outbound or inbound—they send US citizens abroad or they bring foreigners to the United States. This program would do both, first sending teams of US artists to different countries around the world, and then inviting a team of young international artists—one from each country the program visited—to the United States for a two-week residency. This two-way flow was meant to address the abiding challenge of achieving lasting impact. The international artists would be chosen for their leadership qualities and their commitment to serving their communities, with the idea that they would, as the program description states, "extend the multiplier effect of this project through continuing work with young people."[62] The mutuality of the exchange would also help avoid what is seen as the absence of real collaboration or partnership in US foreign aid in general. Plot Mhako, founder of the Zimbabwean non-profit Jibilika Dance Trust that worked with a group of US hip hop artists in early 2015, was expecting what he derisively calls a "give and take program." This is a typical approach in his experience, where "foreigners are coming to give us something they assume we don't have [and] say, 'This is how we're doing it and you take it.'"[63]

On March 13, 2013, the program was announced with what seems to be a purposefully vague name: Creative Arts Exchange: Arts in Collaboration.[64] Based on its title, no one would have reason to assume that this was a hip hop exchange. It's clear that the program was devised with the goal of surviving in an inhospitable environment. Program officers at ECA and the cultural affairs staff in diplomatic posts around the world approach cultural diplomacy with a certain pragmatic idealism. They tend to be sincerely committed to the arts, believing in its power to connect people and effect positive change. Yet they are also savvy, aware of the need to convince the less idealistic, more skeptical, and more powerful to support their programs. The necessity of careful negotiation and maneuvering gives lie to the myth of the monolithic State Department. The birth of hip hop diplomacy is in part the story of a small, passionate, and marginalized group working within a titanic bureaucracy to achieve the unlikely goal of empowering a small, passionate, and marginalized group of citizens to represent the United States through its art. That these two groups had little else in common complicates the story in intriguing ways.

I entered the picture in April 2013 when Pierce Freelon, a Durham, North Carolina–based MC, educator, and social activist told me about the call for proposals. Along with local beatmaker Stephen Levitin (aka Apple Juice Kid), we had previously developed a program called Beat Making Lab. As Freelon wrote to me, the State Department program was "wildly up Beat Making Lab's alley," and he encouraged me to apply.[65] Beat Making Lab was essentially a smaller-scale version of what the State Department was proposing. It began as a two-week residency at the Yole!Africa cultural center in Goma, Democratic Republic of the Congo, facilitated by Chérie Rivers Ndaliko and Petna Ndaliko Katondolo, directors of the center. Freelon and Levitin guided a group of Congolese teenagers and young adults in the art of electronic music composition, which, in hip hop, is called beatmaking, or producing; upon departing they donated equipment to Yole! for the continued use of the local community. A film about the visit, and recordings made by the Congolese youth with Freelon and Levitin, gained the attention of PBS, the US public broadcaster, which sponsored a series of Beat Making Labs to be featured on its website.[66] Freelon and Levitin traveled to Panama, Senegal, Fiji, and Ethiopia for similar residencies in 2012 and 2013.

Given my experience with Beat Making Lab and my previous work with hip hop artists through my teaching and scholarship, I decided to apply, and was awarded the grant in the fall of 2013. But a conflict immediately arose, one that needed to be resolved before the program could even be announced. Jill Staggs, the program officer I would be working with, alerted me that some of her colleagues were uneasy about the proposed name: Beat Academy. One was concerned that it was too close to an existing cultural diplomacy program, OneBeat; another worried that "beat" suggested conflict or violence. Moreover, the chief of the division indicated that "America," "American," or "USA" should be in the name, in line with most outbound ECA cultural programs, such as American Music Abroad, American Film Showcase, or American Arts Incubator. Staggs then passed along some possible alternatives from her colleagues, including "American Street Beat," "Get Hip USA!" and "Youth Engagement through the Arts (YEA!)." "American Street Beat" was a particular favorite. They probably didn't realize that "Street Beat" was very close to *Beat Street*, a 1984 film about hip hop culture in

New York City. In 2013, "Street Beat" sounded out of date and corny. As I explained in a message to Staggs, it "has something of a 1980s ring to it now, and I worry that it would be harder to recruit good people with that name. There's some kind of thing at Epcot called 'Mickey's American Street Beat,' too. We want to be wholesome, but not that wholesome."[67]

Among the circle of artists I consulted there was also pushback about having the name identify the program explicitly as American. Rapper and poet Kane Smego explained the concern in this way:

> I think that it is important for a project whose goal is to har-
> ness, celebrate, and emphasize the cultures of other nations
> to avoid making its thrust seem to be the promotion of its
> own nation. The project is obviously from the United States
> and doesn't need to brand itself as such, but rather should
> seek to be universal enough that the nations involved in
> collaboration feel like the title equally represents them all.
> A Senegalese musician may not feel as proud in mentioning
> and promoting a project that he/she is involved in if it seems
> like it is "property" of another nation not their own. In short,
> a title gives folks a sense of ownership over the work they are
> involved in and should therefore be as universal as possible.[68]

Yet what Smego opposed—explicit national branding—is precisely one of the State Department's objectives in creating international exchange programs. If US cultural diplomacy is to promote the country's image abroad, its programs must be readily identifiable as American.

I requested additional names from ECA and was offered this one: "American Street Beat Academy." I despaired. It was not simply that I thought the names coming out of ECA were weak; it's not just that I would be embarrassed to be director of something called "American Street Beat Academy" (or "Get Hip USA!"). Worse, those names would be received by hip hop artists as evidence of the State Department's lack of respect for hip hop. Those best qualified to propel the program to success, I believed, would be reluctant to participate. I expressed my worries as diplomatically as possible, and to their credit and my relief, they were willing to entertain a new slate of names. Among the names that Freelon and some trusted associates suggested were Hip Hop X, Planet Hip Hop, and Vibe Worldwide. I also threw in my own: Next Level. ECA rejected most of these names; they didn't want "hip hop" in the title and backed away from anything that seemed too edgy. In the end, the only name they embraced was Next Level. I imagine that it was acceptable because of its positive, aspirational tone, and because it wouldn't read to colleagues or legislators as hip hop. Nevertheless, the phrase is common and meaningful within hip hop culture. To take something to the next level is to excel, to surpass expectations, to transcend the expected.

"Next Level" turned out to be a fine compromise, and was readily accepted by the artists who participated in the program. To Jorge Pabon, the pioneering hip hop dancer better known as Popmaster Fabel, the name captured the productive tensions that animate hip hop: "There's a progressive and competitive spirit activated through Hip Hop that constantly inspires us to push towards our full potential as artists and human beings. Artistic battles among each other, and against ourselves, help us to obtain mastery of self by reaching the Next Level!"[69] Fellow dancer Amirah Sackett offered a poetic reading that values the process of striving as much as the achievement of goals. "When we are in between levels we feel uncomfortable, we feel stuck. But transitions are the greatest times for growth. Reaching the next level is the breakthrough, it's the explosion of everything in our past giving way to new creation."[70] Or as Diamond D, a Grammy-winning producer, simply put it, "Next Level = Above and beyond what is considered the norm. To transcend boundaries and/or limitations."[71]

In April 2014, with the new name in place, a group of twenty-five hip hop artists gathered in a Washington, DC hotel conference room, less than a mile from the State Department. Hailing from across the United States, among the fifteen men and ten women were established artists

Next Level design by Sanoizm, a Cleveland-based artist who participated in the 2018 Next Level residency in Cambodia.

and revered pioneers—including Toni Blackman, Popmaster Fabel, and Diamond D—community activists, high school teachers, and a psychologist with a PhD. Some were financially secure, some recently homeless, some had spent time in prison. There were openly queer artists; Christians, Muslims, Jews, and atheists; African Americans, Asian Americans, Latinx, and a handful of white folks.

As a whole, the Next Level "family" (a term the artists use) has been more racially and ethnically diverse, more activist, queerer, more feminist, and less male-dominated than the general population of hip hop artists. Those who responded to the call for applications—which asked them to explain how their art could help promote cultural exchange— were a self-selecting group, and many had an activist bent. In her application, rapper Shirlette Ammons identified herself as a "Queer Black Feminist Woman in Hip Hop." "I am always interested," Ammons wrote, "in pushing the margins of perceptions around who 'belongs' in . . . Hip Hop culture while encouraging audiences to engage Hip Hop from various points of intersection."[72] The presence of Ammons and other queer people in Next Level also pushed back against the State Department's own history of discrimination, most shamefully illustrated by the so-called Lavender Scare of the early 1950s when hundreds of employees were fired solely because of their homosexuality.[73] This first class of Next Level artists, chosen from a pool of more than 150 applicants, would defy the expectations of those who deem hip hop to be irredeemably materialistic, misogynist, homophobic, and violent. This group (and those that followed) tended to be more attuned to the underground than the mainstream, as committed to social justice as they were to their careers. They saw hip hop as a way of life, not simply a lifestyle.

On the second day of the inaugural Next Level orientation, the artists visited ECA's headquarters in the Foggy Bottom neighborhood. They queued up for the metal detector, emptied their pockets, donned visitor badges, and followed staffers up to a conference room. Stacy White, head of the Cultural Programs Division, greeted them enthusiastically. "Thank you for your service to your country," she told them. With slides at the ready, she talked about the history of cultural diplomacy, from the jazz tours to the 1961 Fulbright-Hayes Act. She presented cultural diplomacy in terms of humility and mutuality rather than exceptionalism. "We think about peace. We think about developing mutual trust among people. We don't consider ourselves perfect," she explained. "We think of ourselves as an experiment in progress."[74]

Next Level's State Department visit was a study in contrasts on every level. The hip hop artists didn't look, act, or speak like the bureaucrats that populated ECA's offices. Some wore jeans and hoodies, others sported colorful scarves and copious bangles. They laughed a lot. Sitting around that conference table, waiting for the officials to make their PowerPoint presentations, they started to jam. Elliot "Philipdrummond" Gann pulled a small loudspeaker out of his pocket, connected it to his phone, and set one of his beats going. Others clapped along, chanted "Next Level," or turned plastic water bottles into percussion instruments. "Just getting' started/chillin' up in the State Department," Kane Smego freestyled. "Sittin' at the table like a politician/yeah, but the drama's missin'/Where's Obama at?/I wanna ask him what we're free to do/worldwide." Fabel displayed his signature popping style as he danced in the tight space from the door to his seat. Everyone laughed at Toni Blackman's rhyme about the mediocre quality

Next Level orientation, US Department of State. Left to right: DJ A-Minor, Diamond D, Asheru, Toni Blackman, Junious Brickhouse. Washington, DC, April 28, 2014. Photograph by Paul Rockower.

Next Level orientation cypher, US Department of State. Dancer Ken Fury is in the center.
Washington, DC, April 28, 2014. Photograph by Paul Rockower.

of lunch and her higher hopes for dinner. After the briefing, the music
and dance continued in the marble-floored, flag-lined lobby, where
the artists launched an impromptu performance, known as a cypher.
Standing in a circle, they created a rhythmic track, clapping, stamping,
and beatboxing. One by one, they moved in and out of the center of the
circle, improvising rhymes or steps. In some ways it evoked the early
history of hip hop, when dancers in New York would sneak into posh
apartment buildings to practice their moves on smooth lobby floors.[75]
Here, the security guards watched warily but didn't intervene. The
dark-suited stream of civil servants flowing into and out of the elevator
banks slowed to witness the spontaneous performance, some stopping
to clap along or capture the moment on their phones. Once the cypher concluded the hip hop artists relinquished their badges and filed
out, marveling to each other about the experience, both exhilarating
and odd.

US cultural diplomacy has always been an exercise in harnessing the power of colliding worlds. Collisions can be heedless, violent, and destructive. They can also be purposeful and productive, generating energy like striking flints or smashing atoms. The story of hip hop diplomacy is a story of collisions—between art and diplomacy; between hip hop and the state; among cultures, traditions, and values; between the United States and the rest of the world. But above all it is the story of the people and communities who come together because of the art they create through hip hop.

## CHAPTER 2

# BOOM BAP DIPLOMACY: CONNECTING CULTURES, TRANSFORMING CONFLICT

It's a balmy February evening in the southern Thai city of Surat Thani where we've gathered for a jam session. Professor Thirabhand Chandracharoen is sitting on the floor of the classroom, unpacking his *chakhe*, a Thai zither. Next Level artists DJ Dirty Digits and beatmaker RyNea Soul plug in their gear on two desks in front of the room. Chandracharoen starts playing first, his plucked melody creating a slight buzzing sound characteristic of the *chakhe*. Digits then scratches a record in syncopated rasps, while RyNea taps out a pattern of bass and snare drum beats on her drum machine—"boom bap" in hip hop terminology.[1] We're all excited to see how this mix of analog and digital, traditional and modern will turn out.

It doesn't work.

RyNea and Digits are used to playing together, but they don't mesh with the long, graceful phrases of the *chakhe*. Music may be universal, but there's no singular, universally comprehensible style—we're witnessing a musical version of Babel. I hesitantly offer some suggestions. I ask Digits to scratch along with the Chandracharoen's phrasing, however long or short. I don't speak Thai, so I make a series of hand gestures to suggest that Chandracharoen play and repeat a short phrase. He understands and tries it. In hip hop this is called looping a beat, and it allows Digits to follow him more easily. With my finger as a baton, I start conducting, four beats to the measure, and with a two-bar warning, I count RyNea in. She enters with a commanding *boom bap* on beats two and four, and the three of them lock in tight. They have found their groove. For the next several minutes the musicians trade solos seamlessly, coordinating the strands of their dialogue through sound and gesture. The experience is exhilarating and gratifying.[2]

This encounter captures cultural diplomacy in microcosm, both in its rewards and risks. Two parties with little common culture, history, or language connect with each other. They do this by sharing and combining their cultural expertise, and also by accommodating each other. Art serves as a bridge, closing the distance between them.

Yet the experience unsettled me. I felt uneasy asking Prof. Chandracharoen to simplify his elegant phrases and forego improvisation. As I was conducting, I remember thinking, "My God, am I an imperialist in 4/4 time?" How different was I from the Western missionary who insists that the "natives" abandon or compromise their traditions? Yes, I could defend my intervention—the trio insisted that I continue conducting during the jam session, as well as at a public performance the next day, and Chandracharoen played a solo at the show unfettered by my participation. Still, I had good reason to feel uncomfortable about my role.

Even within a casual jam, hip hop diplomacy is unavoidably political, and consequential. What happens in these workshops, jam sessions, masterclasses, and public performances resounds beyond the moment, and can connect people as well as divide them. But how can making art together further the work of international diplomacy—or derail it?

Something mysterious often takes place when performers improvise together. Communication flows invisibly, and without so much as a word spoken the artists make dozens of decisions. No one knows how it might turn out, and surprises await performers and witnesses alike; yet at the end of a particularly satisfying collaboration it all feels inevitable, as if every moment had been preordained. Such moments of artistic creation may strike us as extraordinary, but they are not separate from our everyday existence. They can, as ethnomusicologist Benjamin Brinner writes, offer "a different way of being and acting together, even serving as a catalyst for social

DJ Dirty Digits, Thirabhand Chandracharoen, RyNea Soul performing in Surat Thani, Thailand, February 19, 2016. Photograph by Mark Katz.

change."[3] This point is a key to understanding how hip hop diplomacy can succeed or fail. Artists who gather to play, dance, sing, or paint are doing more than making art. And when they reach across national, cultural, and linguistic boundaries they can transform barriers into bridges—or widen the gulf that separates them.[4]

Consider a cypher. A central site of hip hop creativity, a cypher is an impromptu performing space—a gathering of rappers or beatboxers or dancers, usually standing in a circle. It may look simple, but a complex set of social interactions guides it at all times. A cypher is leaderless; every individual makes decisions that affect its shape, flow, and success. All of these decisions are influenced by unwritten and evolving norms. Some cyphers meet at specific times and places, with regular participants who connect every week or month over a period of years. Some form spontaneously, whether among friends or strangers. And though every cypher is distinct, there are some basic rules that participants generally abide by,

Cypher in Harare, Zimbabwe, February 2015. Photograph by Paul Rockower.

consciously or not. Only one person may be in the center at a time. Don't interrupt or disrupt someone's solo, don't take too long in the center, don't take too many turns. Freestyle—improvise—rather than reproduce a rhyme or routine you've already created. Avoid unwanted physical contact with others. The rules can be broken, but they exist for good reason: to maintain order, to promote social cohesion, to foster creativity and self-expression.[5]

It's no stretch to say that cyphers reflect social conditions and relationships outside the circle. That's because they evolved as a ritualized form of often aggressive, violent interactions that many youth in New York faced in the 1970s and 1980s during the early years of hip hop. Speaking about this time, Bronx b-boy Trac 2 explained how hip hop allowed young people to express themselves constructively, to discover power that was long denied them:

> In an oppressive society, we had something that we needed
> to say, through this form of aggression. We just adapted,
> overcame, and just excelled. The whole essence of what

people portray as hip hop is basically the youth recognizing who they are through self-expression . . . You know, for a kid that's 10, 11, 12, going into his early teens, it became very empowering. It allowed us to be who we are and express it the way we wanted to express it. And, basically, the whole cultural movement was founded on that.[6]

Decades later and across the continents, people continue to embrace hip hop as a means of self-expression and empowerment.

## CROSS-CULTURAL COLLABORATION, NONVERBAL COMMUNICATION

When b-boy Frankie Perez watches dancers in motion, he is not simply witnessing their performances. He is also reading the performers. "I feel like I can get some insights into their personality, the way that they think, in some cases even how they were brought up," he explains.[7] His own embodied knowledge of footwork, spins, and freezes carries with it the memory of the paths that led him to their mastery, and when he sees others perform he catches a glimpse of their paths, their thought processes, their creativity. Even if they don't say a word, they tell him a great deal.

It's easy to see why nonverbal communication is so important to dancers, but it also matters to that most verbal of hip hop arts: rapping. T.R.U.T.H, a Chicago MC who traveled to Baku, Azerbaijan with Next Level, discovered this when working with young rappers who rhymed in languages—Azerbaijani, Russian, and Turkish—that she did not speak. It was a revelation to discover just how much she could understand and communicate, even without an interpreter's assistance: "When you're just focusing on the energy and how it comes across, it is actually much more powerful."[8] I witnessed this power up close when, in April 2015, I organized a cypher on the campus of UNC-Chapel Hill to connect local MCs with a group of visiting international artists. Black Zang, hailing from Dhaka, spit in rapid-fire Bengali; Dakaroise MC Toussa rhymed in a combination of Wolof and French. The locals understood not a word, but they still understood a great deal, for the visitors' faces and gestures spoke volumes. They told their stories with a hand on the heart, an earnest skyward glance, a clenched fist or a wagging finger, a smile or a grimace. Zlijay, a Sarajevan DJ, directed the flow of the cypher from behind a table full of gear; dancer Angelo from Belgrade impressed everyone with his signature freeze; Malabika, a singer from Kolkata, belted impassioned folk songs in Bengali, and Zimbabwean FTR made beats, rapped in English and Shona, and danced. As the evening wound down, locals and visitors alike remarked that the cypher—fueled by nonverbal communication—was one of the most meaningful they had ever attended.

The success of cross-cultural artistic engagement depends in good part on how practitioners express themselves and communicate with one other nonverbally. The risks and rewards of these encounters were at play when Klevah and Konshens, two US rappers, performed with

Cross-cultural performance. Left to right: DJ A-Minor (United States), Black Zang (Bangladesh), Zlijay (Bosnia), FTR (Zimbabwe), Toussa Senerap (Senegal), Malabika Brahma (India), Angelo (Serbia), University of North Carolina at Chapel Hill, April 13, 2015. Photograph by Mark Katz.

a *gnawa* ensemble in Meknes, Morocco in 2017, first in a jam session
and then at a public concert. *Gnawa* descends from the sacred music
of enslaved West Africans who had been forcibly relocated to Morocco.
Jazz artist Randy Weston, whose tours to Africa in the 1960s were
supported by the State Department, explained the music in this way: "If
you can imagine hearing the black church, jazz, and the blues all at the
same time, in their original form, with all these rhythms coming together, that's what it's like."[9] What he describes as "all these rhythms
coming together" is *gnawa*'s characteristic play of three notes against
two between metal castanets known as *qraqabs* and the lead instrument
known as the *guembri*, a three-stringed bass lute.[10] This rhythm is rare
in hip hop, and it clearly unsettled the visiting US rappers.

The setting for the jam session was the seventeenth-century Palais Al-
Mansour, in a room with red rugs covering the smooth stone floor. The
*m'allem*, the spiritual and musical leader of the group, greeted them. El
Meknassi, as he is known, wore an embroidered green jacket, pants, and
skullcap, his *guembri* slung over his right shoulder. In his mid-fifties,
he was accompanied by several younger band members, both men and
women, decked out in traditional red outfits, who sang, danced, and
kept the three-against-two rhythms alive with their *qraqabs*.

Klevah didn't know what to expect. She listened for a while and then
jumped in. "I tried freestyling, but . . . there was a disconnect. I would
be good for about four, five, six bars, and then I would not even be able
to go past that. It was only a couple of moments where I felt really in the
pocket."[11] The pocket, a term hip hop inherited from jazz, is a state in
which artists lock in rhythmically, connecting with each other almost
effortlessly. Klevah describes being in the pocket as "floating in a way,
because you don't have to try too hard. You don't really have to try at
all. It's just a really natural feeling, and it agrees with you, and it's an
exchange."

But she couldn't quite get in the pocket. "I was standing up, I was
moving around the space. That wasn't working for me, so when I actually sat down, my body was calm. Instead of thinking about it, I just
really tried to feel it. So, I just slowed down, I slowed my mind down.

I would . . . try to actually find a head nod to it, just vibe to it for a while to a point where the words would just come." To find a head nod is to synchronize one's body with a beat, bobbing in time with the music like a human metronome. Hip hop artists try to get their audiences nodding along, sometimes describing the effect it achieves as "headnodic," a play on the word "hypnotic." Klevah never felt entirely comfortable during the jam session, but as she explained, "I was comfortable enough to keep trying." The encounter inspired her: "The experience was a challenge. It makes me want to practice more, freestyling to different time signatures."

Konshens was also at the Palais Al-Mansour that evening. He likewise felt the challenge of connecting his rhyming to the *gnawa* groove. And he also struggled. But whereas Klevah turned inward, sitting down and slowing her mind, Konshens engaged with the musicians on a physical level, literally reaching out to El Meknassi:

> I walked over to the leader of the band. I leaned in his ear and I started patting his shoulder in 4/4-time signature, four beats per measure. As I was tapping his shoulder . . . I started beatboxing. Then, he starts to beat on the guitar [*guembri*]. As he's hitting the guitar at four beats per measure, I'm hitting his shoulder four beats per measure. I started rapping in his ear. Because I'm tapping his shoulder in four beats per measure, he is gathering the cadence, the timing that I'm rapping in. Then he starts playing the same bass line. Then he starts smiling. He stepped back, he nodded his head yes, I nodded my head yes. He pointed his finger up. I said, "Okay, let's go from the top," and that's how it happened.[12]

I asked Konshens why he thought the *gnawa* leader would be open to having him tap his shoulder and rap into his ear, actions that might have offended the *m'allem*, or any performer for that matter. "What I did was I attempted to rap to his music first, to the way he was playing it first, before I interjected anything," he told me. "I just kept trying different cadences, different inflections, different everything . . . so that we got to a point we both started laughing. That's when I walked over to him and started tapping his shoulder." Because they couldn't speak with each other in Arabic, French, or English, they communicated through their gestures and facial expressions. "He just looked at me and started smiling. I want to say that that actually garnered a form of respect, the fact that I didn't come in with like, 'Yeah, okay, so everybody's going to have to conform to this shit right here.'"

El Meknassi had never performed with hip hop artists before. But once he heard Klevah and Konshens rap, he immediately felt a connection: "My opinion is that hip hop is ready made for gnawa," he wrote to me after the encounter.[13] The two traditions, he posited, "have the same roots," referring to the fact that many *gnawa* musicians and African American hip hop artists are descended from enslaved West Africans. He felt enough of a connection that he was confident that they could "resolve the [musical] disagreements between us." And he didn't mind that Konshens tapped out a beat on his shoulder. Although he admitted that "maybe another gnawa would not understand Konshens' gesture," he called it "a gesture of musical fraternity and . . . a way for artists to understand each other."

Later that week, the Next Level artists—Konshens and Klevah along with b-boy Edson "House" Magana and DJ Zephyr Ann—performed with hip hop artists from across the country as well as with El Meknassi's group. The theater was packed with young Moroccans who, dancing on their seats and in the aisles, clearly enjoyed the mix of hip hop traditions and the *gnawa* collaboration, a hybrid that El Meknassi dubbed "Hip Gnawa Hop, H-G-H."

This encounter reveals a range of strategies in which two groups, unfamiliar with each other's music, language, and culture, can find common ground. Klevah and Konshens initially approached the jam session with El Meknassi in the same way. Both sought to understand the music before rapping a word. Both joined in tentatively, trying to groove with the *gnawa* but floundering at first. Then their strategies diverged. Klevah continued to seek ways to understand and accommodate El Meknassi, whereas Konshens proposed—nonverbally—that El

Konshens the MC, M'allem Abdenbi El Fakir (aka El Meknassi), and Klevah performing in Meknes, Morocco, 15 September 2017. Notice Konshens's hand tapping El Meknassi's shoulder. Photograph by Saleem Reshamwala.

Meknassi accommodate him. And when they performed in the public show, Klevah freestyled, matching her syllables to El Meknassi's eighth notes, while Konshens rapped a song that he already written, "Sound of the City." El Meknassi took yet a different approach; he played first, letting the two MCs move in and out of the pocket with him, initially making no attempt to adjust to the visitors. But in the end he did the most accommodation by having the *qraqab* players stay silent and turning his part into a two-bar loop. It was El Meknassi who opened up the pocket that allowed them to groove together.[14]

The process was challenging and sometimes frustrating, but ultimately rewarding. It could have easily failed. Klevah might have called off her search for the pocket. Konshens and El Meknassi might have

B-girl DQ (left) and Edson "House" Magana (right), Meknes, Morocco, September 9, 2017. Photograph by Saleem Reshamwala.

stalked off in frustration, concluding that the other wasn't skilled or willing enough to make it work. But they succeeded, and not simply because they each listened, and each compromised. They succeeded because they were they able to come into physical alignment, moving their bodies in sympathy with each other. There's a formal term for this phenomenon: kinesthetic empathy. Scientists, scholars, mental health experts, and artists alike have become fascinated with kinesthetic empathy, seeking to tap into a form of human interaction that can create bonds as strong as anything that might arise through verbal agreement.[15] Nonverbal communication, especially when it occurs within artistic collaboration, is more than a way to compensate for the lack of a shared language. It can be—and should be—a vital component of cross-cultural exchange and diplomatic practice.

## TRANSFORMING CONFLICT THROUGH HIP HOP

I was walking the darkened streets of Belgrade with Andjelko Pavlovic, a long-limbed Serbian hip hop dancer better known as Angelo

Spaghetti. We had just left a subway station where we watched a group of b-boys and b-girls practicing their spins on the hard, smooth floor. After leaving the subway, I asked Angelo a question that had been on my mind all day: given the region's history of bloody conflicts, was there any tension among hip hop artists from the different Balkan nations? "Not at all," he said, surprised by my question. He constantly collaborated with artists from neighboring countries; in fact, he was organizing the eighth edition of Balkan Fury, a regional hip hop dance festival. But why, I pressed, could these young artists get along when their countries had committed such atrocities against each other? His answer was simple.

"You can't fight when you're dancing together."[16]

This statement reveals profound truths. The mere act of creating art together in the same space has the potential to reduce tensions and foster understanding. As Daniel Fischlin, Ajay Heble, and George Lipsitz claim in their book, *The Fierce Urgency of Now*, improvisation "teaches us to make 'a way' out of 'no way' by cultivating the capacity to discern hidden elements of possibility, hope, and promise in even the most discouraging circumstances."[17]

How and why this works in practice is hardly simple and never automatic. Art has the power to resolve conflict but also to generate it. Music is often thought of as purely a good, but it serves evil as well: Nazis used it to whip up support among the German citizenry; the US military tortured prisoners of war in Iraq and Guantánamo with it; Mexican narcos have celebrated their murderous deeds through it. Hip hop itself has a long history of beefs and disses, and real violence has erupted between rivals, the murders of Tupac Shakur and Biggie Smalls in 1996 being just the most famous examples. Conflict is interwoven with hip hop's history: cyphers and battles simulate violence, and throughout the history of hip hop there have been artists with criminal backgrounds and criminals with hip hop aspirations. And violence has been a recurring theme in hip hop lyrics and videos, notably in gangsta rap, which arose in the 1990s and has flourished in the decades since.

The idea that hip hop can address conflict, then, might seem counterintuitive. And yet, hip hop's very existence can be understood as a form of conflict transformation. When DJs battle each other with their soundsystems or through their virtuosic scratch routines, they transform physical conflict into sonic conflict; when b-boys and b-girls challenge each other within the cypher, their aggressive moves replace fistfights; when MCs diss each other they release their anger into rhyme; when graffiti writers tag public spaces they claim territory through art rather than by force. Since hip hop emerged in the 1970s countless young people have been drawn to it precisely because it offers ways to transform the conflict in their lives.

Conflict resolution was a central interest of the program officers who launched Next Level; part of its stated purpose was "to explore and address conflict resolution strategies."[18] I prefer the phrase *conflict transformation*, which suggests a more holistic approach that is not limited to resolving specific conflicts. Conflict is simply a part of life, something that cannot be eradicated and is not necessarily negative; conflict should be acknowledged and understood, harnessed when it can be productive or transformed into self-expression.

Transformation starts by addressing internal conflict, which requires self-understanding. D.S.Sense, the Detroit MC who represented Next Level in Cartagena, Colombia, claims that "knowledge of self is the most important element of hip hop." "If you don't know yourself first," she asks, "how then can you represent a people? How then can you represent a genre of music if you don't understand yourself?"[19]

There are many paths to self-expression, but all require self-understanding. For b-boy Frankie Perez, understanding his own body allowed him to develop his distinctive style, which in turn allowed him to face conflict in the world with confidence:

> It's really hard to put into words but when you start figuring out how your body naturally wants to move, then it's honest expression that comes with it. Once you unlock that you're able to unlock it in other situations. Once you feel more

comfortable with what you're putting your energy towards in life, conflict is reduced. When you actually come face to face with that conflict you can kind of face it with more easiness because you know yourself, you know the direction you want to go in in life, and you solve that problem in a way that's going to lead towards what will make you happy.[20]

For MC T.R.U.T.H, self-understanding and conflict transformation come through meditation. I witnessed this in action during a workshop in Baku's Harmony Dance Studio, where Next Level held its 2017 Azerbaijan residency. A group of young people sat on the floor of a darkened room, repeating affirmations that T.R.U.T.H uttered in a calming voice, her eyes closed: "I am powerful. I am fearless. Everything I desire I have within me." She starts all her workshops with meditation. "It eliminates just any negative thoughts that may be coming into the room. I don't know what's going on outside of the workshops when the kids enter, so it's for them to come in and just be able to debrief in their own head, in a safe space. It just helps them calm down and get in their creative process, and then we can start rock-n-rolling."[21]

Many times it is only when we try to express how we feel that we really understand ourselves, and art can be a powerful manifestation of our internal states. These states can be joy or serenity or contentment, but often what compels artists is internal conflict. And when conflict is externalized through art, it can begin to transform inner struggles. Konshens the MC grew up in Washington, DC in the late 1980s and early 1990s during the crack cocaine epidemic, when the city was known as the murder capital of the country. The violence took so much from him, leaving him overflowing with rage. "I don't have any friends from my childhood at all," he laments. He turned to poetry, first written and then rapped as a means to manage and transform his inner conflict. "When it came to my friends passing away and things of that nature," he told me, "as opposed to getting mad and wanting to retaliate, I would write about it. I notice that a lot of my writings early on were so angry. I killed so many people in a lot of my early writings."[22]

After developing his craft and his career, Konshens turned to teaching. He studied Theatre of the Oppressed, a practice developed in the 1970s by Brazilian Augusto Boal to promote social and political change through art, and he applied it to hip hop. He began using rap in his workshops to promote what he calls "a sense of self-liberation."

> We focus on storytelling. The person telling the story, if they have the courage to be vulnerable and share their story, they're actually conducting self-therapy. What happens then is that the people who are hearing this person's story, who may have shared a similar experience, they also become liberated as well.

It's not simply the telling of one's story that is vital, it's telling one's story through art. "It's easier for people to be vulnerable through artistic expression," he says. "If you lose yourself in the creative aspect of it, the expression almost comes secondhand. At that point, you're focusing on being creative. You're not focusing on whether people are going to judge you for what you've been through."

Storytelling and verbal expression aren't the only ways to confront and transform conflict through hip hop. As anthropologist Judith Hanna writes, "dance, using the human body with its actual and symbolic energy, can exercise power over self and others."[23] Musical instruments can do the same. Oakland-based Elliot "Phillipdrummond" Gann, a clinical psychotherapist, hip hop producer, and teacher, has witnessed how creating music, particularly making beats with electronic technologies, can help people address trauma and exercise control over their lives.

> A lot of the kids we work with are exposed to a lot of community violence. Maybe there's some chaos in their homes. Intergenerational trauma, unresolved trauma. Maybe they aren't good at school, or it feels out of control

academically or in other ways. But this very structured activity of beatmaking—it has a formula, it's repetitive, it's predictable and that they can master as they gain these skills—that gives them a sense of more control. So if your history is influenced by trauma or anxiety, there's a certain kind of glue that it gives you. And a certain regulation. A repetitive beat is predictable; trauma is unpredictable.[24]

As Frankie, T.R.U.T.H, Konshens, and Gann have found, artistic practice can show us the connection between self-understanding and self-expression; it can lead us to confront and ultimately transform inner conflict.

Grappling with inner turmoil through art is challenging. Using art to try to mediate between multiple parties is altogether more complicated, particularly for outsiders. Those with only a partial understanding of the historical or cultural contexts of the communities they visit should be reluctant to insert themselves into existing conflicts. Sometimes, however, those who practice cultural diplomacy find themselves in the middle of such conflicts. In Next Level's residency in Kampala, Uganda, we learned that there were two opposing factions in our MC workshop. The Ugaflow MCs rapped in English and the Lugaflow MCs rhymed in local languages such as Luganda and Lusoga, and each group felt that theirs was the better way.[25] In Harare, Zimbabwe, language also divided our MC workshop: some rapped in Shona, some in Ndebele. Intensifying the potential for tension was the long history of conflict between the Shona and Ndebele ethnic groups, one that has led to tens of thousands of deaths. In Cartagena, Colombia, we performed with local hip hop artists in Barrio El Pozón at the nexus of several existing conflicts. The park we performed in straddled the territories of two opposing gangs, and was a frequent site of violence. The gangs were also in conflict with other residents, who were fed up with rampant, unpunished crime. Just a few months earlier, leaflets began appearing in the neighborhood calling for

a *Limpieza con sangre* (Cleansing with Blood), a Biblically-inspired ulti-
matum directed at criminals to leave the area on pain of death.[26] The relationship between the police and El Pozón's youth was strained as well.

All of these situations reveal the precarious nature of hip hop diplomacy. On the one hand, outsiders can convene opposing groups
that would be reluctant to meet otherwise; perhaps, in the process of
creating art together, they might even set aside their differences, or
least consider continuing the collaboration. MC Spyda wasn't expecting
to see Lugaflow and Ugaflow rappers in the same space on the first
day of the Next Level workshops, led by Oakland MC Madlines, but
he appreciated the opportunity to confront their differences. "It was
dope," Spyda, a Lugaflow MC, reported. "At the end of the day we
agreed. There are a few brothers fighting . . . [but] that doesn't concern us. What is more important is the culture. So we are just one. And
that's one of the things that Next Level really did."[27] The Cartagena
performance was well attended and unmarred by violence; rival gang
members, police, and other Cartageneros young and old came to the
show, peacefully sharing space at the violence-prone park. In Harare,
a mixed Shona-Ndebele trio of rappers formed in our workshop, performing at the final show in a well-received mix of their different languages and stories.

On the other hand, the presence of outsiders can heighten existing
tensions. During the Cartagena show, where armed officers flanked the
stage, I heard an MC rap something about *la policía*. A representative
from the Mayor's Office was standing nearby, and I asked him what
the young man had said. Visibly nervous, he explained that the rapper
criticized the police for constantly harassing him and then mocked
their intelligence. Although the show was unmarred by any violence
that we could see, the man from the Mayor's Office clearly saw the possibility for future conflict. In seeking to transform conflict, we were also
courting it.

MC Spyda, Kampala, Uganda, June 27, 2015. Photograph by Mark Katz.

## THE B-BOYS AND THE VOGUERS: A CASE STUDY IN CONFLICT TRANSFORMATION

The Rumah Cemara Boxing Club sits off a narrow, congested street in Bandung, West Java, tucked behind a small shop serving *nasi goreng*, Indonesia's ubiquitous national dish of fried rice. For two weeks in November 2016, this was also the home of Next Level's Indonesia residency. Rumah Cemara is more than a boxing club. It's a non-governmental organization that works both to assist young people living with AIDS and HIV and to end the discrimination they face in this country of about 260 million, the fourth most populous in the world. "Indonesia Tanpa Stigma"—Indonesia without stigma—is their motto, their Twitter hashtag, and their ultimate goal.[28] According to Rumah Cemara co-founder Ginandjar Koesmayadi, a former drug addict who lived with HIV until his untimely death in 2018, ending stigma requires mutual respect, which in turn demands active communication. He eschewed well-meaning but ineffective pleas for understanding that aren't linked to direct engagement. "It's not like, 'Oh, you should understand us as a marginalized community.' Or, 'The marginalized community should understand the normative thing in the society.' No. It's supposed to be communication. And then respect. That's my point."[29]

Next Level's residency represented Rumah Cemara's first foray into music, and when I visited the club it was pulsing with hip hop. Los Angeles–based G. Yamazawa was running an MC cypher in the boxing ring; in nearby classrooms Bay Area DJ Erica "Amerriica" Parpan was scratching and mixing, and another California artist, beatmaker Vincent "Gyrefunk" Czekus, stood next to a whiteboard while talking about musical genres and song structure. Detroit dancer Haleem "Stringz" Rasul was set up in a large training space. With mats and mirrors, it was a perfect temporary dance studio. It was here that conflict played out in the week leading up to the residency's final performance in Bandung on December 1, 2016, scheduled to coincide with World AIDS Day.

The twenty or so young men in the workshop represented two very different dance communities. About a dozen were b-boys, most of whom had connections with each other but not with Rumah Cemara. The other group practiced what they called—in English, and apparently without negative connotations—"lady style," a mix of voguing and cheerleading moves that, as the name suggests, have traditionally feminine connotations. No one I spoke with, neither Stringz nor dancer Junious Brickhouse (there serving as residency manager), nor the Indonesian dancers, had ever seen these two communities occupy the same space. The lady style dancers, or voguers as they were more often called, did not consider themselves part of a hip hop community, but were drawn to Next Level because of their ties to Rumah Cemara. And that is how they found themselves dancing alongside b-boys known, here as elsewhere, for their stereotypically aggressive masculine behavior.

"For the most part, it was pretty harmonious," Stringz told me over breakfast on the morning of the final show. "The voguers took to breaking choreography. It might not have been something familiar to them movement-wise, but they tried it. They were smiling. They were trying to pick it up. And likewise the b-boys. We embraced the femme style by including [the voguers'] . . . movement inside of a bigger breaking narrative."[30] He did notice that the voguers tended to crowd out the b-boys during practice, but he didn't observe anything that he would describe as confrontation or conflict.

And then it came time to discuss costumes for the final show. The voguers showed Stringz a photo: "The picture was them fully dressed in drag. Pink women's clothes, really flashy dresses, big hair, make-up, accessories." Supria Budiman, aka Iya, an Indonesian b-boy who served as the workshop interpreter, took Stringz aside. The b-boys objected—they wouldn't participate if the voguers showed up in pink drag. The voguers said that it would be discrimination if they couldn't. They faced prejudice all the time—they were queer and some of them HIV-positive in a society that, as one dancer named Wanda told me, called them "dirty or virus spreaders or contaminants to society."[31] They loved Rumah Cemara because it was a place where they could be themselves—a rare safe space.

The brewing conflict was a surprise to Stringz. "I totally didn't get that vibe when all of this was going down. Deep down they wasn't feeling it," he mused, "but they managed to keep some respectful attitudes, demeanor about it." Because of cultural norms in Indonesia, it would have been nearly unthinkable for the b-boys to make a public show of their displeasure, especially in front of Stringz, an authority figure and guest. *Malu*, a concept generally defined as shame, and the queer identity of the voguers, were also at play. Behavior considered gender nonconforming is traditionally said to elicit *malu* among cisgender men and has been known to provoke mob violence, known as *amok*. (*Amok* is the origin of the English phrase "to run amok.")[32] Roiling emotions likely raged beneath what we outsiders saw as calm and polite behavior. Only Iya's intervention made us aware of the conflict.

Disaster loomed. The groups had much at stake: both wanted to represent themselves and their dance cultures at this important public event, where their friends and families would be watching. Neither Stringz nor Brickhouse had ever encountered this problem before. But with the invaluable help of Iya they came up with an approach that they hoped would defuse the situation.

Stringz gathered the dancers, and through Iya, appealed to authority, tradition, and modesty. Citing a near universal rule within dance communities—that the choreographer, not the dancers, chooses the costumes—and pointing to typical hip hop practice, he informed the dancers that they would all wear black to the show. He also said that because the choreography would (as Brickhouse later put it) "essentially have them flashing the audience," they should not wear skirts.[33] But, and here was the crucial compromise, the voguers could wear whatever black (non-skirt) outfits, make-up, and hairstyles they wanted. This decision reinforced two central values within hip hop: individualism and innovation. Adhering to a particular color scheme still allowed for individual expression, and mixing voguing with traditional b-boy power moves could be defended as the kind of innovative approach that would be respected in the b-boy community. Both groups accepted the compromise, though it did not, as I later discovered, completely resolve the conflict.

The crowd at the concert venue was a mix of hip hop enthusiasts, friends and families of the performers, members of the LGBTQ community there to support Rumah Cemara, and a few US Foreign Service Officers who had driven in from Jakarta. The stage was decorated with an impressive collection of vintage boomboxes backdropped by a floor-to-ceiling Next Level banner with silhouetted hip hop artists striking poses. The small theater crackled with energy.

When the dancers came onstage I was relieved to see both groups together, standing at attention in three rows. A first glance suggested a homogenous group, everyone wearing black and serious expressions. But there were some notable differences. The b-boys dressed in t-shirts and jeans or track pants. Like the b-boys, the voguers sported sneakers and baseball caps, but above and below was a different story—wigs and lipstick, cold-shoulder tops and leather pants, velvet tights, short shorts, and fishnet stockings. Their costuming brilliantly communicated their defiance against social norms and their simultaneous embrace and queering of b-boy style.

The multi-part, ten-minute showcase was a display of conflict transformed into dance.[34] It began with a group number, combining the rapid footwork of Detroit jit, a style Stringz introduced to the dancers, with elements of breaking and voguing.[35] After the opening segment, the dancers, one by one, bowed respectfully to the audience and, with eight bars to themselves, displayed their best moves. High kicks, hip shimmies, hair whips, and cartwheels exemplified the lady style combination of voguing and cheerleading, while the b-boys brought out their best freezes, windmills, and one-armed handstands. There was a nice moment when one of the voguers ended with a baby freeze, head and hands on the floor with scissored legs angling skyward. A new move for the dancer, it was a tip of the baseball cap—and a gesture of kinesthetic empathy—to the b-boys. Another striking moment came when three of the voguers executed a short routine with bright red decorative fans. This was *jaipongan*, a form of music and dance with origins in Bandung, instantly recognizable to most of the audience. A neo-traditional form, *jaipongan* arose in the wake of a ban on Western music by President Sukarno in 1961 and became popular among the middle-class.[36] Accompanied by a hard techno beat and performed by male dancers in b-girl drag, it was both a provocative and affectionate synthesis.

The final segment brought all the dancers together one last time, closing with an homage to b-boy style. Arms folded high on their chests in the classic stance, the groups ended slightly out of synch, but their energy and enthusiasm seemed undiminished. It was a fitting metaphor: the two groups came together, but they were not in lockstep; each worked to close the gap between them but maintained their individuality to the end.

The two groups learned from each other. Although b-boys are known for their swagger, Stringz said that the voguers demonstrated "more confidence and . . . more of a stage presence"; in fact, they modeled self-assurance for the b-boys.[37] Iya told me how the voguers picked up a variety of moves from the b-boys and admired their style.[38] Voguer Wanda, whose stage name was inspired by the African American comedian Wanda Sykes, emphasized the importance of compromise. "Meeting in the middle is something extremely important—you know, the world has differences and we need to coexist." "The b-boys," Wanda continued, "now understand that there are people who are different in terms of style and that they have the same dreams, same hopes, same aspirations of being better."[39]

Wanda's words reveal that there was more at stake than whether two communities of dancers could sort out their stylistic differences. The voguers' insistence that they should dress and dance as they wished was not a matter of comfort or preference, but a form of queer activism. Dance scholar Clare Croft's concept of "queer dance" incisively captures this moment in Bandung. She might well be describing the voguers' routines and costumes when she lists some of its distinctive qualities: "The pleasures *and* difficulties of moving between multiple,

B-boys and voguers performing together on World AIDS Day, Bandung, Indonesia, December 1, 2016. Photograph by Mark Katz.

layered identities. Frustration and diminishment physically reframed as strength. [ . . . ] A slyness, a sexiness, or a joke arriving fast, sideways, and deep all at once."[40] Queer dance, Croft explains, "demands visibility and respect for a range of people and communities *and* demands that receiving respect should not be predicated on behaving in a certain way, a 'normal' way."[41] Especially in a country of state-sanctioned homophobia, where one's queerness can lead to discrimination, arrest, and violence, the voguers were not merely dancing.[42] They were taking a courageous and potentially dangerous stand for their human rights.

In the case of the voguers and the b-boys, conflict transformation did not simply come from sharing a safe space in which to express themselves—it required careful, skillful, and continual negotiation. In fact, the conflict was more heated than I initially understood. A little over a year after I visited Bandung I learned from Iya Budiman that the final dance performance nearly fell apart just before showtime. Shortly before the venue opened to the public, the b-boys came to Iya, angrily complaining about the voguers' "super fancy" and "super sexy" costumes.[43] Iya sought out the voguers backstage and spoke with them as they did their make-up; they insisted that it was their right to dress as they wanted, and wouldn't perform otherwise. Iya went back and forth between the groups. He pleaded with the b-boys for understanding— it was World AIDS Day, an opportunity to "show the people that our scene is a positive scene" by dancing together with this marginalized group. Some of the b-boys still weren't satisfied with the voguers' outfits, but Iya implored them not to disappoint "Mr. Stringz" by walking off. Finally, just minutes before showtime, they all agreed to dance together. Stringz, Muslim like all of the dancers in the workshop, joined them in prayer. "Alhamdulillah," Praise be to God, they began, asking Allah to grant them success in their performance. And then the show began.

Outside of Indonesia, the name Bandung often conjures not simply a city, but a historic event. A little over sixty years before Next Level's visit, a gathering of global significance took place within walking distance of the radio station where we performed. The 1955 Bandung Conference, as it's commonly called, gathered representatives from

Asian and African nations to discuss and promote ideals of political self-determination, non-aggression, and equality in world affairs. The rhetoric of the conference was decidedly anti-colonialist. Sukarno—Indonesia's first president—was blunt in his opening address. "For many generations our peoples have been the voiceless ones in the world. We have been the unregarded, the peoples for whom decisions were made by others whose interests were paramount, the peoples who lived in poverty and humiliation. [ . . . ] Almost all of us have ties to common experience, the experience of colonialism."[44]

The world's two imperial superpowers—the United States and the Soviet Union—were not invited to the conference. But one of the unofficial observers was Adam Clayton Powell, Jr., an African American congressman from Harlem. The conference, which he described as "one of the most important events of the twentieth century," inspired him.[45] Among other things, it motivated him to push the State Department to send prominent black jazz artists on goodwill tours around the world. "One dark face from the US is of as much value as millions of dollars in economic aid," he told President Dwight D. Eisenhower.[46] Sixty years after Dizzy Gillespie departed for his first tour as a jazz ambassador, Haleem "Stringz" Rasul, also African American, was in Bandung, performing with a group of young Indonesians inspired by African American art and culture.

But with due respect to Powell, cultural diplomacy shouldn't be construed as aid. An important lesson to be taken from Bandung 2016—and Bandung 1955, for that matter—is that having common cause doesn't magically eliminate or even reduce conflict. Rather, successful collaboration—especially in a cross-cultural context—requires the active, continuous pursuit of mutual understanding. Or, to use the hip hop term, it demands that people *build*. And that's precisely what happened in Bandung. The success of the dance performance required one part inspiration (from Stringz), one part negotiation (from Iya), and one part dedication (from the b-boys and the voguers). The success of the residency overall was a function of artistic collaboration, one in which kinesthetic empathy accomplished what words alone could not.

There are some specific, pointed lessons to take from this story. Even if their authenticity and credibility is never in question, those seeking to build bridges with communities abroad will almost always lack the local knowledge to fully understand and productively transform existing conflicts, conflicts that they themselves might have set in motion or exacerbated. This is especially true for state-sponsored programs initiated and executed by wealthy, powerful nations like the United States. However well meaning, they cannot charge forward alone, confident in their abilities and authority, and cannot succeed without demonstrating respect and humility. They may step lively, but they must also tread lightly.

## CHAPTER 3

# OPERATING IN A ZONE OF AMBIGUITY: TENSIONS AND RISKS

I am sitting in a hotel room in San Salvador. It is sunny and hot, and as I look out onto the lush, hilly cityscape dotted with church spires and high-rises I hear the improvisations of a solo violinist floating up to my open window. I'm about to head down the street to La Casa Tomada, a funky arts space buzzing with the energy of young Salvadorans dancing, rapping, scratching records, and making beats. I'm inclined to walk, but the US Embassy staff would rather I not. As I sit in the Embassy van for the half-mile drive, I see a familiar sight in this upscale neighborhood: police and security guards standing watch at every corner, each carrying a nightstick, a large knife, and a single-barreled pump shotgun.

San Salvador is a capital twice over: since 1839, the capital of El Salvador, and, in 2015, the year I visited, the murder capital of the world.[1]

In 2015 the country recorded 6,656 homicides, an appalling figure that doesn't even include the many "disappeared" for whom no bodies are recovered. This was twenty-two times the number of murders in one of the most dangerous cities in the United States, Houston, which has the same population.[2] El Salvador's violence, even worse than during the country's civil war of 1979–1992, stemmed largely from the daily bloodletting at the hands of rival gangs MS-13 (also known as Mara Salvatrucha) and Barrio 18 (aka Calle 18 or the 18th Street Gang). This violence was intimately connected to the purpose of my presence in San Salvador. I was there in my role as director of Next Level, checking in on a team of four US hip hop artists conducting workshops for young people in San Salvador and nearby Soyapango.

Next Level's workshops are designed not simply to teach hip hop, but also to use art to help young people cope with the stresses of their lives. Many of the places we visit are riven by conflict, and in El Salvador our presence was directly connected to ongoing violence prevention efforts by both the local government and the US Embassy. Ambassador Mari Carmen Aponte, who watched US and Salvadoran artists perform together at Next Level's final concert in Soyapango, told reporters, "It is a pleasure to know that all this effort is to prevent violence in El Salvador, and that fills me with happiness." The "scourge," she continued, "is so strong that we must unite" against it.[3] Just two months earlier, the severed head of Soyapango police sergeant Baltazar Olayzola Diaz was found on a bridge not far from where our performance was held; he was one of forty-nine Salvadoran police officers murdered in the first nine months of 2015.[4] Daily atrocities like these underlined the urgency of the Ambassador's remarks.

MS-13 and Barrio 18 were not Salvadoran born. They originated, in fact, in the United States. Many of their future members, especially of MS-13, had fled El Salvador during its violent civil war. The United States played a notorious role in the conflict, supporting a repressive regime that murdered untold thousands of civilians, and even trained its death squads. "The United States went well beyond remaining largely silent in the face of human-rights abuses in El Salvador," writes journalist Raymond Bonner. "The State Department and White House often sought to cover up the brutality, to protect the perpetrators of even the most heinous crimes."[5] Starting in the mid-1990s, the United States deported gang members in large numbers back to El Salvador, where their organizations flourished, growing even more violent. So there I was, on a government program intended to promote alternatives to violence sown in part by decades of US intervention.[6] Was the State Department, and by extension Next Level, acting hypocritically? Was the program serving in some way as restitution? Was it doing both at the same time?

Next Level performance in Soyapango, El Salvador, December 14, 2015. Photograph by Daniel Zarazua.

Hip hop diplomacy, and US cultural diplomacy in general, exists within a persistent zone of ambiguity, a state in which palpable, inescapable tensions and uncertainties hang over one's every action.[7] In El Salvador, the same entity that had helped undermine the country's security and stability—the US State Department—was now sponsoring free workshops to help combat violence. Our work to promote peace through music and dance generated an exquisite, unresolvable dissonance.

Occasionally the risks of conducting cultural diplomacy, and hip hop diplomacy in particular, are anything but ambiguous. During the Cold

War, US intelligence agencies covertly supported and manipulated cultural diplomacy initiatives.[8] More recently, the United States Agency for International Development (USAID) tried to co-opt Cuban rappers in a disastrous attempt to destabilize Fidel Castro's regime.[9] These actions undermine the enterprise of cultural diplomacy. Yet for all the attention and criticism they rightfully attract when they come to light, such covert operations are unlikely to be widespread for the simple reason that they demand considerable resources to plan and execute. I'm sometimes asked how I know that Next Level isn't a cover for state-sponsored espionage. I can't be certain, but our activities—mostly workshops and concerts, all of them public—don't provide access to individuals or groups that would be hard to observe or engage in other ways. The school-aged youth and amateur and professional musicians we meet are probably not the assets our spies seek.

The most common risks posed by cultural diplomacy are more pedestrian, often arising from the missteps its practitioners make in response to the ambiguities they encounter on a daily basis. The consequences are very real, for they shape every conversation and relationship, every jam session and every concert. Yet these ambiguities, unresolvable as they may be, are in fact navigable. And as it turns out, understanding how to navigate ambiguity through art offers valuable lessons for operating in the broader world.

One of the principal ambiguities that accompanies US hip hop diplomacy arises from fundamental tensions between diplomacy and the arts. The State Department has traditionally deployed the arts as a response to a threat (whether fascism, communism, or terrorism) or as a means to address the country's image problems. Artists tend not to see their work as part of a solution to international conflict or to public relations problems, and they resist the exploitation of their talents. This asymmetry of orientation and purpose is one that faces every artist who has served in a diplomatic function, from the jazz ambassadors of the last century to the hip hop envoys of today. A second unresolvable ambiguity arises from the asymmetrical relationship between the United States and nearly every other country in the world. The US is wealthier and more powerful than most of the nations that State Department–funded hip hop artists visit; moreover, it has a long history of often unwelcome interventions in the affairs of countries around the world. This relationship, this history, colors diplomatic initiatives in so many, often unspoken, ways.

## ART VERSUS DIPLOMACY

"Trust me, you don't want to go to Zimbabwe," my father-in-law told me darkly. A veteran of the State Department's counterterrorism office, he didn't reveal everything he knew, but what I needed to know, he said, began and ended with a name: Mugabe. Robert Mugabe, Zimbabwe's infamous dictator and—until he was ousted in a military coup in 2017 at the age of 93—presumed President for Life, hated the United States. For years he railed against the superpower, in great part because of the economic sanctions it had imposed on his family, followers, and nation since the early 2000s.[10] Naturally, relations between the two countries were strained. Next Level's connection to the US Embassy in the capital, Harare, would not serve us well, and I was instructed not to mention it on my visa application. I entered the country without incident, but my briefing with the Embassy's Regional Security Officer the next day set me on edge. Don't take photos of soldiers or police officers, he said. Don't take photos of the Munhumutapa Building, which houses the president's offices; it's punishable by a jail term. Watch what you say about Mugabe; better yet, don't talk about Mugabe. Assume that your internet activity is being monitored; don't visit any websites you wouldn't tell your mother about. And so on. I worried that I was being watched. Once when I returned to my ground floor hotel room in the middle of the day, I was unnerved by the sight of the patio door open, curtains waving in the breeze.

At the time I visited, one of the top priorities of the US Embassy in Harare was to "support the fundamental values of democracy, human rights, and the rule of law" in Zimbabwe.[11] This was a veiled reference to the impetus behind the United States' longstanding sanctions—namely,

Zimbabwean rappers TerraFirma (left) and Illerstrator (right) of the group SWK (Streetwise Killaz). Glen Norah, Zimbabwe, March 1, 2015. Photograph by Paul Rockower.

the Mugabe regime's practice of undermining democratic practices, abusing human rights, and flouting the rule of law. What exactly could Next Level do to promote the Embassy's mission, which at the time also included addressing Zimbabwe's HIV/AIDS epidemic and promoting entrepreneurship? We weren't lecturing on democracy, distributing condoms, or offering small business loans. We were making music with each other, we were dancing together.

Here lies one of the central tensions of cultural diplomacy. At heart, it's a tension between process and product. Roberta Levitow, a theater director who has worked around the world to promote peace through the arts, explains it this way:

> Cultural diplomacy, by its nature, preferences using artists towards accomplishing specific predetermined goals. The artistic process works in the opposite way, in that artists pose questions, they don't predict or calculate outcomes. [ . . . ] Not knowing ahead of time where the road may lead can be

frightening and an anathema for the diplomat. But it is the oxygen and inspiration for the artist.[12]

Another theater veteran, Joan Channick, is even blunter. In the hands of the State Department, culture "is merely a tool, or worse, a weapon," she argues.[13] The understanding of culture as a tool is clear from the first report of the State Department's own Advisory Committee on Cultural Diplomacy. The 2004 document notes that the "vibrant traditions of American art, dance, film, jazz, and literature . . . continue to inspire people the world over despite our political differences." "But," it continues

> in the wake of the invasion of Iraq, the prisoner abuse scandal at Abu Ghraib, and the controversy over the handling of detainees at Bagram and Guantánamo Bay, America is viewed in much of the world less as a beacon of hope than as a dangerous force to be countered. This view diminishes our ability to champion freedom, democracy, and individual dignity—ideas that continue to fuel hope for oppressed peoples everywhere. The erosion of our trust and credibility within the international community must be reversed if we hope to use more than our military and economic might in the shaping of world opinion. Culture matters.[14]

Here, culture matters because it can shape world opinion; champion freedom, democracy, and individual dignity; and help reverse a well-earned erosion of trust and credibility. Most likely, this language was meant to convince skeptical government officials of the need to fund cultural diplomacy. However well-meaning, though, rhetoric that so clearly frames culture as a means to political ends promotes a potentially exploitative view of the arts.

In reality, diplomats do care about process and artists seek specific outcomes with their art. The veteran Foreign Service Officer Richard Arndt has described cultural diplomacy in terms that suggest the open-endedness of the artistic process. "Our work as cultural diplomats was carried out in a natural and free-flowing style," he writes in his book, *The First Resort of Kings*, noting that, "with perhaps too little thought to the ultimate results, we cultural officers were opening thousands of tiny windows into other societies, in some cases piercing thick walls."[15] And for their part, the US artists I've collaborated with are generally sympathetic to the mission of the State Department's Bureau of Educational and Cultural Affairs (ECA), which supports cultural diplomacy initiatives: "To increase mutual understanding between the people of the United States and the people of other countries by means of educational and cultural exchange that assist in the development of peaceful relations."[16]

Artists and diplomats often find a middle ground. But sometimes they don't, and we can learn from examples of misaligned goals and values, of poorly conceived or executed processes. In its 2014 residency in Kolkata, India, Next Level encountered a US Foreign Service Officer who seemed not to care about the artists' perspective. The Assistant Public Affairs Officer (APAO) at the Kolkata Consulate repeatedly emphasized "deliverables," notably three video Public Service Announcements (PSAs) that would use hip hop as a way to address issues of importance to the Indian state of Bihar, where most of our residency would take place. Little else seemed to matter. When I mentioned that the US artists would learn as well as teach, she cut me off, saying that she didn't care whether they learned anything; it was not the Consulate's job to provide them with cultural experiences. I learned later that my contacts at State did not share this view. When Stacy White, Chief of ECA's Cultural Programs Division, greeted our artists at an orientation in Washington, DC a few months later, she emphasized exchange: "We hope you get as much as you give," she told us.[17]

As is typical in our residencies, we worked more closely with a locally employed staff member (LES) than with the APAO or another US officer. An LES is a foreign national, often with deep roots in the local community and usually employed for longer than the two- or three-year rotations of the US officers. The Kolkata consulate's Saadia Dayal

US artists Sheikia "Purple Haze" Norris (front left), DJ 2-Tone Jones (rear left), and Knxout (rear right) perform with Indian singer Malabika Brahma (front right) in Kolkata, India, June 2014. Photograph by Anshul Gupta.

was a powerhouse—smart, creative, kind, strong-willed, and culturally sensitive. In fact, time and again during my work with foreign posts the locally employed staff—among them Jonathan Gomes in Dhaka, Kanchalee Jitjang in Bangkok, Aminata Samb in Dakar, Nikolina Paic in Zagreb, Thando Sibanda in Harare, and Carmen Urcuyo in Tegucigalpa—proved to be reliably excellent. Their combination of pragmatism and idealism and their commitment to culture as a means to unite always inspired us.[18] Local employed staff (also called locally engaged staff), however, have little official power in their posts and tend to be chronically overworked. One LES told me that among themselves they pronounce the acronym "less"—a pointed commentary on their place within the State Department hierarchy, and perhaps a dig at the "doing more with less" mantra heard at their underfunded offices.

Difficulties with the Kolkata APAO continued to mount. She refused to extend Dayal's time with us in Patna—where there are no State Department staff—beyond a few days. When she wasn't with us, the team faced a variety of trying situations from the annoying but humorous to the downright dangerous, such as the local official who insisted on singing pop songs at our final concert and the driver who ferried the team around the chaotic streets of Patna one night while drunk.

To the APAO, Next Level was a delivery vehicle for PSAs, which served as an observable, quantifiable product of the residency. From our standpoint, however, the process mattered more. It mattered that the teenagers who created the PSAs weren't just charming—the video "Don't Litta" is irresistible—but that they discussed and reflected on the issues they rapped about—pollution, gender equality, and voting rights.[19] It mattered that Ritika, a young woman in Ansley "Jukeboxx" Jones's workshop, developed the self-confidence to dance in public after years of yearning to perform for an audience larger than her mirror. It mattered that a young man in Sheikia "Purple Haze" Norris's group could finally express—through rap—the anguish that had haunted him since his abuse as a child. It mattered that the students at St. Karen's High School in Patna continued to use the equipment we donated and that so many of them stayed in contact with Jukeboxx and Purple Haze and DJ 2-Tone Jones (Lester Wallace) and beatmaker Knxout (Korin Wong-Horiuchi). Of all the many things that mattered about the India residency, the PSAs mattered least to us.

In her book, *Necessary Noise*, Chérie Rivers Ndaliko discusses a situation similar to the one I encountered in India. An outside organization—in this case a non-governmental organization, or NGO—enlisted young rappers in the Democratic Republic of the Congo to create songs, essentially PSAs, to call attention to issues of local importance. Yet the artists were often uneasy about the process; they felt constrained by the NGO's guidelines, discouraged from really expressing themselves. As Bin G told Ndaliko, "You can't force inspiration. People try to force inspiration, but forcing your heart—that doesn't work, it's not good." Or as Emma Katya put it, "What's really true is that they wanted my music but not my message; yeah, the music without the message."[20] Common to both the US Foreign Service Officer in Kolkata and the NGO in

Congo was a failure to develop processes that truly heeded the voices and accounted for the needs of the communities they engaged.

When product trumps process, even the most well-intentioned programs can generate tension and ill will, as a story about a hip hop diplomacy initiative in Morocco reveals. This comes from ethnomusicologist Kendra Salois, who tells of a performance by Brooklyn's Chen Lo and the Liberation Family as part of a 2010 American Music Abroad tour in Morocco. Moroccan MCs Nores and Jeny Ko were invited, presumably by the US Embassy in Rabat, to join the show for a rousing final number that would bring together the citizens of the two countries. It did not work out as planned. Because they didn't speak the same languages and had differing views about onstage collaboration and audience interaction, they ended up confusing and irritating each other. The incident achieved exactly the opposite goal of the event, and of diplomacy in general: it increased the mutual *mis*understanding between the people of the United States and the people of other countries.

For the artists, the performance should have been part of a process by which they came to know each other, personally and musically, neither their first nor last encounter. According to Chen Lo, the group's rapper and leader, the US and Moroccan musicians were given little chance to connect. As he told Salois,

> The one thing I saw time and time again . . . was that real collaboration happened very rarely. We should have been in contact before the show, and coming up with something the three of us could do that was meaningful for the people that were there. . . . I felt like a lot of the sentiment around collaboration was not really about collaboration as much as it was for an annual report or a television station. . . . That happened time and time again, cameras are ready and we're going on with these half-hearted collaborations with people.[21]

For the Embassy, the performance was the product, a visual symbol of diplomacy at work. It offered good optics for television and social media and helped supply metrics for the Public Affairs Section's reporting—another cross-cultural collaboration, another audience to tally. I don't mean to paint the Foreign Service Officers that Chen Lo encountered as cynical. They might have been completely unaware that the encounter was *not* a success; yet even with the best of intentions, a lack of understanding of the artistic process can thwart the goals of cultural diplomacy.

In July 2010, Secretary of State Hillary Clinton spoke to *CBS Morning News* with great enthusiasm on the subject of hip hop diplomacy, and Chen Lo's work in particular. Asked why the State Department would fund international hip hop tours, she explained:

> It may be a little bit hopeful because I can't point to a change in Syrian policy because Chen Lo and the Liberation Family showed up. But I think we have to use every tool at our disposal so we move a lot of different pieces on the chess board every day. It's multidimensional chess, if you will.[22]

"Hip hop can be a chess piece?" the interviewer asked. "Absolutely," Clinton replied. Clinton probably didn't intend to suggest that hip hop was a mere pawn to be used and sacrificed; still, the words *chess, tool,* and *disposal* reveal an instrumental view of art. Scholar Hisham Aidi, among others, has criticized this view, noting the potential for exploiting hip hop's art and artists and expressing skepticism about the possibility that hip hop diplomacy could promote democracy or improve the image of the United States abroad. It's likely that "perceptions will remain poor," he writes, "and no dose of black music or 'diversity talk' will change that."[23]

This talk of hip hop as a tool should not surprise us. When the State Department funds music or dance or painting or theater it is in service of its mission: to support and protect US interests abroad. Hip hop will always be a tool for the State Department, even if, as I have heard from program officers, they now consciously avoid using the word "tool" when referring to art and artists. And deploying hip hop as a tool poses risks, both for hip hop and for US statecraft. The frustrations and indignities experienced by the Next Level team in India and Chen Lo in Morocco are just two examples.

What matters most, then, is that any form of people-to-people engagement actually serves the interests of the community in which it operates. The question remains: can a process-oriented arts approach that honors open-ended exploration succeed in promoting specific State Department priorities? I'll return to this question, but first, I want to explore another tension that complicates US-sponsored hip hop diplomacy.

## IMBALANCE OF POWER

Among rows of low-slung cinderblock houses on a dusty street in Rufisque, just outside Dakar, Senegal, stands a small recording studio known as Key I Am. Dominated by vivid murals of Tupac Shakur and Bob Marley, the front room doubles as a waiting area and rehearsal space; a small recording booth lies just beyond. Situated in a residential area, children play in the street just outside; chickens squawk and goats bleat in the neighbors' yards. I visited the space in October 2014 during a Next Level planning trip—the purpose of the visit, with Paul Rockower, who would be managing the residency, was in part to identify a local organization that would host our workshops and provide logistical support. Key I Am was one of several spaces we visited. After a short tour of the studio we stood chatting outside; one of the group sported a camouflage baseball cap with the letters USA appliquéd to the front. Among the group were two well-known rappers, P.P.S. the Writah (Paul Pissety Sagna), the founder of the studio, and Maxi Krezy (Amadou Aw), a revered pioneer of Senegalese hip hop and a social activist. One remark particularly stayed with me. "The Embassy," Maxi declared in English, "is a godsend."[24] He was referring to the US Embassy in Dakar, which, I later learned, had assisted him in a variety of projects in the past, including an initiative that used hip hop to help Senegalese youth learn English.[25]

Maxi's remark surprised me. I wasn't accustomed to hearing hip hop artists warmly laud the government, any government. But P.P.S., Maxi Krezy, and other artists across Dakar had enjoyed the support of both the Embassy and the State Department in recent years. P.P.S. was a OneBeat fellow, spending several weeks touring the United States in 2012 with an eclectic group of international musicians, the bill picked up by the State Department. That same year Ambassador Lewis Lukens gave a speech at the opening of the Hip Hop Akademy at the Africulturban center in the suburb of Pikine, accompanied by embassy-donated musical gear.[26] A year later, local rapper Toussa Senerap became a OneBeat fellow as well, and later participated in Next Level. The United States government wasn't the only source of patronage for the Dakar hip hop community: also lending their support were embassies, NGOs, and private foundations from Europe, as well as a variety of municipal and governmental offices in Senegal. Corporate, foundation, and government grants represented a significant source of funding for hip hop in Dakar. It only made sense for the local artists to make nice with me, and anyone else representing the US Embassy.

Here we see another fundamental tension within cultural diplomacy: the asymmetrical power relationship between funding agencies and the communities they serve. This tension is hardly unique to state-sponsored cultural diplomacy: it affects the work of NGOs, charities, and private citizens from the United States and other wealthy nations. The US government, however, has distinctive powers to help and to harm: it can grant visas and asylum and it can impose economic sanctions or wage war.

Why does this matter? It matters because this power dynamic always informs and influences interactions between the US visitors and members of the local community. If it is not in the background, it is very much in the foreground. To complicate this dynamic, we are simultaneously powerful *and* vulnerable. We rarely speak the local languages with any fluency, so we require interpreters to help us do everything from lead workshops to order meals at a restaurant.[27] We don't know our way around, so we need transportation, and sometimes

Toussa Senerap at Rockteam Music, a recording studio she established for women, Guédiawaye, Senegal, October 13, 2014. Photograph by Mark Katz.

we even need help crossing the street. We aren't used to the water and food, so we need the occasional trip to a pharmacy or hospital. All of this burdens our hosts. And even when the State Department or a US embassy or consulate foots the bill, a significant amount of time and attention may be taken away from the main purpose of the program to attend to the needs of the foreigners. The ironic combination of power and vulnerability is a legacy of centuries of colonialism; US cultural diplomacy programs serve as a reminder of that historical taint.

This dynamic can make it difficult to unpack seemingly straight-forward exchanges. On the one hand, Maxi Krezy's praise may have been completely sincere. As Aminata Samb, the US Embassy's Cultural Affairs Specialist and a Senegalese national, told me, "Senegalese love American culture. They love American culture, American people. We

have a common history, you know, especially with Afro-Americans."[28]
She also explained the concept of *teranga*, a Wolof word that means
hospitality, but which is more than that—both something of a self-
identified national characteristic and an ethical obligation to treat
guests with respect and generosity. Maxi's warmth, then, may have reflected his genuine admiration for US hip hop as well as his commitment to *teranga*.

At the same time, he may have felt compelled to express his admiration in the strongest way. Perhaps he didn't feel free to criticize or
bargain with us, or even to offer feedback. And it wasn't simply that
he was being savvy in complimenting the Embassy. There was more
at risk than funding for his studio. The welfare of many Senegalese
living in economic precarity depends a great deal on what are known

Aminata Fall Samb, Cultural Affairs Assistant at the United States Embassy in Senegal. Dakar,
Senegal, October 13, 2014. Photograph by Mark Katz.

as remittances—transfers of money by a foreign worker to an individual or family back home. In some countries, remittances are the principal source of external financing for that nation's economy. In Senegal, remittances far outstrip foreign investment and foreign aid in total value.[29] For many families, they are all that keeps poverty and homelessness at bay. Remittances depend on one's ability to travel and work abroad, and visas are effective means for finding well-paid work outside of Senegal. They are also expensive and difficult to obtain. And because I am connected to the US Embassy, I am seen as a means to securing a visa.[30]

United States visas are prized throughout the world, and the pursuit of them is accompanied by a mix of hope, trepidation, frustration, desperation, and despair. Nigerian writer Chimamanda Ngozi Adichie captured that complex of emotions in her 2009 short story, "The American Embassy."[31] A line of 250 Nigerians snakes outside the Embassy's gates, the first petitioners queuing up before dawn to plead their case before a pair of consular officials. As they wait in the stifling heat, one of the hopefuls is overheard talking about "a special church service called the American Visa Miracle Ministry." Another, who wants to visit his brother in Texas, offers this advice: "Just make sure that you look the interviewer straight in the eye as you answer questions. Even if you make a mistake, don't correct yourself, because they will assume you are lying. I have many friends they have refused, for small-small reasons." An asylum-seeker is counseled: "cry, but don't cry too much." One small but telling detail in the story is the embassy official's whiteness—suggested by her "limp auburn hair" and green eyes, a reminder that race, and by implication, colonialism, is inextricably implicated in this asymmetry of power. I once met a US Foreign Service Officer—also white—who ruefully described her job as a consular officer as that of a "dream killer."[32]

Petna Ndaliko Katondolo, a US-based Congolese filmmaker who has documented several Next Level residencies, related to me a remark his father once made to him many years earlier: "There will never be a small white man in Africa."[33] The observation was a warning, no doubt born of long experience. One must take great care when dealing with *mzungu*—a Swahili word referring to white people and foreigners in general—because of the power that stands behind them, power that historically has been wielded *against* the interests of Africans. As I've come to realize, I am no small white man in Africa, especially when I represent Next Level.

An encounter in Zimbabwe drove this point home for me. It was February 2015, and the setting was Chillspot, a club in Mabvuku, outside of Harare. I was there with US hip hop artists DJ Juan Gomez and b-boy Ken Fury; our host was Plot Mhako, at the time heading up the Jibilika Dance Trust, a local NGO. We were there to meet Fantan, a well-known DJ, producer, record label owner, and proponent of Zimdancehall, a wildly popular dub- and reggae-influenced local genre. As we made our way to the small DJ booth to meet Fantan, I felt self-conscious and conspicuous—I was told later that no white person had visited the club before. Fantan's fans pressed against the booth, reaching in with outstretched arms—I shook hands, bumped fists, and politely declined to buy sneakers offered to me. Others pounded the scratched Plexiglas of the booth in a raucous gesture of appreciation for the DJ. The energy in the low-ceilinged space, packed with sweating dancers, was palpable.

As we left the booth, the crowd of dancers immediately engulfed us. One woman moved in close, pushing herself into me. She advanced, I retreated; soon she had me up against a wall. And then she turned around, grinding her backside into me. Squeezing out between her and the wall, I turned and brandished my wedding ring in protest. Undeterred, she grabbed my hands. "Don't you like me?" she shouted imploringly over the throbbing beat. Plot then intervened, allowing me to slip away.

For a very brief moment I had little power over my own body. And yet I never worried for my safety, never felt the terrifying realization that I would have to submit to the will of another, a privilege the woman might well not have enjoyed. In fact, the woman—whom Plot suggested was a sex worker—likely propositioned me precisely because of my whiteness, assuming that I was richer than her other prospects. No matter how small I felt in that instant, I was *still* no small white man in Africa. The evening lingers in my memory, reminding me that however sensitive, aware, or respectful I try to be, I cannot escape the history that I, as a white man working on behalf of an imperial power, carry with me.

Given this power dynamic, our interactions on the ground are always more layered than the surface level reveals. This fundamental ambiguity can take a toll, for we can never be certain of the consequences of even our best-intentioned efforts. More consequentially, this ambiguity affects the host community. In Dakar, Next Level did not, in the end, choose Key I Am studio as its main local partner. The studio didn't have the space or facilities necessary to host the number of participants we were expecting. Nor did we partner with Africulturban, another hip hop organization we visited, the one that had received US embassy support in 2012. Instead we worked with G Hip Hop, a large community-based organization in Guédiawaye; it was G Hip Hop, then, that benefitted from the free workshops, the media attention, and the equipment worth a few thousand dollars. We did our best to involve members of the other groups in the workshops and donated modest amounts of equipment to them as well. Still, serving some more than others and others not at all, potentially generating unfulfilled hopes and lingering resentment in the process, is an unavoidable reality.

In Senegal, we chose our local partner, but in some residencies the US embassy makes that decision. In these cases, we have sometimes found ourselves in situations thick with tension, distrust, and resentment. This was the case in Zagreb, Croatia. Our contacts at the embassy chose a local dance studio to host our workshops, which in turn received a grant as well as equipment worth several thousand dollars. Many in the local hip hop community resented the studio, deriding it as "commercial," lacking in the expertise and authenticity of Zagreb's "underground" dance community. It wasn't even a hip hop studio—hip hop was just one of many styles taught there. Worse still, the studio had received several embassy grants in the past and seemed to have a monopoly on US funding. The embassy's indomitable Cultural Affairs

Assistant, Nikolina Paic, was aware that the studio and its management were not well liked by Zagreb's hip hop community, but unfortunately there seemed to be no other organizations with the capacity to host our workshops.

Jaci Caprice, the residency's manager, and I established good relationships with local underground hip hop artists and were fortunate to gain the assistance of Filip Ivelja, aka Phat Phillie, a hip hop promoter and radio host who has influenced Croatian hip hop as much as anyone. We were also lucky to have a veteran team—dancer Asia One, beatboxer Baba Israel, DJ and MC J-Live, and MC Toki Wright—who were already known to many of the Croatians we met. Yet we could not escape the tensions that permeated Zagreb's hip hop scene. We knew that some who might have embraced our presence avoided the workshops and final show. Although our visit forged strong relationships between the US artists and the Croatians who did participate, our presence also brought old tensions to the surface.

The simple fact that hip hop was born in the United States adds another layer of complexity. Our hosts often place a great value on our connection to the birthplace of hip hop, a connection that earns us good will and can smooth our way in places where anti-US sentiment is strong. On the other hand, our special status can make it difficult to establish mutually respectful relationships. When veteran hip hop diplomat Toni Blackman spoke to a group of artists preparing to leave for their first Next Level residency, she offered this word of advice: "Don't be too American. We're most effective when we are humans."[34]

Power imbalances play out at every moment in cultural diplomacy. We have the power to disrupt established relationships when we work with young people whose local teachers and mentors might see our presence as intrusive or threatening to their authority. In Dakar, we learned of a respected local dancer who refused to collaborate with Next Level and warned his students against joining our workshops. We do everything we can to identify and involve local hip hop teachers or pioneers in our workshops—often inviting them to teach alongside us, and always offering an honorarium—but a certain amount of suspicion or wounded pride is both unavoidable and understandable. These concerns persist through to our final show. Where will it be? Who will be featured? What local dignitaries will make speeches? Every decision we make has the potential to irritate or alienate.

And then we leave. The State Department spreads its cultural funding widely, meaning that residencies are relatively short, and there's no built-in funding for return visits. The consequence of this approach is palpable. In Senegal, Junious Brickhouse couldn't escape the feeling that he was about to abandon the young people with whom he had grown close over the previous two weeks. Compounding his unease was the knowledge that he was departing for a more privileged life than they could ever hope to enjoy. As we sat on the patio of our upscale Dakar hotel, looking out over the Atlantic expanse, he shook his head

Junious Brickhouse in Dakar, Senegal, January 14, 2015. Photograph by Mark Katz.

and said, "I'm an asshole. A rich asshole who gets on a plane and leaves. We always leave."[35]

## NAVIGATING AMBIGUITY

If art and diplomacy have such different goals, and if power asymmetries unavoidably shape cross-cultural encounters, can hip hop build community and understanding *and* address specific policy goals? There's reason for skepticism. Sure, a workshop could help youth participants create and record songs that promote voting or HIV prevention, which could then be disseminated throughout the local community. Presumably these songs would satisfy the embassy's request for deliverables that address the post's priorities. But in a narrowly goal-oriented workshop, would the participants really have the opportunity to express themselves freely and fully? Would writing songs with pre-determined messages foster the connections that build local and global community? Taking a lesson from Chérie Rivers Ndaliko's work, probably not. Moreover, the US artists, unlikely to be experts on these matters, might sow misinformation, and in addressing particularly sensitive issues—human trafficking, for example—would risk reducing participants to their victimhood or re-traumatizing them.

What about the other side of the equation? What if the US artists avoid focusing on any particular policy priorities, and simply aim to *build* without regard to policy priorities or messaging? Would this approach actually satisfy an embassy's Public Affairs staff? Some might feel that the workshops would still address the State Department's goal of fostering mutual understanding and collaboration. "Part of why we do these programs is to build bridges and personal connections," says Michele Peregrin, the State Department program officer who worked with Next Level between 2014 and 2017.[36] When she mused about her favorite aspects of working with the program, she cited the opportunity to observe the budding cross-cultural and transnational friendships.[37] But certainly others would be disappointed. No doubt that would have been the case with the PSA-loving consular official in Kolkata; or the

Foreign Service Officer in Algeria who had observed our workshops and complained, "I thought I was getting a conflict resolution program, not a hip hop program."

Does serving the goals of diplomacy diminish the integrity of hip hop, and art more broadly? Does honoring the creative process and the agency of artists thwart the goals of diplomacy? The answer to both is not necessarily, but success requires compromise. The compromise between hip hop and diplomacy, however, should not be an equal one. It is diplomacy that needs to yield. If a State Department–sponsored hip hop program is truly to act as a form of people-to-people diplomacy, people must be treated as individuals, not as stand-ins for broader issues or problems, whether democracy or disease.

Some State Department staff might resist this argument, but others explicitly agree. During the Washington, DC orientation for the Next Level's second cycle in 2015, Bruce Armstrong, Director of the Office of Citizen Exchanges at the State Department, made this clear when he addressed a room full of hip hop artists. He acknowledged that the presence of State Department staff is not always needed or helpful and he recognized the expertise of the artists they send abroad. "We have the intelligence," he explained, "to get the hell out of the way."[38] In my experience with Next Level, most State Department personnel, from the program officers in Washington, DC to the public affairs and cultural affairs officers at embassies and consulates abroad, take a hands-off approach. This approach, however, is in part a function of the structure of Next Level, which has a staff—none of whom are government employees—that plans and manages residencies, and which acts as a liaison, and sometimes buffer, between the artists and the State Department. Oftentimes traveling US artists work directly with State Department staff, who may not be used to engaging with artists, and either cannot or do not wish to get out of the way.

Ideally, the cultural envoys sent abroad by the State Department are both well supported and are left to do their work without undue interference. Yet the ambiguities remain ever present; the tensions persist undiminished. At the intensive orientation where all the US hip hop

Kevie Kev leading a Next Level workshop in Ankara, Turkey, October 9, 2018. Photograph by
Saleem Reshamwala.

artists gather prior to leaving for their residencies we distribute a document called "The Next Level Principles: Some Suggestions for Being
and Acting During International Residencies." The suggestions—drawn
from the advice of dozens of experienced artists—are as follows:

- Show respect
- Be humble
- Be self-aware
- Be present
- Be flexible
- Stay safe
- Share yourself
- Be professional
- Recognize your privilege
- Listen as much as you speak
- Learn as much as you teach
- Value process over product
- Do your homework
- Stay in touch

We reinforce each of these principles through discussion, role-playing exercises, and conflict transformation workshops led by experts.

However obvious these guidelines might be, they can be extraordinarily difficult to enact for the simple reason that we as Americans may assume that we embody these qualities (when we don't) or believe that we are somehow exempt from them (which we aren't). Perhaps the most important of these exhortations, then, is to be self-aware. In her 2017 book *Notes on a Foreign Country: An American Abroad in a Post-American World*, journalist Suzy Hansen points to the consequences of this lack of historical and geopolitical self-awareness: "Americans are surprised by the direct relationship between their country and foreign ones because we don't acknowledge that America is an empire; it is impossible to understand a relationship if you are not aware you are in one." She further suggests that accepting American exceptionalism essentially demands entering into a state in which self-awareness is nearly impossible:

> How could I, as an American, understand foreign people, when unconsciously I did not extend the most basic faith to other people that I extended to myself? This was a limitation that was beyond racism, beyond prejudice, beyond ignorance. This was a kind of nationalism so insidious that I had not known to call it nationalism; this was a delusion so complete that I could not see where it began and where it ended, could not root it out, could not destroy it.[39]

For Hansen, the only cure for her lack of self-awareness was to spend time abroad, to engage with non-Americans until she was able to see her country through the eyes of others.

Next Level's principles, then, are mere abstractions until we put them into practice. Even before the workshops start, we've met local artists and others, whether on advance trips by the residency manager or through informal meet-and-greet sessions before the first day. On the first day of our workshops, we convene the participants and try to learn as much as we can from them before we begin. We ask questions: What does hip hop mean to you? What is hip hop like in your community? What do you want from this experience? And we often open or close the session with a call and response or a cypher—performing and not just discussing the type of relationship we hope to develop. With this approach we are both gathering information and making a statement. We learn why hip hop matters to them; how hip hop operates within their communities; what goals they want to pursue though hip hop; where our experiences and histories intersect and where they diverge. Our statement, often articulated explicitly, is that their voices and concerns matter to us, that we come not to teach but to build.

Hip hop theater director Daniel Banks puts it well when he explains that:

> Cultural diplomacy, at its most human and aware, would be self-reflective: constantly striving for better ways to interact; consciously working to deconstruct multiple levels of hierarchy in a room; and seeking the space of pure presence where participants paradoxically celebrate the implicit humanity that connects all people, while learning about significant differences.[40]

Hip hop diplomacy, done right, is hard. The mental and emotional energy required of self-reflexivity; the burden of carrying the history of one's country; and the unease in knowing that one inevitably misses important nuances when interacting with those of other cultures: all of this can be exhausting. Yet art, though it can neither bypass nor eliminate ambiguity, can create common ground, transforming difference from a source of conflict into a foundation for mutual respect. Moreover, navigating ambiguity through art may lead us, as US-based visitors, to tread more considerately, weigh consequences more carefully, and carry ourselves with humility rather than arrogance. To probe ambiguity is to discover the principal challenges of cultural diplomacy and to appreciate what makes art—and hip hop in particular—such a powerful medium through which to build community and understanding. Responding to ambiguity by operating in a critical, self-aware, historically-informed and culturally-sensitive manner is, simply put, a valuable way of living in the world.

## CHAPTER 4

# SONGS INSTEAD OF MISSILES:
# AGENCY AND SUBVERSIVE COMPLICITY

Complicity was big news in the United States in 2017. Raised most pointedly in connection with Donald Trump and his circle, the new president was accused of being complicit in, among other things, Russia's interference in US elections and in the resurgence of white nationalist violence across the country. In a *Saturday Night Live* skit from March of that year, First Daughter Ivanka Trump (played by Scarlett Johansson) peddled a perfume called *Complicit*. Its tagline: "the fragrance for the woman who could stop all this, but won't."[1] A month later, the real Ivanka Trump attempted to redefine the word: "If being complicit is . . . wanting to be a force for good and to make a positive impact, then I'm complicit."[2] In October, Arizona Republican Jeff Flake announced his retirement from the Senate, explaining, "I have children and grandchildren to answer to, and so, Mr. President, I will not be complicit." He exhorted fellow Republicans to speak out against wrongdoing, arguing that "silence can equal complicity."[3] Complicity was constantly in the media, and not solely in connection with the new president: it came up in stories about the role of Facebook and Twitter in the sowing of misinformation and the National Rifle Association's link with mass shootings. No wonder *complicit*—defined as choosing to be involved in an illegal or immoral act—was called the word of the year.[4]

Complicity was also a concern of the US hip hop artists who crisscrossed the globe in 2017 on the government's dime. Given how thoroughly rappers had publicly dissed Trump, any association with the federal government risked tainting the work and reputation of hip hop diplomats.[5] But this tension was not new to the Trump administration. The first State Department–supported hip hop tours began in 2001 under George W. Bush, a president hated by many in the hip hop community. Before Kanye West infamously aligned himself with Donald Trump in 2016, he famously complained in 2005 that "George Bush doesn't care about black people."[6] Barack Obama may have been the first hip hop–loving president, but that was not enough for artists to forgive the government's history of violence and oppression against people of color.[7] As rapper Guru rhymed in 1993, during Bill Clinton's presidency:

> It doesn't matter who's the president
> I hate to tell ya, but slavery is still in effect
> Haven't you checked, us black folks we ain't free yet
> I make a bet, if you don't let the truth out
> Huh, evil will rule without a doubt[8]

Injustice, as Guru suggests, is systemic, embedded in the very history and structure of the United States and its institutions.

Hip hop has long been defined by its resistance to the structures that perpetuate injustice. The story of hip hop's birth in the Bronx, New York of the 1970s is often told as a response to urban dysfunction, to pervasive crime, poverty, and despair. National headlines, such as the *New York Times'* "South Bronx: A Jungle Stalked by Fear, Seized by Rage" (1973) and frequently-cited songs like "The Message" (1982)—"It's like a jungle sometimes/It makes me wonder how I keep from going under"—paint a lurid picture of hip hop's hometown. Resistance has been a mainstay in hip hop lyrics from "The Message" to N.W.A.'s "Fuck tha Police" (1988) to "Police State" by dead prez (2000) to Kendrick Lamar's protest anthem "Alright" (2015) and Childish Gambino's caustic "This is America" (2018). And these are just American examples. The terms *resistant, oppositional,* and *political* are commonly used to describe hip hop artists and traditions around the world. This kind of discourse became especially common in connection with hip hop in North Africa and the Middle East during the Arab Spring (2010–2012).[9]

Seeing hip hop through the lens of resistance, however, has its problems. As Cristina Moreno Almeida explains in her book, *Rap Beyond Resistance*, "defining rap as a response to power downplays the ability of artists to imagine and create their own new narratives."[10] Rayya El Zein, writing of hip hop in Lebanon, Palestine, and Jordan, notes that distilling the diversity of hip hop into "a simple symbolic 'resistance' fails to assess the actual, sometimes contradictory political energy in these city streets."[11] When resistance becomes hip hop's driving narrative, we may neglect the agency of the artists who create this work—as if they had no choice but to fight the power—and overlook the complexities and even contradictions within actual hip hop practice.

To answer the question of how hip hop artists have squared their participation in state-supported cultural diplomacy programs, we must understand that this is not a simple either/or proposition, a choice between maintaining or compromising one's integrity, between keeping it real or selling out. Hip hop diplomacy exists not in a world of *either/ or* but one of *both/and*. To recognize this reality is to gain insight into why artists decide to participate in cultural diplomacy programs. These insights, in turn, shed light on how hip hop artists exercise agency and autonomy, how they navigate within power structures, and, at root, how their values give life to their art.

## RESERVATIONS

In the 1989 Public Enemy song, "Black Steel in the Hour of Chaos," rapper Chuck D dismisses the idea of serving the government:

> I got a letter from the government the other day
> I opened it and read it, it said they were suckers
> They wanted me for their army or whatever
> Picture me giving a damn, I said never[12]

Even the US hip hop artists who accept State Department invitations to teach and perform abroad often have reservations about the opportunity, and many had already felt uneasy about the government in general. Speaking of Next Level, DJ Zephyr Ann Doles recalled, "I was slightly skeptical because it's run by the State Department. So, to what extent am I representing the US government? I'm not a fan of *this* [the Trump] administration, but I'm also pretty anti-US government in general in terms of my politics. So I was just like, ehhhhh . . . I wanna do it, but at the same time, what am I signing myself up for?"[13] Referring to his West Indian heritage and quoting Bob Marley, rapper Asheru explained, "I was very nervous to be honest because I'm old school. 'Rasta don't work for no CIA,' that's how I was taught. So I was like, I don't know about this, it's a great opportunity, but this might be some propaganda bullshit."[14] Also coming from a family of immigrants, DJ Juan Gomez likewise had good reason to be wary of the US government:

> You have to understand, I came to this country as a direct result of US policy. I was born in Nicaragua during the end of the revolution and the counter-revolution that was being secretly backed by the US government. [US] Latin American policy time and time again has fucked over my family and fucked over a lot of people that I know and work with. So yeah, I think there's reservations working with the US government.[15]

What does it mean that nearly every artist I have interviewed about signing on to a State Department program initially had reservations about participating? It would be easy enough to tar them as hypocrites or sellouts. But these are not people who decided to hold their noses and take the money. Listen to their reasoning and what comes across is a mixture of pragmatism and idealism, and an understanding born from lived experience that ideological purity is a myth.

Asheru, Dhaka, Bangladesh, November 16, 2014. Photograph by Anshul Gupta.

Sure, there's been some grimy stuff that's happened. That's real talk, but what do you do? Do you just not learn how to work with each other? When opportunities come for us to work together, I jump at those opportunities. I give mad love and kudos to the State Department for wanting to open up channels of communication and also to the hip hop artists who want to open up channels of communication so that we can move together. (Beatmaker Jaci Caprice)

I know my head and my heart is in the right place. I know what I'm doing, and I appreciate that there's funding for this. I'm not the government. I don't think the same thing that the government thinks, and I don't always agree. I don't have to. I'm an American. That's the luxury. Being American, I don't have to agree with my government. Some of the places we go in some of these underserved communities, they don't

have that privilege. I come from a privileged place, and I remember that privilege when I'm in service. (Dancer Junious
Brickhouse)

After finding out that it [Next Level] was a federally funded
program, I thought for a minute: what better way to utilize
this kind of funding for something great and something
beautiful that I believe in? As an indigenous person, I'm
from a reservation [Diné] that's very underserved. I love hip
hop, love to share the gifts of hip hop that I've been given.
And the fact that it is a federally funded program kind of
blows my mind. I felt like if I were going to be involved with
anything to do with the US government, this program is it.
And I am willing to provide my service completely for this
program, because I believe in it, I love hip hop, and everyone
here is such a great asset to the team. (MC Def-i)

I'm into hip hop so of course I have reservations about our
own government. I've been fortunate in that most people that
I've met in different countries, they have enough common
sense to differentiate between who makes the decisions for
certain countries and who doesn't. They have a disdain for
their own governments in many ways. And so they recognize too when the US has done certain things that people
would frown upon. They know to say, "I don't like your government. I like Americans in general, though. Y'all come
over." (DJ 2-Tone Jones)

This was the first time I've ever seen a government agency
logo attached to anything that was related to hip hop. My
history as a graffiti writer, I typically was running away
from the establishment like that, and the only time I saw
those logos was in court buildings. [But] I understood that
there could be some opportunities here above and beyond

opportunities I may have access to in my normal world.
(Graffiti writer CHINO BYI)[16]

One consistent response is that the artists feel that they can do this work without compromising their artistry or integrity. This is a key requirement, a crucial assurance that they are not selling out. Once artists feel that they can be true to themselves and to hip hop, they seem to follow a line of reasoning that goes something like this: the government *should* be funding hip hop, which is a positive and powerful use of taxpayer money; if the government is going to support hip hop it needs the right people to represent it; I am one of those people; therefore, I should take this opportunity. Once they are on the ground, teaching or performing, they often find that they are treated not so much as

Def-i performing at Next Level's Lincoln Memorial cypher, Washington, DC, June 5, 2018. Photograph by Mark Katz.

representatives of their country or government, but as kindred spirits, not only because they love hip hop but also because they are often similarly marginalized in their homelands.

## MOTIVATIONS

Back to the question at hand: why would any hip hop artist work with the government? The broadest answer is that the US State Department offers rare, paid opportunities to create both art and community around the world. In the van ride back from the final show in Next Level's residency in Villa Neuva, Guatemala, b-boy Kareem Gwinn, a 20-year veteran of the competitive breaking scene, exclaimed, "I've never been a part of something as hip hop as this." This is a surprising thing to say about a government program, but he contrasted this experience with "the street side of hip hop," which often comes with "negative situations and negative energy." "I only felt good energy," he said of his time leading a workshop of young Guatemalan dancers, and felt that his work allowed him to "pay it forward to anyone in need."[17]

Most artists I've spoken with express inwardly and outwardly directed reasons for signing on for this work. Listen to producer Diamond D, who spent two weeks teaching and performing in Serbia in 2014:

> What intrigued me about it was just the chance to share some of the knowledge that was shared with me as far as the art of production, the art of beatmaking. Also, using that talent to bring cultures together, you know what I mean? It was just something different for me to do. I've basically done a lot of things that producers strive to attain. Platinum records, gold albums. I've won a Grammy, I've won awards. So it was just something different, and something to add to my resume, of course, but at the same time, you know just to give back. 'Cause like I said, I've been blessed.[18]

Diamond D begins and ends by talking about serving others. Established artists speak frequently about "giving back." For them, this means passing along their knowledge in order to pay forward their debt to their mentors and to keep the culture thriving. But he also expresses inwardly-motivated reasons for participating: the pleasure of teaching, the expansion of his professional experience.

Diamond D wasn't especially drawn by the pay, and he may well have earned more had he accepted performance gigs instead of going to Serbia. Money *is* a motivating factor for many other artists. Most make a living by stringing together one-off or short-term gigs, and many also have jobs unrelated to hip hop. (Among the Next Level artists I've met, these have included architect, driver, hair braider, nurse, receptionist, schoolteacher, social worker, and television show producer.) Some of these artists had recently been students and were carrying considerable debt, many have families they support, and a few I've met had been homeless or incarcerated at various times in their lives. For most of those who participate in these programs, the pay is decent, and welcome. Between 2014 and 2018, for example, Next Level paid artists a daily honorarium of first $150 and then $200, as well as a per diem for meals and incidentals; travel and lodging were also covered. Over a two-week period, the total compensation was often equal to or better than what the artists might have made otherwise.

This money is important to artists, not simply because they have bills to pay, but because they are getting paid for their art. Zephyr Ann Doles put it this way: "For me, coming from a broke, artist, hustling background . . . it was kind of an incredible opportunity to be like, 'Oh no, we value what you bring to the table as a teaching artist and we're gonna pay you well for it.' And I was like, this is fucking crazy!"[19] Speaking only partially in jest, producer Suzi Analogue described her pay as a form of reparations when she spent two weeks in Kampala: "Black Americans joke, 'Hey, I want my reparations. I want to be sent back to Africa.' And once I got chosen for Uganda I realized, hey, I'm getting my reparations. I'm going back. It's on the government's dime. Dream come true."[20] *Getting paid* is a powerful hip hop trope. Critiques that hip hop culture flaunts crass materialism and ill-gotten gains tend to miss the symbolic significance of money to those who face systemic racism and entrenched poverty. When Guru raps about earning money illegally in Gang Starr's "Code of the Streets" (1994), he's not celebrating his life of crime—he's lamenting that crime is the only way he can use his talents and escape destitution.

> What about the system, and total corruption?
> I can't work at no fast-food joint
> I got some talent, so don't you get my point?
> I'll organize some brothers and get some crazy loot
> Selling D-R-U-G-S and clocking dollars, true
> Cause the phat dough, yo, that suits me fine
> I gotta have it so I can leave behind
> The mad poverty, never having always needing.[21]

Again, it's the struggle between agency and system playing out. There's a similar dynamic when hip hop artists decide to work with the government. One way they overcome their misgivings is to see this work as the government's acknowledgement of their talents as hip hop artists. Can this be a form of self-serving rationalization? Can one claim empowerment and still be exploited? Of course. Operating in a zone of ambiguity means that there's not always a clear line between co-optation and self-empowerment, between complicity and independence, between selling out and getting paid.

Financial gain, however, is rarely an end in itself for these artists. The strongest internal motivators for taking on a State Department gig are connected to opportunities for personal, professional, and artistic growth. This growth might be represented by the partnerships they develop and the gigs that come from it; the unfamiliar cultures they are exposed to and the new art they create in response to it; and the personal friendships that arise and continue well after they return home.

For many artists, international travel is a vital catalyst for this growth, both a personal dream and a professional goal that cultural diplomacy can satisfy. Asheru, hailing from Washington, DC, has visited more than twenty-five countries, performing in most of them, often supported by government funds.

> Graduating as an anthro major [from the University of Virginia], I wanted to work in the Smithsonian or Discovery Channel, and I wanted to travel and eat exotic foods and find out about other cultures. And I'm doing that, but I'm doing it as an MC, not as an anthropology scholar. And that right there is the best reward for this kind of work. I've never been able to sustain myself solely off of music, but I've been able to travel all over the world. I've been able to make a lot of great connections, have incredible opportunities that most people haven't had. So I don't take any of that lightly or for granted. This is just yet another affirmation that I'm doing the right thing, I'm doing what I'm supposed to be doing.[22]

For Asheru and so many others, some of the most meaningful aspects of their work for the government have little connection to the State Department or its diplomatic goals.

International travel often satisfies deeply held personal goals and needs. "As a little girl, my biggest dream was to travel and see the world," pioneering hip hop diplomat Toni Blackman recalls. "And because of programs like this [Next Level] I've been able to do that, while still being able to be an artist. Two things I've done all my life since I was sixteen is teach and perform. And so those are the two things I need to do to feel sane, and to feel grounded, and to feel emotionally and mentally well."[23] Medusa the Gangsta Goddess, a legendary west coast MC and dancer, sees a spiritual element to her travel as a hip hop artist. As she explained one evening after a workshop in San Salvador, "It's necessary for me to travel and give. It is exactly what the Creator's plan was for me to do. It's not just about the money, homie, it's about the healing. So it's a give and give situation, and you don't realize that until you do some traveling."[24] Blackman and Medusa both connect travel to their well-being. Here, they tap into a stance within black feminism that asserts self-care as a radical act when practiced by those whose selflessness is regularly exploited, whose needs are deemed unworthy of attention. As poet Audre Lorde wrote in 1988, "Caring for myself is not self-indulgence. It is self-preservation, and that is an act of political warfare."[25] For women, people of color, and other long-oppressed minorities, unashamedly fulfilling one's individual needs can be a political act; to have the government pay them to do what they love may be nothing less than a triumph, a form of long-denied justice.

During a break in a Next Level workshop in May 2017 I stood chatting with Atlanta-based DJ and MC J-Live near the banks of the Sava River in Zagreb, Croatia as he mused about the power of travel. During our conversation he offered this improvised verse:

> From the depths of the deepest
> Darkest black hole in the core of the berry
> Where the sweetest juices get buried
> Climb out of the light and get married
> To the brightest, hottest stars before they burn out
> Light goes far
> Transcend ancient, but still bizarre
> Got other worlds figuring where they are
> In other words, navigating through the night
> Because a word's thoughts are able to take flight
> Because a beat's words are able to grow wings
> Because a thought's beats are able to move things
> Arm, legs, head, feet, hands and what they bring
> Objects, places, people, perspective
> See we selective, 'cause we're protective
> That's the objective for this collective, but it's subjective

"This music," he explained, "is taking me all around the world, and it's allowed me to share my thoughts through my words, so it's like my thoughts have value because of the words. The words have value because

Medusa, San Salvador, El Salvador, December 5, 2015. Photograph by Mark Katz.

of the beat, and the beat has value because it inspires more thought. You know what I mean? So it's a kind of cyclical relationship."[26]

When J-Live speaks of the "darkest black hole . . . where the sweetest juices get buried," he also hints that travel allows him to leave behind a place where his art is unappreciated or even suppressed. For African American and other marginalized artists, the duality of international travel as a means of escape and a form of validation is nothing new. Ever since bugler and composer Francis "Frank" Johnson and his ensemble sailed to London to perform several concerts in 1837, black musicians have found refuge, opportunities, and enthusiastic audiences abroad.[27] The same has been true for the blues, jazz, rock, and hip hop artists in the generations that followed.

In traveling abroad, America's artistic ambassadors of color don't just leave behind demeaning critiques of their music; they also find refuge from more menacing forms of discrimination. Houston-based dancers Javier Garcia and Rocc Williams of the Soul Street Dance Crew told me how they, as Latino and African American, are treated in their own country: "We literally get pulled over every single tour because the way we look."[28] When they travel for cultural diplomacy tours, the profiling and harassment follow them to the borders and greet them on their return; they are regularly held for additional searches and questioning at airports. "We've been going through it our whole lives. It's something we'll never like or get used to, but you get kind of numb to it. It's just something that we understand from growing up in the hood." Their reception changes once they step foot outside the United States. "Aw man, it's crazy, it's like we're superstars out there," Garcia marvels. This open-armed welcome has greeted them in Armenia and Azerbaijan, Estonia and Latvia, Malta and Haiti. Akim Funk Buddha, a multifaceted artist who beatboxes, dances, and raps, notes a change the moment he leaves the United States, where he feels that others see him as a criminal simply because he is a black man. "There is an immediate weight off my shoulders. I don't feel like I'm being watched. I actually feel like I'm moving around freely. When I see cops or authorities, I feel a lot more relaxed. It's nice just moving around the stores, and the attention you get is usually that of curiosity."[29]

Many US artists report the same curious attention, and most of the time they take it in stride. For African American MC Mahogany Jones, "the idea of being the 'exotic other' does not sting. It doesn't offend, maybe just because even back home I'm used to being different, my difference usually being a thing that causes a shunning or being ostracized." But when abroad, "being different, it's just like, you know, I'm a celebrity for being 'other.' Works for me!"[30] Still, there can be a trade-off, especially when artists visit places where few people look like them. DJ Marc Bayangos, aka Mista B, recalls an encounter in Podgorica, Montenegro, when some schoolchildren called out: "Oh yeah, Jackie Chan!" and gave him the thumbs-up sign. "Another group of kids," he reports, "when I passed by them they were doing martial arts sounds." He heard comments like this enough times that he finally

responded in exasperation to one group: "Me Filipino. No Chinese."[31]
Dancers Garcia and Williams reported being treated "like exotic an-
imals" in the Baltics where people want to touch their skin and hair
and take photos of them. Akim Funk Buddha had the same experience
in Azerbaijan. "Wow, is it just the fact that they've never seen a person
of color like myself? What is actually behind the intrigue? Is it because
we look like images that they've seen on TV? Am I being seen like a
trophy?" Although it's not much of choice, he prefers exoticization over
discrimination. "I'll take being seen as a trophy, I'd take that over being
seen like you're a criminal."[32] These encounters remind us that hip hop
diplomats constantly operate within a zone of ambiguity. They can
never be certain what is intended and what has been lost in translation.
As marginalized citizens of a global superpower who are perceived both

Mahogany Jones and new friends in Samarkand, Uzbekistan, June 1, 2018. Photograph by
Mark Katz.

as tradition-bearers of authentic hip hop culture and as exotic others, the power relationships become too complex to disentangle.

A depressing aside: participants in Next Level's US residency, who come from each of the countries the program visits, have reported the inverse experience of being apprehensive about being people of color in the States. Salvadoran DJ Cue Bass said that he was warned that in the United States "you have to be careful with the cops. They don't play around."[33] When Tanzanian rapper Kiche Legend came to the United States in 2016, his mother feared for his life and insisted that he check in every day. When I asked why, he said, "I think, more or less, it's because I am a black man, and I am in the US."[34]

Despite these unresolvable tensions, uncertainties, and ambiguities, hip hop diplomats often speak of their work as life-changing in the most positive ways. The personal, artistic, and professional growth that they experience, however, is only part of what drives them. They also cite external, outward-directed motivators: the ability to serve and represent something larger than themselves; the promise of building global hip hop community; the power to do good in the world through one's art. Reflecting on his motivation for participating in a hip hop diplomacy program, beatmaker Charles Burchell recalled how, when he was a teenager, a visitor to his high school asked him what he wanted to do with music. "I remember at that moment feeling this weird pressure to say what I really, really wanted to do, to speak it into existence. So I said, 'I want to change the world.' Through my career I've seen just how impactful music can be to different communities. And for me my entry point into music was hip hop."[35]

## REPRESENTATIONS

Representing is a powerful theme in hip hop discourse.[36] Hip hop hails individual success, but it also celebrates affiliation and belonging. In the US, hip hop artists frequently shout out their neighborhoods and hometowns, their area codes, their crews or gangs; they also invoke broader or more metaphorical affiliations, whether the hood, the ghetto, the street, the underground, or their gender, race, or ethnicity.

Representing is related to getting paid in that both may be a response to exclusion, motivated by the desire to find meaning, value, and power outside "the system." Hip hop diplomacy allows artists opportunities to represent, often in ways that are difficult to achieve otherwise. Representing one's country through hip hop is both a novel and attractive proposition for some artists. Diamond D's father was a Vietnam War veteran, and he suggested that he was both following in his footsteps and forging a more peaceful form of representing. When I asked him if he felt like he was representing his country during his time in Serbia, he didn't hesitate: "Yes, because I am. All of us are. We're not out here shooting at people, but we're out here representing the country."[37] Well before venturing on his first State Department–supported trip, dancer and later Next Level director Junious Brickhouse represented his country as a soldier. He spent a decade in the US Army, serving in the Balkans as a Supply Sergeant with NATO peacekeeping units. Part of the appeal of representing the United States as a dancer was that it allowed him to continue his peacekeeping work in conflict areas around the world. "I am a soldier. I am a warrior spirit. I knew that being a soldier was something that I have to continue to do. If not as soldier in the capacity of a war fighter, there had to be other causes that needed attention. Those two things, being a soldier and being an artist, they're connected for me in a lot of ways."[38]

Yet representing one's country is irreducibly problematic for those whose communities and cultures have been marginalized or actively oppressed by their government. This is not unique to hip hop diplomacy. In the 1961 album *The Real Ambassadors*, Louis Armstrong sings of the pressures of serving as a US cultural envoy in "Remember Who You Are":

> Remember who you are and what you represent
> Always be a credit to your government
> No matter what you say and what you do
> The eyes of the world are watching you

The pressure to "be a be a credit to your government" remains, even if the State Department has moved toward working with less famous artists and promoting less publicly visible activities, like workshops. The song continues to be relevant, as when, in a later verse, Armstrong advises:

> Remember who you are and what you represent
> Never face a problem, always circumvent
> Stay away from issues
> Be discreet—when controversy enters, you retreat[39]

More than a half-century later, the State Department's cultural programs officers are quick to tell hip hop artists that they shouldn't feel responsible for addressing matters of US foreign policy. More or less as Armstrong suggests, they are encouraged to retreat from controversy when asked about sensitive issues by speaking from their personal or artistic perspectives. They frame this advice as a means to relieve artists of any pressure to speak outside of their area of expertise. At the same time, it's a canny way to avoid public embarrassment.

Most of the hip hop artists I've worked with are happy *not* to speak on behalf of the government, yet most feel that they are representing something more, something larger than themselves. Beatboxer and MC Baba Israel, a white artist and committed social activist, spoke for many when he related that representing his country meant "being able to represent a *different* kind of America." As he explained in 2017, early in Donald Trump's presidency, "this is the America that I know and participate in, which I don't always feel is reflected in mainstream media and most people's experiences of how America is perceived, particularly now."[40] MC Toki Wright offers some specific examples. "For me, it's one thing for me to speak on behalf of the United States. But it means so much more for me to speak on behalf of Minnesotans, and to speak on behalf of black men, and to speak on behalf of black Minnesotan men, black Midwestern men, black artists that aren't creating ultraviolent, sexist music."[41] When I asked MC Pinqy Ring who or what she represented when she went to Cambodia she answered with this list: "Women, for sure, first and foremost. Especially because we're so underrepresented in hip hop. And then I feel like I was representing Chicago specifically. You know, we get such a bad rap about our city and the violence in it. And then, just representing people of color, Latinx people, Puerto Rican people."[42] Pinqy Ring and Toki Wright, like all artists, represent multiple related categories, all of which contribute to their identity.

Toni Blackman embodies yet a different form of representation. During a radio interview in South Africa, where she had been performing on behalf of the State Department, she rebutted a caller's accusation of complicity by invoking her ancestors' contributions to her home country.

> This guy calls into the radio station and he had a whole speech prepared. He couldn't believe that a woman as educated as me, who had gone to the esteemed Howard University, the mecca of black education, could rationalize working for the US of A. And I was like, are you asking me how I rationalize the fact that my grandfather and great-grandfather helped build the country of the US of A? Are you asking me to rationalize that I have a history in that country, and yes the beginning of that history began with the brutalization of my people and my ancestors, but I come from a legacy of survivors who are also builders and contributors, and one of the reasons the culture and music around the country is good? I said every time I show up my grandfather is being represented and honored. It's his legacy, his history and I have a right to stand up and be a part of it, so which country would you have me represent? And it was silence. I said this is who I am, yes it's a painful past, but so is the past here in South Africa. And we can't reject all of who we are, all of our history. We can dislike it, we can hate it, we can be pained by it, but it is what it is and we have to figure

out how to own it and make it our own, and I think I do that quite powerfully.[43]

Hip hop artists traveling abroad for the State Department are representing at all times: they are representing themselves, their government and their country, their hometowns and their families and ancestors, their race and gender and ethnicity, their hip hop art and culture. Representing, as much as performing or teaching, is vital to this work. Largely invisible, it is a form of emotional labor—Kendra Salois describes it as "affective labor"—and an underappreciated part of people-to-people diplomacy.[44]

Like representing, building—community, relationships, or understanding—is a form of emotional or affective labor that hip hop diplomats provide. Building is also, as many artists attest, deeply meaningful to them. Sometimes the results of this labor are immediately gratifying. Over the course of a few days or a few weeks the artists may become fast friends with those who had recently been strangers. Often, however, the process of building unfolds over months and years. Relationships may deepen and new collaborations blossom. I have witnessed almost every possible combination of collaborative partnership: US artists and international participants, US artists and other US artists; international artists and other international artists. Most often these arise out of their direct interactions, but in other cases it was the network of artists—or "family," as some call it—created by a particular program that led to these collaborations between artists who hadn't previously worked together. Next Level MCs G Yamazawa and Kane Smego came together for the infectious summer 2017 track, "North Cack" (referring to their home state of North Carolina), whose viral video was directed by Saleem Reshamwala, a videographer for several Next Level residencies.[45] In 2016, Next Level MC Shirlette Ammons produced the *Family Affair Mixtape*, a CD compilation featuring tracks created by Bosnian, Senegalese, Serbian, and US rappers, DJs, and beatmakers.[46] Perhaps most often, however, building yields invisible structures, whether friendships, networks, or communities, and sometimes one builds without knowing what might come of it. As DJ Juan Gomez put it when he was finishing his Zimbabwe residency in 2014, "It takes a lot of work to see the fruit of your labor, it takes a long time for that. I feel there is something to be said about the idea of planting seeds and seeing what comes from that."[47]

## SUBVERSIVE COMPLICITY

Hip hop artists who work as cultural diplomats sometimes worry that they will be censored or asked to spout "propaganda bullshit," as Asheru put it. State Department personnel, however, tend to champion free speech, and not only tolerate dissent but hold it up as proof of the great value of democracy. This was true when certain jazz ambassadors lashed out against their government during the Civil Rights Era, and it remains true in the age of hip hop diplomacy. Yet, as Su'Ad Abdul Khabeer suggests, there may be an element of cynicism in the State Department's deployment of hip hop as a vehicle for free expression, particularly in its efforts to reach Muslim populations around the world. "In refiguring hip hop as a bridge builder," she writes, "the dissent of racialized and marginalized communities becomes a marker not of where the state has failed but of where it is succeeding. Like the power inequities between the United States and Muslim-majority nations, the power inequities within the United States voiced by hip hop cannot be heard over the roar of US American triumph."[48] What Khabeer calls "the administration of dissent" can be a way of championing free speech without addressing the injustices that such dissent reveals.

What, then, is a hip hop artist to do when faced with the possibility of working with the State Department? Some suggest that any relationship with the State Department is simply too problematic for a person of conscience. Hip hop journalist Harry Allen put it this way when I asked him about the prospect of artists participating in a State Department program: "I think that our government, our United States government is such an enormous entity, and has its hands in so many things, that arguably anything one does on its behalf, in that context, is selling out."[49] Yet refusing to participate and selling out are not the only choices. There is another possibility: subversive complicity. Following sociologist Ramón Grosfoguel, scholars have used this term to describe a stance in which a traditionally marginalized or subjugated group participates within an exploitative system in order to resist or reform a hegemonic power. Grosfoguel developed the concept to explain why Puerto Ricans have consistently voted for statehood rather than independence from the United States, a choice that has been caricatured as the product of a passive, ignorant, or colonized people. To the contrary, Grosfoguel argues, it is a pragmatic stance that, as he bluntly puts it, recognizes that "exploitation with some benefits" is preferable to "exploitation without benefits."[50] The concept of subversive complicity also illuminates why hip hop artists may choose not to fight the power but, on occasion, to collaborate with it. As Kane Smego put it, "I'm taking that money. They're going to use it to build rockets and missiles anyway, so I might as well take it and build songs instead."[51]

Consider the example of the Los Angeles–based group Ozomatli, a band known for its activist, often anti-government lyrics. Between 2007 and 2011 the group performed in more than a dozen countries in Africa, Asia, Europe, the Middle East, and South America on behalf of the State Department. Given that, in their 2001 song "Embrace the Chaos," they asked, "Are you a soldier who fights against fraud/Or pawns in this game on this government's chess board?" we might wonder whether they themselves became pawns when they accepted the invitation to serve as cultural ambassadors. But as Cruz Medina suggests, there's a different way to view their State Department work. "As cultural ambassadors," Medina argues, "Ozomatli performed subversive complicity. [Their] incorporation of *banda, cumbia,* and *merengue* appeals to neoliberal celebrations of diversity, thereby facilitating Ozomatli's appearance as complicit ambassadors; however, the danceable beats and rhythms mask the political messages transmitted in lyrics that contest governmental authority."[52] Percussionist and founding member Jiro Yamaguchi recalls being perplexed by the invitation to perform on behalf of the State Department. "We were against the war, very against George Bush and pretty vocal about it. So when they asked us we were like, do you know who we are? Do you know what we represent? Have you been to our website? Do you know what we do? They were open to that, they loved the music and wanted us to represent America."[53] The musicians of Ozomatli didn't seek out this work, but when the invitation came they accepted, knowing that they could share their messages about justice and injustice to people around the world that they would otherwise never encounter.

When Pinqy Ring, a Chicagoan MC of Puerto Rican heritage, was invited to perform for the US Ambassador to Cambodia as part of Next Level's April 2018 residency in Phnom Penh, she chose "Revolución," a song she wrote in response to Donald Trump's election. An announcement accompanying the 2016 release of "Revolución" explained its genesis and its goals:

> Last week Donald Trump was announced President-elect of the United States, and there is no denying that a lot of people are upset, hurt, confused, scared, and angry. Pinqy uses her platform to prepare the *paleteros*, the Chicago Bucket Boys, our ancestors and so many more . . . She is chanting and rapping for women, people of color, the undocumented, the disabled, the LGBTQ community, the religiously persecuted, and all allies to mobilize and create the future WE want and need.
>
> It's time for equality, it's time for equity, it's time for social justice. It's time for Revolución.[54]

The song is a call to action, an honor roll, a memorial, and a shit list. She praises the *paleteros* who sell ice cream from pushcarts; the Chicago Bucket Boys, percussionists who perform using only drumsticks and five-gallon plastic buckets; Oscar López Rivera, the Puerto Rican activist and militant. She blesses "fallen soldiers," victims of police brutality such as Sandra Bland and Philando Castile. And she calls out the president and the police: "Lemme hear the people holla—Fuck Trump!"; "Fuck the boys in Blue." She sang all this at the well-appointed residence of the US Ambassador in Cambodia. When members of the Embassy's Public Affairs Section heard the song they requested that she not perform it at the residency's final, and public, show a few days later. But she and her team pushed back, insisting that she be able to express herself in solidarity with those in the audience who were not as free as her. She only made one change for the all-ages audience by replacing the obscenities. But she did not temper her message. She felt that the performance was well received. "The Universal message of creating a better world & speaking your truth is always welcomed," she later explained, proud that the youth "were raising their fists and really taking in the energy of the song."[55]

Solidarity can be a form of shared resistance, directed toward oppressive systems, inequality, and bigotry. Since late 2016, solidarity also emerged around a more specific object of resistance: Donald Trump.

Pinqy Ring in Phnom Penh, Cambodia, March 28, 2018. Photograph by Juan Gomez.

When Next Level visited Tunis, we commissioned a group of local graffiti artists to paint a mural near where the final show would take place. In stylized letters spelling "Next Level Tunisia," they painted "Next Level" in red, white, and blue stars and stripes and "Tunisia" in red with the white crescent and star from the national flag. Flanking the words were two hats, a baseball cap on one side and a Fez on the other. Connecting "Next Level" and "Tunisia" was an image of a traditional studded blue Tunisian door. The symbolism of solidarity was hardly subtle. The final touch was an example—one of many—of shared resistance and subversive complicity. In smaller print, below the American flag lettering, one of the Tunisians added two words: "Fuck Trump." The US and Tunisian artists bonded gleefully over the shared sentiment. Moments like these became an undeniable form of cross-cultural bridgebuilding in the age of Trump.

Hip hop diplomacy has been subversive in a variety of other, often informal ways. The impromptu cypher in the State Department lobby during Next Level's first orientation invoked the spirit of the New York b-boys and b-girls who commandeered the marble-floored lobbies of upscale apartment buildings. But simply the existence of government funding for hip hop artists is potentially subversive. The continued operation of hip hop diplomacy into the age of Trump may in fact have been due to a quiet subversiveness on the part of the State Department's program officers. Soon after the election they fast-tracked the renewal process for Next Level so that funding could be secured before cuts threatened by the president could be enacted. They moved Next Level's orientation cypher out of the State Department, where they worried it would be noticed by higher-ups with little sympathy for hip hop or cultural diplomacy. After Trump's proposed "Muslim bans" they suggested ambiguous talking points for responding to questions from the media—for example, that cultural diplomacy is more important than ever to demonstrate the diversity of our country. Behind the scenes, too, they defended these programs, touting their effectiveness in ways that would be palatable to skeptical officials in the State Department or in Congress.

Cultural diplomacy became an act of subversion in the age of Trump. These programs were often designed to engage and support groups—women, the disabled, refugees—whom the president openly mocked or whose concerns he dismissed. Conflict resolution, an activity explicitly mentioned in the earliest documents connected with Next Level, was at odds with a president who publicly embraced conflict. "I like conflict," he said in March 2018. "I like watching it, I like seeing it, and I think it's the best way to go."[56] Consider a striking, almost absurd juxtaposition of events from November 2018. MC Def-i was leading a State Department–sponsored workshop in Abuja, Nigeria with a group of rappers from different ethnic groups and regions of the country, all of them sharing their languages and cultures. In a Facebook post he wrote, "Today's writing workshop focused on 'Cultural Heritage.' We learned some new vocabulary from [one] another and then applied pieces of #DinéBizaad, #Hausa, #Igbo, #Yoruba, and #English languages into the rhyme. Learning so much each day and am very honored to help build connections between our local community."[57] That same day, just a few miles away, the Nigerian army was killing dozens of protesters who were armed only with stones. Defending the massacre, army officials posted a video of Donald Trump suggesting in a speech that he would authorize deadly force in a similar situation at the US–Mexico border. "They want to throw rocks at our military," Trump said, "our military fights back."[58] While Def-i was using words to build community with Nigerians, the Nigerian Army was using Trump's words to justify slaughtering protesters.

With the change in administration it became less clear if hip hop diplomacy was still consistent with the mission of the State Department. In late 2017, Secretary Rex Tillerson instituted an explicit change in the Department's mission statement. Compare the older and newer statements:

> The Department's mission is to shape and sustain a peaceful, prosperous, just, and democratic world and foster conditions

for stability and progress for the benefit of the American people and people everywhere.[59] (2016)

The US Department of State advances the interests of the American people, their safety and economic prosperity, by leading America's foreign policy through diplomacy, advocacy, and assistance.[60] (2017)

Notice the change in priorities. Not only are certain words absent—*peaceful, just, democratic, stability,* and *progress*—the new statement clearly asserts an America First mission, one that advances the interests of the United States rather than the interests of people everywhere.[61] Where did that leave mutual understanding and collaboration? What did it mean for hip hop diplomacy? Did the act of *building* with others through hip hop suddenly become off-mission? Did it become subversive?

Subversive complicity may seem like a contradiction, an impossibility, but in hip hop diplomacy it is standard operating procedure. The artists who participate in these programs tend to recognize the tradeoffs of this work and have decided that standing on the sidelines is not an acceptable option. Kuttin Kandi put it this way: "When . . . I come in to working with the United States Department of State, it may seem like a contradiction, but maybe it's really a form of resistance in a different way." Explaining her perspective, she flipped the concept of hip hop as tool of diplomacy. For Kandi, diplomacy was a tool of hip hop: "I think we have to utilize every tool. This one is literally the tool of being under the United States Department of State, which is completely different, and it's contradicting, and people can argue that with me, and that's fine. I learn as I go along. If it's a mistake, it's a mistake, but I won't really know that until I step into the country and begin that dialogue."[62] Or as I once heard another hip hop artist say, "If you want to stay pure, stay home."

"I'm not anti-government," says hip hop theater artist Will Power, who has conducted workshops on behalf of the State Department. "I'm very aware of the great things that the US government has done," he explains, but he is also well aware "of some of the wicked things that the US government has done or does." So I asked him, does he feel in any way complicit with this wickedness? His answer came without hesitation: "Absolutely."

He did not agonize about the definition of complicity. He simply accepted the inescapability of complicity even for the most principled among us:

> I have one of my son's toys in my hand. It's a grim reaper toy and it's made in China. It's plastic, which is not good for the environment, and it was made probably in a sweatshop. So I kind of feel like we all are complicit. I'd like to think that I'm more part of the solution than part of the problem, but I don't know 100 percent. You try to do the best you can. So in the State Department I feel like the work I was doing was complicit with some of the evils that it's done, but I also feel like it was in line with some of the good that it's done. I think the United States government does do good, too. Whether it does more good than bad I don't know. I feel like right now the work I'm doing in the world, I'm serving better than I would if I just moved to the country and was just like, "I'm not going to be complicit in those type of things." Plus, I want to take care of my family.[63]

When Power accepts his complicity, how exactly does his work with the State Department align him with his government's most dishonorable acts? There's no easy answer. But as he points out, he could hardly pretend he was blameless in that sphere or any other. At the time he was teaching at Southern Methodist University in Dallas, an institution made rich by the oil and gas industries, and by extension, through environmental degradation. I was calling him from my home outside Chapel Hill, where I teach at the University of North Carolina, an institution built in part by slave labor, and thus built upon human degradation. The real question we need to ask ourselves, he suggests, is not if one is complicit, but whether one can do good in the world despite the unavoidable complicity of modern life.

Talk to US hip hop artists who decided to participate in a State Department–funded program and you'll find a nuanced understanding of the challenges and rewards and tradeoffs of this work. These artists are not naïve. They realize that the US government can oppress and empower and destroy and build. They recognize that they need not embrace the State Department to work with it nor reject it to maintain their integrity. They believe that they can be skeptical of their government while serving it, that they can despise aspects of their nation's history while loving—and embodying—elements of its culture. They know that to live with these ambiguities without seeking to resolve them is no sign of an unprincipled nature but the mark of a good citizen, precisely the kind of citizen who should represent their country to the world.

## CHAPTER 5

# BUILD AND DESTROY:
# HIP HOP, US DIPLOMACY, AND ISLAM

"Alhamdulillah!" the singers called out, "Praise be to Allah!" Behind them a large hand-painted banner proclaimed in English, "Hip Hop is Universal," with the Wolof words for *peace, love*, and *unity* written below. The audience at the Théâtre National Daniel Sorano, including the great Senegalese musician Youssou N'Dour and his family, raised their arms high, fists clenched in solidarity. At the skirt of the stage, another banner, emblazoned with the United States flag, advertised the US Embassy in Dakar. It was January 16, 2015, the final night of the two-week Next Level residency in Senegal.

The next day I was chatting with Pape Mamadou Camara in the library of the G Hip Hop community center in the nearby city of Guédiawaye. I was surprised, I told Camara, the center's program manager, at how often the performers invoked Allah at the concert. That was nothing unusual, he said, noting that Senegalese hip hop shows and albums typically featured one or more songs praising Allah, the prophets, or a *marabout* (a local religious teacher). Curious, I asked him what he saw as the relationship between hip hop and Islam. "I actually see the conception, the philosophy of hip hop in Islam," he replied. "And I actually see the philosophy of Islam in hip hop. "[1]

Two years later I stood in front of a room full of beatmakers in Algiers. The young men were eager to start the second day of their workshop with US producer Nicholas "Decap" Piantedosi, but first I had some questions. What, I asked, would they want non-Muslims to understand

Final concert, Next Level Senegal, Dakar, Senegal, January 16, 2015. Photograph by Mark Katz.

about their religion? "Salam," several said simultaneously, explaining that Islam is a religion of peace. What, I then asked, was the connection between Islam and hip hop for them? One replied that the Qur'an says that music—and, by extension, hip hop—is *haram*, or forbidden.[2] Another suggested that, as good Muslims, if they were to make hip hop music it had to be clean. But mostly I was greeted with annoyance. One beatmaker curtly responded that hip hop is a culture and Islam is religion and that he doesn't mix the two. Another agreed, saying that he prays five times a day and makes beats in between. A third called out, "Why do you keep asking about Islam?"[3] I realized that, as a stranger and non-Muslim, I was rude to ask such forward, personal questions, especially in a public setting, and I regret my insensitivity.[4] Their irritation made it clear, however, that they did not share Pape Camara's view of the intimate relationship between Islam and hip hop.

These experiences in Senegal and Algeria are just two of the varied perspectives I have encountered among Muslim hip hop artists in

Africa, Asia, and Europe, as well as among US Muslim artists. Some were pious. Some expressed a cultural connection to Islam but weren't observant. Others said that they were not very good Muslims. This is exactly what one should expect from the world's Muslims, who, numbering about 1.8 billion, make up almost a quarter of the world's population.[5] All religions have devout followers as well as indifferent or estranged ones. As scholar Peter Awn has said, "Let's get over thinking that Muslims are more pious than anyone else."[6] In looking for the connection between hip hop and Islam, I found many, and sometimes I found none.

In reflecting on these conversations I came to realize that it was almost always I who initiated them. In a sense, I have served as a stand-in for my country's perspective on Islam. Even taking the most charitable view, the attitude of many non-Muslim Americans reveals a mix of anxiety, curiosity, fetishism, and ignorance. For decades, and especially since the terrorist attacks of September 11, 2001, the United States has had a fraught, almost obsessive relationship with Islam. This relationship has shaped hip hop diplomacy, which has operated almost entirely in the post-9/11 age, when much of the work of cultural diplomacy implicitly or explicitly focused on the question of how to engage Muslim communities around the world. US Foreign Service Officers had long been aware of the popularity of hip hop among young Muslims; when footage of young protestors chanting politically charged rap anthems played throughout the world during the Arab uprisings of 2010–2012, the possibility that hip hop could be a force for political change, even for the spread of democracy, took hold among many observers. It's no coincidence that the State Department has sent scores of US hip hop artists to more than two dozen Muslim-majority countries since 2001.

Non-Muslim Americans get a lot wrong about Islam. Well-meaning, open-minded people speak about "the Muslim world" and "moderate Muslims" without realizing why the concepts are problematic. In her 2017 article, "The 'Muslim World' Does Not Exist," Zareena Grewal explained the problems:

[The "Muslim World" is] a Western idea built on the faulty racial logic that Muslims live in a world of their own—that Islam is an eastern, foreign religion that properly belongs in a distant, faraway, dusty place. If the Muslim world is a euphemism for the Middle East [ . . . ] what to make of the fact that 80 percent of the world's 1.6 billion Muslims live outside the Middle East, including American Muslims like me?

The "moderate" Muslim is the Muslim who will endorse a version of his or her own religion that has already been endorsed by the US government. The "moderate" Muslim is the Muslim who will uncritically toe the line when it comes to US policy.[7]

Both of these concepts reduce Islam to a monolithic and potentially menacing other, viewing this vast, diverse religion through the lens of foreign policy. The "Muslim world" is actually a legacy of nineteenth-century European imperialism that conceived of Islam as a geopolitical unit that could be brought under outside control. At the same time, many Muslims embraced the concept themselves, but for the purpose of unifying communities against European hegemony. As historian Cemil Aydin explains, "starting in the late nineteenth century, pan-Islamists and Islamophobes have used the assumption, ideal, and threat of Muslim unity to advance political agendas. Together, and in tension, they created the Muslim world for their own strategic purposes and positioned it in everlasting conflict with the West."[8]

Misunderstanding about Islam also arises from confusion about the terms *Muslim* and *Arab*. When referring to people, *Muslim* denotes a follower of the religion of Islam and *Arab* typically refers to someone whose native language is Arabic. The majority of Arabs are Muslim.[9] Most Muslims are *not* Arab, however. The five countries with the largest Muslim populations—Indonesia, India, Pakistan, Bangladesh, and Nigeria—are not Arab.[10] Whereas the "Muslim world" is a concept, the Arab world is a geographic reality, constituting twenty-two nations in North Africa and the Middle East with a combined population of around 415 million in 2017. (There is also a significant Arab diaspora spread throughout the world.) Confusion about the terms *Arab* and *Muslim* and all that they represent seems to have persisted undiminished in the years since 9/11.

US cultural diplomacy, particularly after 9/11, has operated on the assumption of a monolithic Muslim world—not always clearly distinguished from the Arab world—and a moderate Islam that can be cultivated. These assumptions have guided the State Department's interest in hip hop. We see this when former US Ambassador to the Netherlands Cynthia Schneider wrote in 2008 about the "tremendous potential of hip hop for building connections between the United States and the Muslim world," and encouraged "greater exploitation of this natural connector to the Muslim world."[11] We see this when Hillary Clinton, as Secretary of State, spoke in 2010 of hip hop as one of the "tools at our disposal" in US relations with Syria.[12] Both represent an understanding of hip hop as valuable and exploitable, a distinctively effective means of connecting with audiences that have been alienated by US foreign policy.

## US CULTURAL DIPLOMACY, 9/11, AND THE "MUSLIM WORLD"

Although the United States received a great deal of international sympathy after the 9/11 attacks, global public opinion soured in the wake of human rights abuses committed by the US in its War on Terror. As the State Department's Advisory Committee on Cultural Diplomacy explained in its 2005 report,

> [L]arge majorities in Egypt, Morocco, and Saudi Arabia, for example, view George W. Bush as a greater threat to the world order than Osama bin Laden; favorability ratings in Turkey, Pakistan, and Jordan steadily declined in 2002, 2003, and 2004; a poll taken in ten countries in October 2004— in Canada, France, Britain, Spain, Japan, South Korea,

Australia, Mexico, Israel, and Russia: some of our closest allies—revealed the same trend.[13]

The United States had an image problem, one of the worst in its history. As Ronan Farrow explains in his book, *War on Peace*, the State Department was historically ill-equipped to deal with the situation: "So it was that on September 11, 2001, the State Department was 20 percent short of staff, and those who remained were undertrained and under-resourced. The United States needed diplomacy now more than ever, and it was nowhere to be found."[14] The State Department faced a nearly impossible task, and not only because of depleted resources. The true problem wasn't so much one of image but one of reality, a reality created by US foreign policy. A 2003 report made it plain: "Surveys show much of the resentment toward America stems from our policies. It is clear, for example, that the Arab-Israeli conflict remains a visible and significant point of contention between the United States and many Arab and Muslim countries and that peace in that region, as well as the transformation of Iraq, would reduce tensions."[15] But short of changing policy, what could be done?

The first response was a public relations campaign. Charlotte Beers, a successful advertising executive, was appointed to the newly created position of Undersecretary of State for Public Diplomacy, and quickly launched a $15 million "Shared Values Initiative." Consisting of videos, radio spots, print ads, fliers, websites, and lectures aimed at Muslims around the world and promoted during the holy month of Ramadan, the campaign was intended, according to a government report, "to demonstrate that the United States is an open society, and that Americans and Muslims [i.e., non-American Muslims] share certain values and beliefs."[16] In one video segment, the Muslim American owner of a Lebanese bakery in Toledo, Ohio, is shown enjoying a family outing to a local carnival; in a voiceover he says, "Religious freedom here is something that is very important, and no one ever bothered us. Since 9/11, we've had an overwhelming sense of support from our customers and clients."[17] However sincere those featured in the campaign were,

"Shared Values" was widely criticized as an ineffective and ethically compromised propaganda campaign. As one analysis put it, "The campaign's utilization of truth, its treatment of Muslim audiences as means to achieve broader policy objectives rather than as a population to be engaged on its own terms, and its use of 'palaver,' or innocuous talk, all suggest that the campaign had serious ethical shortcomings."[18] Beers resigned from the State Department after eighteen months and "Shared Values" was discontinued.

The Freedom Promotion Act of 2002, introduced in the House of Representatives by Henry Hyde, took a different tack, recommending over $800 million in funding for public diplomacy:

> As part of a broad and long-term effort to enhance a positive image of the United States in the Muslim world, a key element should be the establishment of [State Department] programs to promote a greater familiarity with American society and values among the general public and select audiences in countries of predominantly Muslim population.[19]

The bill did not pass. A few months later, the "Cultural Bridges Act of 2002," proposed by Senator Edward Kennedy, authorized $75 million in annual funding to "expand the activities of the State Department's existing educational and cultural programs in the Islamic world."[20] It also did not pass.

Some early US diplomatic initiatives had more success. Radio Sawa (*sawa* means "together" in some spoken Arabic dialects) and the television network Al Hurra ("the free one") began broadcasting throughout the Middle East in 2002 and 2004. The networks offered Arabic language news and entertainment with the purpose of promoting democratic values and improving the image of the United States. They remained on the air as of 2019, although their effectiveness and credibility have been questioned over the years.[21] In September 2002 the State Department established the Advisory Committee on Cultural Diplomacy. Its first report urged the Secretary of State to "expand international cultural exchange programs, inviting more Arab and Muslim artists, performers, and writers to the United States, and sending their American counterparts to the Islamic world."[22] The State Department–funded Kennedy-Lugar Youth Exchange and Study (YES) program, established in October 2002, invited high school students from countries with significant Muslim populations to spend an academic year in the US.[23] In its first fifteen years, the program brought more than 11,000 young Muslims to the United States. In 2003, the State Department sent US dance companies for one-month residencies in Egypt, India, Malaysia, and Turkey specifically to work with Muslim communities; although this was a one-time government investment through its Cultural Specialists program, some of the companies continued their work on their own.[24]

For the most part, however, the recommendations for people-to-people exchanges were little heeded. The best funded initiatives were in the form of public relations or propaganda campaigns—one-way flows of communication. Yet this mode of image-shaping is rarely successful on its own.[25] The most effective methods of shaping opinion demand an understanding of local contexts and sustained engagement. A 2003 US Government Accounting Office report observed an "absence of an integrated strategy" around public diplomacy.[26] Given that global opinion about the United States worsened considerably in the few years after 2001, it would be hard to argue that these initiatives succeeded.

The State Department's Bureau of Educational and Cultural Affairs did rather little by way of hip hop exchanges in the early years of the millennium. After rapper Toni Blackman's 2001 visit to Senegal and Ghana, the next State Department–sponsored hip hop tours were probably not until 2004. When Ozomatli toured Egypt, Jordan, and Tunisia in 2007, the Public Affairs Officer in Amman raved about the power of their presence:

> At a time when Jordanians maintain a largely hostile attitude toward US foreign policy, through this program they saw the best of America—that diversity and mutual respect makes

us stronger and feeds our ideals. Not just with their music, but also with their words and actions, Ozomatli promoted American culture and values and suggested to the audience that peace and tolerance can bring people closer together.[27]

Still, despite post-9/11 recommendations to conduct more intensive engagement with Muslim populations, and despite positive responses to the hip hop exchanges that State did sponsor, it was not until the so-called Arab Spring of 2010–2012 that hip hop diplomatic activity picked up. From the State Department's perspective, this would seem to be a missed opportunity, not only because of the popularity of hip hop among global Muslim youth, but also because of hip hop's historical connections with Islam.

## US HIP HOP AND ISLAM BEFORE 9/11

"Rap's got a religion and that religion's Islam."[28] So proclaimed Charlie Ahearn, journalist and director of the landmark hip hop film, *Wild Style*, in a 1991 issue of *Spin* magazine. Ahearn was not saying that most hip hop artists were Muslim, but rather that a growing number of prominent acts practiced Islam and incorporated its teachings and values into their music. His article profiled Brand Nubian, King Sun, Lakim Shabazz, Poor Righteous Teachers, and Rakim, just a few of the high profile artists who have identified with Islam.[29] Whether they know it or not, most hip hop fans have encountered the music of Muslim American artists. "Given that Islam has been a normative practice in Black America for centuries," writes linguist and hip hop scholar H. Samy Alim, "and that Black American popular culture from the Blues to Be Bop has always contained strong elements of social protest, the dynamic presence of Islam in the HHN [Hip Hop Nation] should come as no surprise."[30]

When Ahearn and others speak about the connection between hip hop and Islam, they are usually referring to the movement known as the Five Percent Nation.[31] Also known as the Nation of Gods and Earths, the Five Percent Nation was founded in Harlem in 1964 by

Clarence 13X, a former student of Malcolm X. Both men were associated with the Nation of Islam (NOI), an African American religious
and political movement that had been founded in Detroit in 1930. (To
be clear, however, Islam had been a part of American life since the time
of slavery.) Clarence 13X (later known as Allah the Father, or simply
Allah) split from the NOI to create the Five Percent Nation. The name
of the movement derives from the NOI concept that 10 percent of the
world's population understands the truth of human existence but use
their knowledge to keep 85 percent of the population ignorant and
under their control; the remaining 5 percent are the "poor righteous
teachers" who know the truth and use it to spread enlightenment. The
sharing of knowledge—"dropping science"—is central to the teachings
of the Five Percent Nation.

A rich source of the Five Percenters' knowledge comes from the
Science of Supreme Mathematics, which assigns specific meanings to
numbers and is used to reveal truths about the world. Two of these
number-concepts come up over and again in hip hop diplomacy, and
have been central to my understanding of hip hop's ability to foster
global community: 0 (cipher, also spelled cypher) and 8 (build or destroy). The cypher, that core improvisatory practice in hip hop and
one that can be so powerful in creating cross-cultural connections,
derives directly from Five Percenter numerology. Here is one expla-
nation: "Cipher is a circle, a completion of 360 degrees, consisting
of 120 degrees Knowledge, 120 degrees Wisdom, and 120 degrees
Understanding. The cipher has no beginning or ending point so that
we may rid our cipher of all negativity."[32] Whether or not hip hop artists are aware of the connection to Five Percenter theology, cyphering is
widely considered a positive, generative force.

And then there's the notion of building. In Five Percenter thought, to
build is to enhance knowledge and understanding, to add positivity to
the world. In the 1992 Brand Nubian song, "Allah and Justice," which
invokes all the numbers of the Science of Supreme Mathematics, Sadat
X raps, "God came to teach us/Of the righteous way/How to *build*
and be born/on this glorious day."[33] Building is always twinned with

its counterpart, destruction. "With my staff I walk through the wil
derness/*Build* on math, and *destroy* all the villainous criminals," Lord
Jamar, Sadat X's colleague, raps in "Dance to My Ministry," another of
Brand Nubian's many Five Percenter–inspired tracks.[34] Destruction is
typically undesirable, but it can also be a positive force, a means to rid
oneself and the world of negativity. Five Percenter MC J-Live describes
his art as "music that *builds* bridges and *destroys* barriers."[35] This sentiment echoes the broadest goals of hip hop diplomacy, which seeks to
build bridges and destroy barriers between communities and nations.
J-Live himself has participated in hip hop diplomacy, spending two
weeks in Zagreb teaching DJing to Croatian youth. He was willing to
work with the State Department precisely because it allowed him to
build. "I would never serve this country from a military standpoint because of how I feel about US foreign policy and its militaristic, imperialist nature," he explained. "But to be a cultural ambassador . . . it's like
by any means, whatever gets this done, I'm going to take it. I didn't have
any qualms about working for the State Department, but I was obvi-
ously on alert."[36]

The paired concept of building and destroying captures the uneasy
realities of cultural diplomacy. Every diplomatic act, however positive its goals, has the potential to destroy—to generate ill will, weaken
relationships, sow misunderstanding. Even if the destruction is meant
to be cleansing—by eliminating hate or confusion—it's not always clear
what has been built and what has been destroyed.

## HIP HOP AND ISLAM: INTERTWINED OR PARALLEL?

Most Five Percenter hip hop artists would view the relationship between hip hop and Islam as inextricable. Hundreds of songs allude
to Five Percenter concepts or explicitly articulate its theology.[37] Many
hip hop artists, like those I encountered in Senegal, would agree. But
many feel equally strongly about keeping their faith and art separate.
Both perspectives tell us about the values and aesthetics of individual
artists and the families, communities, and cultures that shape them.
Understanding these different perspectives also offers insights into how

diplomacy might serve as a builder—or destroyer—of bridges across nations.

Those who see hip hop and Islam as intertwined typically defend their view by pointing to shared values or practices. Early in hip hop's history, Afrika Bambaataa founded the Universal Zulu Nation to channel the energies of Bronx youth into positive, productive activities. Its unofficial motto and its core values are "Peace, Love, Unity, and Having Fun," and it is these values that I have heard many Muslim artists invoke. Pape Camara said this explicitly: "The best about hip hop are peace, love, unity and having fun. The best of hip hop are also knowledge, wisdom, understanding. The best of Islam are that."[38] This alignment of values is not coincidental; Bambaataa has said that he was "heavily influenced" by the philosophy of the Nation of Islam.[39]

Nesto, a graffiti artist in Baku, Azerbaijan, focuses specifically on love as the common element. "Love for the creator. Love for the creation. Hip hop is the same thing. It's about love."[40] The Cairo-born MC known as El Khayal speaks of Islam and hip hop in terms of wholeness and rationality: "Hip hop is about being a unit. Islam is about being a unit. Hip hop is about reason. Islam is about reason."[41] Moroccan MC Soultana sees both Islam and hip hop as agents of positive change, and defends hip hop against the charge that it, like other forms of music and art, is *haram*, forbidden, as some Islamic traditions and communities believe. As she contends, only that which brings *fitna*—strife, affliction, or temptation—is truly *haram*, and hip hop need not be a source of *fitna*.

> Mohammad, sallallahu alayhi wasalam [peace be upon him], he was asking for change for his people. In Islam they say that if your music is bringing fitna . . . it's haram. But if music is about changing, it's about something that is social [i.e., a social good], it's about a message, it's not haram at all. Because what you are doing, prophets did it before. Just they did it without music. You, you're doing it with music.[42]

Other Muslim hip hop artists have similarly argued that hip hop has the potential to do good, and thus be acceptable, or *halal*. Ahmed El Hareedy, a rapper from Alexandria, Egypt, put it this way: "We have a famous Imam who was called Sheik [Muhammad Metwali] Al Shaarawy. He told that music is like any other form of art. It's like a cup, you can fill it with alcohol, or you can fill it with water or medicine. So, it [hip hop] can be used for marketing, for sex and drugs, and whatever. Or, it could be good for the community. It could be haram. It could be halal. It could be forbidden, it could be okay."[43]

Some of Senegal's most prominent rappers are adherents of the centuries-old Tijaniyya Sufi order. Maxi Krezy, one of Senegal's most revered MCs, is a follower. Not only does he see hip hop and Islam as intertwined, he argues that his art is a powerful vehicle for disseminating religious values. "Those who listen to us," he explained in a television interview, "don't go to the mosque. They don't listen to sermons. So the ones they can listen to are those who are of the same generation, who do the same things, who frequent the same places." He may perform in nightclubs, but he isn't there to drink alcohol or be drawn into anything *haram*. He goes to the clubs "to fix people [and] to fix society," which, after all, he says, is the mission of Islam.[44] Consider "Baye Your Side," a 2008 song by Maxi Krezy, with Fadda Freddy and Ndongo D. The track, whose title is pronounced like "By Your Side" in English, combines hip hop and reggae with traditional forms of Arabic and West African poetry while extolling the virtues of Shaykh Ibrahim Niasse, the founder of the Tijaniyya Sufi order, whom followers call Baye, "father" in Wolof.[45] It's an extraordinary mixture of multilingual wordplay, Qur'anic references, heartfelt pleas for piety, and headbobbing grooves that exemplifies a view of hip hop and Islam as profoundly intertwined.

From the very beginning, hip hop has been a partner in rhyme with older oral traditions, whether with the dozens, an African American form of verbal battle, or the Jamaican practice of toasting—lyrical chanting over a beat. Like the Sufi rappers of Senegal, Muslim hip hop artists around the world find powerful connections with traditional poetic forms. Syrian American rapper Omar Offendum put it this way: "The Qur'an is such a lyrical, poetic text. Therefore, there's this tradition of real, deep respect for the word and for spoken word and for recitation in Islamic culture. I think that carries forth with hip hop."[46] Or as Egyptian MC El Khayal stated simply: "The Qur'an is poetry, hip hop is poetry."[47] The Muslim MCs I've met often cite the high esteem in which poetry is held by their families and in their communities as a key to gaining acceptance. Mohammad Indra Gandhi, an Indonesian rapper and producer who goes by the name Dom Dom, pointed out the similarity between hip hop rhymes and *pantun*, a poetic form popular in Indonesia, Malaysia, and Singapore. Its four-line stanzas and *abab* rhyme scheme make it easy to blend the old and the new in a way that Dom Dom has said finds favor among some who otherwise would reject hip hop.[48]

However much these artists might cherish the common ground between hip hop and Islam, the potential for friction between their creative and spiritual lives is ever present. For the Chicago-based dancer Amirah Sackett, this tension is heightened because of her gender and because she wears hijab, a traditional head covering. In 2014 she traveled for the first time to a country with a majority Muslim population, Bangladesh, where she spent two weeks leading a dance workshop. She has movingly related the experience of hearing the Muslim call to prayer in Dhaka as well as the tensions she felt during her visit:

> On my first morning in Dhaka, I woke up to the sound of the Adhan for Fajr prayer, it was still dark out. I leapt out of bed with energy I have never had for the earliest morning prayer. Hearing the Adhan ringing from different mosques in the stillness of that moment before dawn was the most emotional experience of my life. I prayed my two rakats (cycles) of prayer and as I put my forehead to the ground in prostration to my creator, tears fell from my eyes uncontrollably onto the prayer rug. I thanked Allah for this dream come true. I stayed looking out the window of my hotel room as

the sun rose above Lake Banani and I watched as rickshaws
and people headed to work. I realized I was halfway around
the world, doing what I love, with the people that share my
faith. Tears just flowed freely as I said "Allahu Akbar" (God
is Great) over and over again.

But during her time in Dhaka, Sackett felt the pull of opposing forces.
"I was very much aware of this conflict every day. The dancers [in the
workshop] didn't care at all. But other people outside of the hip hop
world made many comments to me on the appropriateness of what
I was doing. Even asking me why I am dancing as a career when I am a
good Muslim woman. So it was not easy. And it will not be easy. "[49]

Some artists feel that they have to make compromises to be a hip hop
artist and a "good" Muslim. I heard this from Fares "Fforsan" Forsan, a
Belgian producer of Moroccan heritage, who was introduced to hip hop
as a child in the 1980s. As we sat drinking mint tea and eating honeyed

Amirah Sackett (rear, with hijab), with Bangladeshi b-boys, Dhaka, Bangladesh, November 2014.
Photograph by Anshul Gupta.

sweets in a Brussels café that could well have been in Casablanca, he mused about these compromises:

> If you are a true believer, for example, God says to you "Do the good, be good with people." I can't be a part of gangster rappers, I can't sing "Let's kill everybody, let's deal [drugs], let's put the women in the street as prostitutes and they bring me money." I can't do that. It doesn't work with me because my principle is above my art. It's above my art because I was raised as Muslim, [and] then art came to me, so I have to find a balance. Can I at the same time deal drugs and be Muslim? It doesn't work. So a part of hip hop I have to erase.[50]

Supria "Iya" Budiman, the Indonesian b-boy and interpreter Next Level worked with in Bandung, started to distance himself from certain aspects of hip hop culture as he became more devout. "I am now learning to reduce to listen to music because the Al-Qur'an and my Prophet Muhammad PBUH [peace be upon him]," he wrote. "I realized that whenever I listen to music and or memorize the lyrics, the more I get it hard to remember the verses from Al-Qur'an. I found there is a good brotherhood in hip hop, and hip hop also teach the Peace Love Unity and Respect thing (+Having Fun). But the Having Fun side is contradictive with what I know now."[51] Other artists, on the other hand, have said that they are not sure that they are, or can be, "good" Muslims. Although what it means to be a "good" Muslim varies, often the implication is that they do not observe all the "pillars" of Islam, such as praying five times a day and fasting during Ramadan. "I'm not a real real real Muslim," one rapper told me. "I'm not doing prayers. I'm not doing a lot of things."[52]

Some artists maintain that there is simply no connection between how they practice hip hop and how they practice Islam. This came out clearly in my conversation with the roomful of Algerian beatmakers when the interpreter explained one of their responses: "He said that he was raised in [the] environment of hip hop, so all his family are involved

Sarah Shalaby, Alexandria, Egypt, December 2017. Photograph by Petna Ndaliko Katondolo.

in hip hop music. But religion is important, and Islam is the religion he has. It's two different things. For him hip hop is a way of life. It's culture, and he doesn't want to mix between religion and the way of his life."[53] Amine Wakrim, who organizes hip hop festivals throughout Morocco, invoked the metaphor of a divided highway—hip hop and Islam may be close, they may run parallel, but they never intersect. As I chatted with him in his office in Meknes, the muffled sound of thumping beats leaked through the door as dancers practiced outside. "It's like a road," he told me over the pounding bass. "They don't cross."[54]

Whether artists see hip hop and Islam as intertwined or parallel, they find ways to maintain their identities both as artists and as Muslims. This balancing act, which often demands deep self-reflection and difficult compromise, reveals these artists as complicated, thoughtful, passionate, and often conflicted people, and demonstrates just how contingent—on culture, history, geography, and personal and family values—the relationship between hip hop and Islam really is.

## HIP HOP, ISLAM, AND REVOLUTION

In 2011, hip hop was making international headlines. At the time, a wave of demonstrations and protests, civil wars and coups collectively referred to as the Arab Spring was sweeping through parts of North Africa and the Middle East. The international media quickly discovered that some of the more prominent voices of dissent and opposition came from hip hop artists. "Is Hip Hop Driving the Arab Spring?" the BBC asked, and its answer was a qualified yes.[55] NPR highlighted five of "the best" revolutionary tracks in its feature, "The Rap Songs of the Arab Spring," which, it claimed, "have played a direct role in popular uprisings."[56] Earlier in the year *Time* profiled Hamada Ben Amor, the Tunisian MC better known as El Général, and cited his 2010 song, "Rais Lebled" (a play on the phrase "President of the Republic"), which was chanted by protesters both in Tunis and Cairo.[57] In her book *Rock the Casbah*, journalist Robin Wright wrote, "Throughout the Islamic World, rap is now providing the rhythm of resistance. Its songs are the twenty-first-century anthems against both autocrats and extremists." "'Rais Lebled,'" Wright argued, "had a transformative influence. It set the stage for the Jasmine Revolution that broke out a month later [in Tunisia]."[58] Claims like these were later shown to overblown or incorrect, but for a time hip hop artists had become the stars of the Arab Spring.

The possibility that these artists and their songs might have stoked revolution was irresistible to the Western media and raised the possibility that hip hop was the "natural connector to the Muslim world," as diplomat Cynthia Schneider put it. If so, it would be an opportune time for the State Department to send US hip hop artists to connect with young Muslims around the world. And that's what happened. Between 2010 and 2012, hip hop artists—some of them Muslim, but not all—performed, lectured, and offered workshops in Algeria, Indonesia, Jordan, Lebanon, Libya, Malaysia, Pakistan, Palestine, Saudi Arabia, Syria, Tunisia, and Turkmenistan.[59] This was not a coordinated initiative; many of the artists were invited by individual US embassies and consulates, others took part in State Department programs such as

American Music Abroad. Some were created and promoted specifically as Muslim-to-Muslim exchanges, while others were people-to-people programs without Islam as a focus.

We can see the more direct approach in the tours by Native Deen and Remarkable Current. Native Deen, a trio of three African American Muslim men from Washington, DC, formed in 2000 with the goal of "spread[ing] an uplifting message of Islam."[60] In 2002, the group was featured in the web series, "Muslim Life in America," part of the short-lived "Shared Values" campaign headed by Charlotte Beers. An article highlights Native Deen's wholesomeness, contrasting their inspiring "Muslim Rap" with "the dark themes of drugs and violence that permeate most rap." A final quote from member Joshua Salaam captures the campaign's anodyne approach: "Our music is American, it's hip, and it's something everybody can be comfortable with."[61]

The group was initially ambivalent about working with the State Department. As Abdul-Malik Ahmad told the *New York Times*, "We had a debate in the community. 'Should we do it?' 'Should we not do it?' Some people were saying, 'Y'all are going to be puppets, going over there saying: 'Everything's O.K. We're bombing your country, but we have Muslims, too!'" They decided to convene a *shura*, a community consultation. Based on the advice they received, they decided that they shouldn't accept just any invitation by the State Department, but, as Ahmad said, "if it's our mission to spread tolerance and faith, it can be O.K. to take this offer."[62]

Video clips from Native Deen's 2004 tour of Mali, Nigeria, and Senegal show them speaking to audiences about the positive power of Islam and performing songs like "Remember the Days": "As a son of a crescent, I'm not an adolescent/I've done a lot of growing I consider it a blessing/Hmm, I think about my situation/I need to increase my Islamic education."[63] Their messaging remained consistent through their 2011 and 2012 tours. They sang "I'm not afraid to stand alone if Allah is standing by my side" in Ramallah, Palestine and announced the theme of a showcase in Malaysia as "Reaffirming the Belief, Inspiring Good Deeds."[64]

Traveling with Native Deen on some of their earlier tours was Californian Anas Canon, a DJ and producer who was serving as the group's sound engineer. Canon, founder of the hip hop collective Remarkable Current, saw the demand for Muslim American artists overseas and started promoting his own group to US diplomatic posts as "hip hop ambassadors of the 21st century." "My intention," he explained, "is really to help develop a Muslim American culture, something that is uniquely American and also Muslim. The art that we create puts us in a position to define ourselves to the world, be it Muslim or American, and create an identity that is uniquely Muslim and uniquely Western or American."[65]

Canon and his group performed in several Muslim-majority countries between 2006 and 2011. They visited several cities in Tunisia in May and June 2011 in the wake of nationwide protests that forced President Zine El Abidine Ben Ali out of office and launched the so-called Jasmine Revolution. They were there explicitly, as Canon put it, to "get people excited about voting" in the run-up to the elections in October, Tunisia's first free election since its independence in 1956.[66] During his visit he met rapper El Général, of "Rais Lebled" fame, and even recorded a track with him and Canon's colleague, rapper Kumasi Simmons. Their song, "Pick up the Pieces," promoted solidarity in this time of both chaos and hope: "Empires rise and empires fall, the people are left to pick up the pieces. One heart, one mind, one body, we're standing tall, together united, we'll pick up the pieces."[67] Remarking on Canon's tour, Tunisian activist Achref Aouadi, who had recently launched a "Go Vote" campaign, declared that "Remarkable Current has more of an impact on Tunisia than Secretary Hillary Clinton."[68]

The State Department's deployment of Native Deen and Remarkable Current took an explicitly peer-to-peer approach: send US Muslims to meet with young Muslims of other countries to demonstrate America's religious tolerance, to emphasize the peaceful, community-building facets of Islam, and to do so through a globally-beloved American art form. These connections, according to some State Department officials, could do more than enhance the image of the United States; they could potentially improve its security. Stanley Harsha, who led the US Consulate in Medan, Indonesia, declared that Remarkable Current's 2010 tour of North Sumatra "reached the hearts of over 10,000 Muslim youth with messages of peace and tolerance, more deeply than any program PO [Principal Officer] Medan has witnessed in 11 years of reaching out to Muslims in Indonesia. RC's was a timely serum against radicalism which is trying to poison Sumatran youth."[69] Abdul-Malik Ahmad of Native Deen agreed that promoting Muslim solidarity through hip hop could discourage anti-American rhetoric, and by extension, violence against the United States:

> There's some American Muslim rappers that are proud to be who they are, and they practice their religion freely, and you didn't know about them 'til now. So before you go saying USA is all evil, listen to these guys . . . [In our music] we're just talking about our faith. We're talking about what we believe, and we believe Islam is peace.[70]

The idea that Muslim American hip hop artists might help counter violent extremism exposes both the potential value and risks of hip hop diplomacy. From one perspective, it serves a core State Department priority, and therefore represents a valuable return on investment. In a 2018 document, State's Bureau of Educational and Cultural Affairs (ECA) identified "combatting radicalization" as one of its four main goals:

> In response to the Administration priority of combatting radicalization, ECA offers exchange programs that encourage participants to share information on the drivers of violent extremism, to promote messages that counter extremist narratives and recruitment tactics, to explore educational approaches to building resilience, and to engage tribal and religious leaders, youth, women, and civil society.[71]

At the same time, framing hip hop diplomacy as a "serum against radicalism" raises the specter of exploitation. When artists are considered tools, instruments of foreign policy, it is easy to ignore or neglect their agency, to see their well-being as secondary or unimportant. In my experience, however, I have yet to hear State Department staff encourage hip hop artists to "share information on the drivers of violent extremism" or "promote messages that counter extremist narratives and recruitment tactics." And as Anas Canon explained in a 2012 interview, "I don't think it's an exploitative relationship from the State Department's position; it's more of an opportunity to break down multiple walls."[72] Still, it remains vital to be "on alert," as J-Live put it, and to acknowledge the risks of hip hop diplomacy and the concerns of its critics.

## HIP HOP DIPLOMACY AND ISLAM: CRITICS AND RISKS

The State Department's post-9/11 interest in Islam generated controversy from the beginning. Critics across the political spectrum condemned the Department's use of hip hop artists to connect with Muslim communities as variously dangerous, exploitative, manipulative, offensive, propagandistic, and superficial. Political and social conservatives denounced hip hop diplomacy as a waste of taxpayer dollars and hip hop artists as poor representatives of the United States. In the conservative magazine *American Thinker*, comments following a 2015 article on popular music and diplomacy unleashed a torrent of racist and Islamophobic vitriol. "Rap is the rhythm of savagery," said one commenter. "Of course it appeals to the jihadis." Another complained: "This sewage is completely mainstream in the black world and honored at the [Obama] White House. Your government is exporting this same sewage and with Arabic lyrics it is fertilizing the fields of jihad."[73] It's easy to dismiss this vile rhetoric, but it is still true that there are hateful, violent, and narrow-minded aspects of hip hop art and culture. Moreover, from the perspective of traditional conservative concerns about small government, hip hop diplomacy can reasonably be criticized as a form of governmental overreach.

Critics of hip hop diplomacy are also found among left-leaning activists, journalists, and scholars. One of the most visible has been scholar Hisham Aidi. He has rightly questioned the link between hip hop and the 2011 revolutions, a presumed connection that helped fuel the enthusiasm for US diplomatic engagement with Muslim youth: "Hip hop did not cause the Arab revolts any more than Twitter or Facebook did. [ . . . ] And the countries in the region with the most vibrant hip hop scenes, Morocco and Algeria, have not seen revolts. Western journalists' focus on hip hop—like their fixation on Facebook and Twitter—seems partly because, in their eyes, a taste for hip hop among young Muslims is a sign of moderation, modernity, even 'an embrace of the US.'"[74] Journalist Torie Rose DeGhett has probed the faulty logic of this latter assumption:

> The mistake many in the West often make in interpreting Arab hip hop is to assume that rap represents an embrace of Western philosophies and ideals of government, or a Western sense of reform and modernization. If these rappers are embracing anything Western in their choice of musical genre, however, it's the history of conscious African American hip hop and dissidence, often rejected in America as violent, radical, or libertine.[75]

Anthropologist Su'Ad Abdul Khabeer has criticized the State Department's use of hip hop as a means "to manage young Muslims who are perceived as potential terrorists." She has suggested that Muslim peer-to-peer hip hop diplomacy can both promote US imperialism and exploit the citizens it deploys: "in this management of an imperial relationship with the 'Muslim world,' US Muslims have become a strategic asset for the state's efforts to 'reform' Islam outside the United States."[76] British scholar Omar El-Khairy concurs, calling out "the hip hop soundtrack of American imperialism," implying that in pursuing the goal of spreading democracy around the world, the United States has, ironically, imposed a "hegemonic imagination of freedom."[77]

These are serious, legitimate critiques. There is simply no way to disentangle the State Department's efforts to build bridges and foster mutual understanding through hip hop from its history of imperialist intervention. The potential consequences of this tension are varied and vast, but most broadly they generate resentment. Peter Kovach, a US Foreign Service Officer and champion of Native Deen's international tours, related how "a Malay critic quipped to me at the time [ . . . ]: 'The subliminal message will be, now Americans are even telling us how to be good Muslims.'"[78] In his 2011 song "Tahya Tunis" ("Viva Tunisia") MC El Général rapped (in Arabic), "We must solve our problems before America enters," expressing antipathy towards US intervention.[79] To speak of resentment may seem to underplay the consequences of US foreign policy. But resentment can generate a spectrum of responses, everything from simmering annoyance to world-changing acts of terrorism.

And so commentators on the left and right concur: US hip hop diplomacy, as a means to build bridges with Muslim populations, is problematic. In the face of such rare agreement, why should we think it possible for hip hop diplomacy to facilitate cross-cultural, transnational collaboration and understanding with Muslim communities around the world?

## SOLIDARITY AND RESISTANCE

"I love America—I dream of going to America!" Exclamations like this greeted me over and again from the Algerians and Tunisians I had just met. Their warmth and good will surprised me. It was February 2017, hardly two weeks since President Trump had issued Executive Order 13769, widely criticized as a ban on travel to the US by foreign Muslims. Ostensibly intended to protect the United States from terrorists, the order was seen as part of a pattern of xenophobic policies and rhetoric coming out of my country.[80] Given such palpable hostility, why would people of these Muslim-majority nations so admire the US, why did they yearn to visit its shores?

During my North African trip I interacted with dozens of young, working-class Muslim men and women. They were passionate about the United States, but not because of its government. (Several times I heard variations of this statement: "I love America—but your president is crazy!") They expressed a love for American culture and the ideals of freedom and opportunity that it embodies. And for so many of the young people I met, hip hop is at the center of US culture. "I fell in love with the music, the way they dress, the way they dance, the way they speak, the way they do their thing," 25-year-old Tunisian DJ Rami Mhazres, aka Supaflava, told me. Hip hop, he said, has "played an important role in my life."[81] When Supaflava and Next Level DJ Nick Neutronz stood side by side, scratching and mixing records together, their respective religions had nothing to do with the strength of their connection; they were connecting as hip hop artists.

To be sure, hip hop diplomacy can facilitate building together *as* Muslims. Native Deen and Remarkable Current communicated their commitment to Islam during their State Department tours and no doubt generated some good will because of it. I've seen and heard of many small moments of peer-to-peer exchange in Next Level residencies as well. Haleem "Stringz" Rasul, who participated in Next Level's Indonesia residency, explained that his Muslim identity allowed him "to connect with the participants right away because there was already a common ground established, regardless of if everyone was a practicing Muslim or not." But this connection was only occasionally articulated or even visible. "Islam is very important to me and I always like to be an example and represent. However, I chose to let my actions speak. I prayed with some, gave my Islamic greeting to many, and let my character attempt to do the rest."[82] For US rapper One Be Lo, who led MC workshops in Algeria in Tunisia, this common ground was equally important. "Islam wasn't my focus, but the great part about Islam is that we believe in a book called Al Qur'an. In the Arabic language, the entire book rhymes. Because I knew everybody was Muslim, I could use examples from the Qur'an. These rhymes are for everybody,

DJ Supaflava (Rami Mhazres) and Nick Neutronz (Nick Low-Beer), Tunis, Tunisia, February 12, 2017. Photograph by Mark Katz.

and they cover real subject matter from community, to family, to food, to business."[83] In Dhaka, Amirah Sackett, DJ A-Minor, and I went to visit a beatboxer named Shohan in the apartment he shared with his extended family. At one point during our visit, Shohan's sister-in-law, who had earlier presented Amirah with a carved wooden Qur'an stand, shyly remarked on how stylishly Amirah wrapped her hijab. The two women then disappeared into another room. When they emerged a few minutes later, Shohan's sister-in-law was beaming as she sported her hijab à la Amirah. It was a lovely moment, an unscripted and meaningful exchange for these two Muslim women.

It is one thing to witness and appreciate such connections, but it's risky to try to engineer them. The "We have Muslims, too!" approach demonstrates understanding and tolerance no more than white people prove that they aren't racist when they proclaim that they have black friends. Sending US Muslims to engage with Muslims in other countries is also risky. Deep tensions and searing conflicts emerge within families over shared religion. We cannot expect that co-religionists will

One Be Lo and Ezer Ghariani, Tunis, Tunisia, February 12, 2017. Photograph by Petna Ndaliko Katondolo.

automatically connect in meaningful ways, especially across the divides of culture, geography, and language. An American Five Percenter MC told me he would be careful about how he would connect with other Muslims abroad. There are aspects of Five Percenter practice—for example, taking Allah's name as one's own—that might be offensive. "It could be oil and water," he explained.

The lives of Muslims around the world vary dramatically. The Rohingya in Myanmar and Uighurs in China are both persecuted Muslim minorities, but their experiences are both different from each other and completely unlike the lives of the ruling classes of the Arab Gulf States. Islam in Azerbaijan has been shaped by the history of religious repression in the Soviet Union. Since the 1980s, Indonesia, the country with the world's largest Muslim population, has been experiencing what has been called the "Arabization" of Islam, in which Saudi Arabian religious practices have increasingly influenced contemporary culture. Life for Muslims in India and Israel is deeply affected by their relationship with the Hindu and Jewish majorities. In Tunisia, the practice of Islam changed drastically after the 2011 revolution; in the United States, the lives of millions of Muslims changed drastically after the 2001 terrorist attacks.

The distinctive histories and cultures and lived experiences of the world's Muslims affect how they think about everything from the arts and education to gender roles and international relations. They also influence how Muslim hip hop artists conceive of the relationship (or lack of one) between their religion and their art. The difference in perspective I encountered in Algeria and Senegal, for example, had a good deal to do with differing views on the public and private roles of religion, views shaped only partly by Islamic doctrine. Given this reality, Muslim-to-Muslim engagement in cultural exchange programs or any approach in which Islam is a focal point carries with it the potential to destroy rather than build connections and good will. And then there is the tension, especially acute since 9/11, between foreign policy and diplomacy. When US foreign policy treats Islam as a threat, when it creates conditions that promote or allow violence and hardship to be visited upon Muslims around the world, when it closes its borders to Muslims seeking a better life in America, then a coherent and honest diplomatic approach to connecting hip hop and Muslim youth may be impossible.

To return to my earlier, unanswered question: can hip hop diplomacy facilitate cross-cultural, transnational and meaningful collaboration with Muslim communities around the world? I believe it can—by building solidarity that is not (or not necessarily) connected to Islam. Solidarity among participants emerges as they discover shared challenges and pleasures: making a career as an artist; convincing families of the positive value of hip hop; translating inchoate emotions into art; the exhilaration of a good cypher; the pride in mastering a technique; the adrenaline rush of cheering crowds. This does not require a colorblind approach, where religion is conspicuous for its absence, where we pretend that Islam is not, in fact, often top of mind among those who devise US foreign policy and plan public diplomacy initiatives. Islam can be part of the conversation, but it should emerge from the artists themselves, built out of a mutually respectful call and response. The most effective way to use hip hop diplomacy to create meaningful relationships with Muslim populations around the world, then—and, to take a broader lesson, any population—is to connect with them first and foremost as people.

It might well be, however, that these diplomatic initiatives are most valuable for their impact on the US participants. Many of these artists had never experienced life in a majority Muslim community or country. Hearing the Muslim call to prayer resounding across a cityscape five times a day or learning the ubiquitous Arabic phrase, "insha'Allah"— "If God wills it"—can have a profound effect. "I realized I appreciate the call for prayer," dancer "Big Tara" Crichlow says. "I think everyone should take a couple of pauses in the day to meditate, reflect, pray."[84] DJ Nick Neutronz, Crichlow's teammate in Algeria and Tunisia, told me how he "picked up the phrase Inshallah, which I love. It attributes much of our destiny to an unseen force of fate, which I believe even controls our wills and hopes. So the spirit in which this term went around resonated deeply with me."[85] Konshens the MC put the handful of Arabic words that he learned in Morocco to good use when he returned home to Washington, DC. Many of the shop employees in his neighborhood are native Arabic speakers, and Konshens was pleased to see how much good will he elicited even with his *shway* (little bit of) Arabic. "I went to the [convenience] store greeting them with *salaam*, meaning peace. After a brief convo and asking them where are the *kabir ma'an*—big water [bottles]—I turn to walk out of the store and say *bisalaam*, meaning 'Go in Peace.' Every visit to this corner store now upon walking in I'm greeted with *As-salamu alaykum*, 'peace be unto you,' as I happily respond, *Wa alaykumu as-salam*, 'and unto you peace.'"[86]

These US visitors also come to realize that the media they consume typically depicts Islam narrowly, often prejudicially. Spending time in Algeria and Tunisia made Big Tara "aware of how media scare tactics can instill fear when you haven't gotten the chance to see something first hand. There was a fear in me that was based on the lies and exaggerations that was ingrained in me even though I am an open minded global citizen."[87] Producer and MC ADUM[7], who led workshops in Uzbekistan, pushed back against the "narrative that American media has created that Muslims are terrorists and almost barbaric in behavior." His experience, like many other artists I've spoken with, was "powerfully eye opening."[88]

In the end, the State Department's deployment of hip hop to the "Muslim world" may be best understood as a mirror, reflecting back perceptions and misperceptions about Islam, revealing the power and limitations of hip hop as a means to build global community, and exposing the ever-present tensions between diplomacy and foreign policy. The most powerful lesson of these initiatives, perhaps, is that mutual understanding—that vaunted diplomatic ideal—begins at home.

# CONCLUSION

Black men in baseball caps holding microphones. White men in suits shaking hands. These are the most common images associated with internet searches for hip hop and diplomacy. The contrast is stark: informal/formal, loud/quiet, the resistance/the establishment, black/white. No wonder the phrase "hip hop diplomacy" sounds jarring to many, even if both hip hop and diplomacy are more complex and diverse than these stereotypes suggest.

There are historical reasons for the improbability of the collaboration. In the early years of US cultural diplomacy most officials agreed that the best way to represent the United States was through its "high art," whether classical music, ballet, or modernist literature and painting. Even when the State Department cleared jazz for diplomatic export, there remained a strong and often racialized prejudice against it. When, in 1956, Senator Allen J. Ellender of Louisiana learned that Dizzy Gillespie was serving as a cultural ambassador, he was shocked. "I never heard so much noise in my all my life. I can assure you that instead of doing good it will do harm and the people will really believe we are barbarians."[1]

Nearly sixty years later political scientist Michael Curtis decried the latest wave of US musical envoys in the online magazine, *American Thinker*, arguing that "The rappers are not jazz giants or have star power like Gillespie."[2] Gillespie was now a giant; the rappers were the new barbarians. One commenter heightened the irony: "That [a rapper] even believes that they are comparable to a Dizzy Gillespie is appalling." But of course they are comparable. Just like Dizzy Gillespie and the other jazz ambassadors of the Cold War era, hip hop artists have been dismissed, derided, and reviled. It's the same refrain: they represent the worst that the United States has to offer, and besides, they aren't even real musicians. A representative remark from another commenter could have been recycled from the days of ragtime or jazz: "Rap and hip hop 'music' is potty mouth garbage spewed from emotionally challenged 'people' who cannot express themselves with intelligence."[3]

Another historical tension can be traced to the State Department's very motivation for launching modern cultural diplomacy. US cultural diplomacy has always been justified as a threat response, whether that threat has been fascism, communism, or terrorism. As historian Frank Ninkovich has pointed out, the constant national security justifications for cultural diplomacy have required "a willingness to cry wolf." "In agreeing to institutionalize the programs," he notes, "Congress also institutionalized various tensions between culture and information, elite and mass targets, nationalism and internationalism and short-term and long-term approaches."[4] This history has meant that the arts have been instrumentalized for diplomatic purposes—we might even say weaponized in the fight against America's enemies. The tensions between the goals of art and diplomacy potentially render any partnership between hip hop artists and the US government anathema to both.

And yet. Despite the tensions that make hip hop and diplomacy such an apparently odd couple, there are so many ways in which the partnership has worked. I maintain that hip hop can be a tremendously valuable, positive, and effective means to promote meaningful and productive relationships among people, communities, and nations. In defending this conclusion, I ask: what good is hip hop diplomacy and do we know that it works? How can it be both effective and ethical? And finally: What might the future hold?

# WHAT GOOD IS HIP HOP DIPLOMACY?

The great and overarching value that hip hop diplomacy offers is the opportunity to build community and develop mutual respect and understanding through artistic exchange. These artistic encounters can be empowering, energizing, fulfilling, and validating. They can create lasting friendships, challenge assumptions and stereotypes, promote empathy, and inspire ambitions. More practically speaking, they can facilitate artistic, entrepreneurial, and technical skill building. Over and over I have heard participants in these programs describe their experiences as *life-changing*. And in changing the lives of individuals, these exchanges also affect their communities. They can start to heal rifts, connect groups that once had tense relations or none at all, and they can foster a sense of global interconnectedness. When people feel a personal and meaningful relationship with those who share a common love but are otherwise so different, they may feel a closer connection to the countries, cultures, languages, and religions they represent.

To anticipate a reasonable question, why do hip hop–based workshops need to be conducted by outsiders, particularly from the United States? Artists anywhere might be well qualified to teach microphone control to rappers, windmills to dancers, chirp scratches to DJs, or the pros and cons of quantization to beatmakers. It's also possible for local artists to teach the history of hip hop. However, one of the most frequently lauded aspects of these workshops is the opportunity to learn this history from US artists, some of whom were present during the early years of hip hop or were prominent in its "golden age" in the late 1980s and into the 1990s. As Brazilian b-boy Samuka told me, "It was in the United States that hip hop was born—it's the cradle of hip hop. There's nothing more important than the creators of hip hop coming here to plant the seed."[5] B-girl Key from Kampala, Uganda likewise explained how "everyone was so eager" to study with visiting US artists "because when someone comes from the actual source, we want to learn."[6] Such statements, however, can lull visiting US artists into accepting American exceptionalism and ignoring the exhortation to learn as much as they teach, both of which can limit the possibilities of true collaboration. At the same time, this view generates the warm welcome that so often greets the US visitors and prepares the ground for productive building. This is simply one of the ironies of operating in a zone of ambiguity.

Hip hop practitioners around the world tend to self-segregate by discipline, meaning that dancers and MCs, DJs and graffiti artists, beatboxers and beatmakers don't regularly collaborate. The presence of outsiders can provide an excuse for these groups to come together, and the same is true for rivals with longstanding beefs—recall the Lugaflow and Ugaflow MCs of Uganda and the Ndebele and Shona artists in Zimbabwe. A first step to ending or de-escalating these rivalries is simply to bring the different sides into the same space, something that might only happen if they are invited by a third party. Community building can occur on a larger scale when artists from across a region or even an entire country come together to work with visiting artists. Rapper Soultana painted a vivid picture of the exuberant atmosphere in the Meknes hostel where young Moroccan artists converged for Next Level's 2017 residency:

> If you just come to the hostel where we are staying with all those dancers and rappers, you will see the love that they have for each other. Nobody know nobody. They just came here for Next Level and they just meet the others. And they build something between them. I have a lot of them, all of them, in my Facebook. We take pictures and we get tagging each other and [we say] "Next Level, Next Level, Next Level, Next Level." It's kind of like, "Yeah, this is the next level." Do you see?[7]

Young people will often travel for hours across their countries to take advantage of these free workshops; an unexpected and powerful benefit of their dedication to hip hop is the new connections and friendships they develop with their fellow citizens.

Soultana, Meknes, Morocco, 14 September 2017. Photograph by Mark Katz.

An academic critic of hip hop diplomacy once asked me why a university or a corporate sponsor couldn't fund this kind of exchange instead of the State Department. This can happen and sometimes does, but state-sponsored programs are often valued by participants precisely *because* they are state sponsored. The participation of the local US Embassy, or the US government in general can be a validating force for hip hop artists and their communities. Soultana describes the US government support she has received in this way: "It's so big. It's not just support, it's an honor."[8] When I asked Salvadoran b-boy Stimpy how he felt about working with a US government–sponsored program, he was unequivocal: "I'm proud. I felt really good and happy that a government of a country that is so recognized as the United States would be interested in coming especially to San Salvador. It's giving importance to what we work on in hip hop here, in a way that it's really difficult for the local government to give." He also said that the program's connection with the US government forced the older generation to rethink their low opinion of hip hop. "Our parents are old fashioned and so they think that we might be doing vandalism . . . or that we're running around smoking marijuana. But really, [hip hop is] a discipline, and the fact that the United States would come here to promote this type of work, they're really surprised by this."

Given the notorious involvement of the US in his country's civil war, I was surprised to hear such praise. Surely many Salvadorans must think poorly of the United States, I suggested. "I don't understand," Stimpy responded. So I talked about the civil war and the deportation of Salvadoran-born US criminals back to El Salvador in the 1980s and 1990s. "Really, I'm not too familiar with the topic of the deportations you were talking about," he said. "I feel like we're a new generation. I mean, I'm really happy that the United States is investing in us artistically, pedagogically, and economically."[9]

Stimpy's response was a reality check. I realized that my concerns, and those frequently expressed by academics, are not always shared by the people with whom these programs engage. The civil war was not part of Stimpy's living memory and apparently not a topic of conversation among his peers. He was much more focused on his struggle to make a life in hip hop, and it only made sense that he would appreciate my government's assistance. Of course, past (and present and future) US intervention may affect Stimpy's life whether or not he knows it, and a skeptical perspective on state-sponsored cultural programming has helped me be a more sensitive partner in the communities Next Level has visited. Still, Stimpy teaches us an important lesson about honoring the agency of others and heeding their voices. In her aptly titled article, "The Problem of Speaking for Others," philosopher Linda Alcoff puts it this way: "When one is speaking about others, or simply trying to describe their situation or some aspect of it, one may also be speaking in place of them, that is, speaking for them." In the end, she exhorts, "We should strive to create wherever possible the conditions for dialogue and the practice of speaking with and to rather than speaking for others."[10] This dialogue, and the collaboration that can come from it, is the ideal to which these programs should strive.

Stimpy wasn't the only Salvadoran artist I spoke with about the country's civil war. Another was rapper Blaze Uno. He was older than Stimpy and well aware of the war—his family had lived in exile in the United States for several years during that time. But like Stimpy, he praised Next Level without hesitation, lauding the US government for providing the credibility and support he sought for his beloved art. "So if they see the USA embassy supporting this it's like, 'Hello!' That's the key we need to get to people. Because remember hip hop also has been stereotyped as being from the streets, from the ghetto. You know the respect the USA has over here." When I pressed, reminding him about the civil war, he replied, "I'm glad that you brought that to the table because we keep it real." He continued, "We need to see the intention of, 'Ok guys that was bad . . . but now we want to help you.' So it's really important to change people's mentality about the USA embassy. I'm not into politics, but it's important to change that view, and I think we're all helping together doing these types of things."[11]

This was a generous, perhaps too generous response, but it also revealed a pragmatism born out of lived experience. Blaze could condemn Next Level as a too-little-too-late gesture by the State Department. He could reject the program and scoff at the team of gringo artists brought in by the US Embassy. But he had the savvy and the will to make the opportunity serve him and his community. For those living in precarity, life is too short to refuse opportunities simply because they arrive from the zone of ambiguity. Sadly, life was too short for Blaze, who passed away at the age of 34 in 2017. His epitaph reads "Siempres vivirás en nuestros corazones. Desde el cielo escucharemos tu hip hop"—"You will live always in our hearts. From heaven we will hear your hip hop."[12]

Although some of the goals of hip hop diplomacy can be accomplished without the involvement of the United States government, its support of these exchanges is often seen as sincere, powerful, and positive. This fact helps answer the question of what the State Department

Blaze Uno, San Salvador, El Salvador, December 5, 2015. Photograph by Mark Katz.

gets out of sending hip hop artists abroad. While hip hop diplomacy risks generating resentment among those it seeks to engage, the converse can also be true—it can generate good will. And just as resentment may lead to a range of responses from mild to catastrophic, good will, too, manifests itself across a broad spectrum. The most obvious manifestations come in the form of positive program evaluations and heartfelt expressions of gratitude for the visiting artists on social media. Good will, like resentment, is a seed whose growth is impossible to predict; still, there's reason to be hopeful about what might germinate.

When I spoke with Calvin Hayes, the Cultural Affairs Officer at the US Embassy in Dhaka during Next Level's 2014 residency in Bangladesh, he offered an example of such a seed and how it might someday bear fruit. He told me of an encounter with a rapper who was attending the workshops:

> One of the MCs showed up very angry, tears were coming down his eyes. I asked him, "Hey, what's wrong? Are you okay?" He shared with me that earlier that day his friend had died. He says, "Calvin, I didn't know where to turn, so I turned to Next Level." Somebody hearing this [story] might say, "This is very small," but in a sense Next Level and hip hop was able to be a place of refuge for this young man. If he did not have this option, who knows what would've been the outcome? This is people-to-people connection that I think can't be duplicated in any other way. We may not be able to measure [the impact of] this in the next year, two or three years, but what we can say is that when the Next Level program leaves here the relationship between America and Bangladesh is deeper and stronger. If there was any young person here that had any doubt about America, and doubts about US interest in Bangladesh, they now know that there are Americans that are just like them, that have had struggles of their own. Because of this program, some of the students are already talking to me about studying in the US. We hope that as they grow older they not only remember this program, but remember some of the lessons learned. This program is not just about what goes on in the workshops, it's also about what goes on in the conversations in between the workshops, and we hope that those conversations will stick with our participants, so in turn they'll have a more favorable view of the US.[13]

Although Hayes was right that we cannot precisely measure the impact of the 2014 program, there's evidence to suggest that it has been welcome and sustained. Participants in those workshops have mentioned a variety of positive outcomes: new artistic and professional opportunities, greater visibility for hip hop in Bangladesh, continued connections with the US team.

A year after the final show—which was held in front of an audience of 3,500 and covered by national media—rapper Bigg Spade gathered dozens of the participants from the original workshops, and many newcomers as well, to mount a reunion show. Other reunion gatherings and shows followed. It has been common for the Next Level Bangladesh participants to post nostalgic sentiments about their experiences. Beatboxer and MC Arghya Mandal wrote this on Facebook in November 2017:

> Talking about movements? Biggest movement in Bangladesh Hip Hop Scenario was Next Level. If you were not part of it then you have no idea how big it was. Missing those days of our workshop. Golden days indeed.[14]

Over the next several days more than a dozen related posts followed, including a photo showing him proudly holding his certificate of participation alongside Asheru, the US Next Level MC.

Next Level selects one workshop participant from each country it visits to participate in a two-week professional and artistic development program in the United States; the Bangladeshi representative was MC Black Zang. I checked in with Zang a little over a year after his 2015 visit to the US. "Next Level Bangladesh started a movement," he told me; it empowered the hip hop community to "change our situation through art or culture." For him personally, the experience both in Dhaka and in the US was life-changing. "This was so inspiring for me—after working hard for seven or eight years, I got the opportunity to fly to the States and have this lifetime experience. I literally got that if I work hard I will get what I deserve, and after that I started working more hard. Inshallah, we'll see what happens."[15]

These are nice stories, but why should the US Department of State get involved in the lives and careers of young Bangladeshis? Bangladeshi youth matter because they are a key to their country's future, which is of great interest and concern to the United States. Bangladesh is

Final concert, Next Level Bangladesh. Bangladeshi rappers (left to right), V.X.L., ABD, Shift, and Black Zang. Dhaka, Bangladesh, November 17, 2014. Photograph by Anshul Gupta.

the world's third most populous Muslim-majority nation and one of the few with a democratically elected government. It has traditionally been a strong ally, with a 76 percent approval rating of the US in 2014, among the highest in the world.[16] But the country has been in a precarious state. Its young democracy is fragile, having endured coups, failed elections, and two years of military rule. Religious extremism has been on the rise.[17] Civil unrest flares up regularly. The influx of about one million persecuted Rohingya refugees has strained the country's thin resources. Climate change is likely to render significant portions of the country underwater in the near future. To be blunt, the United States needs allies among the major Muslim populations in the world, and it has very few. Instability in Bangladesh makes it vulnerable to the influence of groups and nations antagonistic to the United States, and the prospect of a nation of 160 million Muslims turning against it no doubt keeps many US government officials awake at night. It simply makes sense for the United States to cultivate good will among Bangladeshi youth, and hip hop programs have proved to be an effective way to do so. Having the good will of young Bangla hip hop artists might seem to be a small thing, but it serves the State Department's overall mission.

Cultivating good will is also cost effective. The State Department's 2002 Shared Values initiative, which failed to generate much good will in the wake of 9/11, cost $15 million, an amount that would have sustained Next Level for a decade and a half. And even the most expensive State Department diplomacy programs pale in price next to most military options. Counterterrorism expert Michael Jakub, who worked for many years at the Defense Department and the State Department, explained the necessity of soft power approaches to difficult international relations:

> The smart operatives, the smart policy officers, the smart deputy secretaries are going to understand there's a role to be played by all different elements of power. And to eliminate one of them—public diplomacy—that is ridiculous.[18]

To put some numbers to this, consider that in 2010 a Tomahawk cruise missile cost $1.4 million dollars. On a single morning in 2018 US forces fired sixty-six Tomahawks on three Syrian targets.[19] The cost of administering Next Level over a two-year period: $1.1 million. As General James Mattis (later Secretary of Defense under Donald Trump) told the Senate Committee on Armed Services in 2013, "If you don't fund the State Department fully then I need to buy more ammunition."[20]

## DOING IT RIGHT

Cairo traffic scares the *khawaga*, the foreigner. It was December 2017, and there I was, in all my *khawaga* glory, staring forlornly across eight lanes of unceasing traffic, no crosswalk or traffic light in sight. Seeing my consternation, a local man approached and kindly asked if I would like some assistance. I gladly accepted, and he calmly guided me across the street as cars whizzed within inches of us. The experience, like a video game come to life but with no extra lives, was terrifying, exhilarating, and humbling.

During my travels with Next Level I've had occasion to traverse some of the most fearsome traffic in the world, and these experiences have taught me valuable lessons about navigating unfamiliar systems. First, I have to acknowledge my ignorance of local rhythms and unwritten rules, as well as the histories behind them. Second, I have come to realize that when faced with a treacherous path, my instincts—to sprint or to freeze—rarely serve me well. Third, I've discovered that the fastest and safest way from point A to point B is never a straight line, and is rarely uninterrupted. I've nervously watched people walk into what I imagine is certain death, only to avoid harm because they know when to stop and start, when to pause and pivot. Finally, I've concluded that my best chance of success and survival is by putting my trust in locals and taking their lead. All of these lessons apply both literally and figuratively, whether I'm trying to negotiate a traffic circle or a bureaucracy in Cairo or Rio, Bangkok or Kolkata.

The larger point is that the success of US cultural diplomacy programs—and the well-being and even safety of all participants—requires collaboration. In a 2008 article, Geoffrey Cowan and Amelia Arsenault describe three "layers" of public diplomacy: monologue, dialogue, and collaboration. They acknowledge the vital role of monologue and dialogue, but make the case that collaboration, too often overlooked, can be "a more effective approach to engaging foreign publics." As they explain, "Whether working together on small projects or on large ones, participants can learn from each other's skills; they learn to respect each other; and they may find that they have common ground in at least one area of importance to them."[21] One lesson I have learned through organizing and observing hip hop diplomacy programs around the world is that successful collaboration demands demonstrating respect, humility, and self-awareness. Such an approach is especially important given that collaboration has not been the hallmark of US international relations. There is, in fact, a hip hop term for collaboration conducted with respect, humility, and self-awareness, and it captures in a single word an effective and ethical way to achieve the goals of cultural diplomacy: building.

## THE RECENT PAST AND THE CLOUDY FUTURE

At the beginning of 2019 hip hop diplomacy looked healthy. Next Level, now in partnership with Meridian International Center, a well-respected non-profit that has overseen cultural diplomacy programs for decades, was renewed for a seventh cycle, stretching its activities into 2021. Next Level had already engaged thousands of people on six continents through its intensive workshops and many thousands more through performances and media appearances. Next Level's sibling programs— American Music Abroad, Center Stage, and OneBeat—continued to work with domestic and international hip hop artists as part of their cultural exchanges. The State Department's Arts Envoy program and individual US embassies and consulates still funded local hip hop artists and their organizations, and regularly invited US artists for short-term residencies and tours. These programs have garnered plaudits from within ECA (the State Department's Bureau of Educational and Cultural Affairs), which funds them, and have generated great enthusiasm from communities abroad. The future, at least the near future, looked bright.

But there was every reason to assume the contrary. Early on in Rex Tillerson's fourteen-month tenure as Secretary of State it became clear that the Trump Administration intended an unprecedented reduction in the Department's staff. Diplomats from both political parties sounded the alarm, using words like decimation, exodus, gutting, slashing, and decapitation to describe the situation. A November 2017 *New York Times* editorial minced no words: "The Trump Administration is Making War on Diplomacy."[22] The outlook for cultural diplomacy was bleak. In January 2017, a representative of the newly-inaugurated president declared, "A lot of the stuff that State does, like promoting the arts and minority groups . . . is just pandering to Democratic Party domestic constituencies in the United States. It's not about serving any identifiable American interest."[23] Since the early twentieth century, "promoting the arts and minority groups" has been a modestly-funded but significant part of the Department's enterprise, from the international tours of renowned jazz artists (initiated under Republican President Dwight Eisenhower) to the hip hop diplomats of today. Although these programs had always had their critics, it was unusual to see them characterized and derided as purely partisan projects. I fully expected that State's cultural programs would be slashed, if not eliminated.

And then nothing happened. Most of ECA's exchange programs, from Fulbright to Next Level, kept humming along. Their continued survival was due in part to the very gutting of the diplomatic leadership at State. ECA, like the Department's other bureaus, is typically overseen by a politically appointed Assistant Secretary of State, and when Evan Ryan, President Obama's appointee, exited on January 6, 2017, it was more than a year before President Trump named Marie Royce as a permanent replacement. In the interim, ECA's tireless civil servants kept the programs running, and with bureaucratically uncharacteristic speed even pushed the renewal process up by months to ensure that programs would have continued funding. And Royce did not seem inclined to reduce ECA's cultural diplomacy efforts. "I am a passionate champion of people-to-people exchanges," she explained at her confirmation hearing, promising that, "If confirmed, I would aim to strengthen our people-to-people ties even further."[24]

It is fitting that the institution of hip hop diplomacy should exist in a persistent zone of ambiguity, where unresolvable tensions keep the enterprise in a state of precarity. But that's hip hop. Most hip hop artists and educators hustle 24/7, never knowing when or if they will see another gig or grant. It is this constant hustle, and the nimbleness, strength, and humility required to endure it, that makes hip hop diplomacy so robust. Hip hop, as a mode of cultural exchange and diplomacy, can be an inspiring, effective teacher. It can help us understand—and even refine—how more traditional forms of government-to-government diplomacy operate. The cypher and the jam session model attentive listening and creative self-expression; they reveal the rewards of recognizing and embracing difference, of seeking compromise and transforming conflict, of setting aside ego and sharing the stage. Konshens the MC captured the potential of hip hop diplomacy for artists, their communities, and their nations when, inspired by his interactions with an international group of artists in Morocco, he freestyled, "Came to build/Makin' it real/So knowin' they on it/I'm steadily growin' beyond borders."[25]

Art may be the product of an artist's inner life, but self-expression is rarely the sole end. So often, the goal of self-expression is other-connection. We express ourselves to see if others feel as we do, find meaning as we do, to prove that we are not alone in the world. It is this connection-seeking that makes art a powerful ally to diplomacy. And although hip hop is not the only means of creating connections it is distinctively powerful. Hip hop is accessible and popular. It draws people from all walks of life, but its appeal is especially strong among those who live on the margins, among those whose creativity is neither encouraged nor rewarded by the powers that be. It is an art for those who were not given a seat at the table, but have the nerve to show up with a folding chair. Hip hop is idealistic but not purist. It appeals to those who do not have the privilege of living a life without contradictions. And when those who identify hip hop as their culture come together they can make a world of limited options seem like—and become—a world of infinite possibility.

# NOTES

## INTRODUCTION

1. Quotations from Mark and Frankie come from the following interviews: Mark Kaweesi, interview with the author, Chapel Hill, NC, August 9, 2016; and Frankie Perez, telephone interview with the author, September 13, 2016.
2. For more on Abramz and Breakdance Project Uganda, see the 2010 documentary *Bouncing Cats*, https://www.youtube.com/watch?v=L99OIJk6zoc and the accompanying site http://www.bouncingcats.com/breakdance/.
3. For Mark Kaweesi's fellowship profile, see http://wagner.edu/intercultural/uncategorized/meet-mark/.
4. See https://www.nextlevel-usa.org/.
5. Richard T. Arndt, *The First Resort of Kings: American Cultural Diplomacy in the Twentieth Century* (Washington, DC: Potomac Books, 2005), x. For more on cultural diplomacy, see Advisory Committee on Cultural Diplomacy, *Cultural Diplomacy: The Linchpin of Public Diplomacy* (Washington, DC: US Department of State, 2005) and Simon Mark, "A Greater Role for Cultural Diplomacy" (Antwerp: Netherlands Institute of International Relations "Clingendael," 2009), 1.
6. For more on jazz diplomacy, see Penny Von Eschen, *Satchmo Blows up the World: Jazz Ambassadors Play the Cold War* (Cambridge, MA and London: Harvard University Press, 2004).
7. Bureau of Educational and Cultural Affairs, "About ECA," https://eca.state.gov/about-bureau.
8. Michael Curtis, "Rock, Rap, Hip Hop and All that U.S. Jazz Diplomacy," *American Thinker* 7 (November 2015): http://www.americanthinker.com/articles/2015/11/rock_rap_hip_hop_and_all_that_us_jazz_diplomacy.html.
9. Su'ad Abdul Khabeer, *Muslim Cool: Race, Religion, and Hip Hop in the United States* (New York: New York University Press, 2016), 180, 212.
10. "Hip-Hop é o fio condutor de uma luz que resgata jovens da criminalidade e que faz eles pensarem que através da cultura há uma saída." Rafaela Romualdo Belo Guse, email message to the author, June 19, 2017.
11. D.S.Sense, interview with the author, Cartagena, Colombia, August 19, 2016.

12. Konshens the MC, telephone interview with the author, December 10, 2017.

13. Christopher Hooton, "Hip hop Is the Most Listened to Genre in the World, According to Spotify Analysis of 20 Billion Tracks," *Independent*, July 14, 2015, http://www.independent.co.uk/arts-entertainment/music/news/hip    hop-is-the-most-listened-to-genre-in-the-world-according-to-spotify-analysis-of-20-billion-10388091.html.

14. Samuel Henrique da Silviera Lima, aka B-Boy Samuka, interview with the author, Ceilândia, Brazil, March 15, 2017. For a short feature on B-Boy Samuka filmed during Next Level's Brazil residency, see "Samuel's Next Level Story," April 3, 2017, https://www.youtube.com/watch?v=QU-UccGLs9U.

15. https://www.illabilities.com/.

16. Dumi Right, Facebook post, February 7, 2018. Quoted with permission.

17. *Slingshot Hip Hop*, dir. Jackie Reem Salloum, Fresh Booza DVD, 2008.

18. For an excellent study of the impact of filesharing on hip hop creativity and activism, see Adam Haupt, *Stealing Empire: P2P, Intellectual Property, and Hip-Hop Subversion* (Cape Town: HSRC Press, 2008).

19. For more on the origins of hip hop, see Jeff Chang, *Can't Stop, Won't Stop: A History of the Hip-Hop Generation* (New York: Picador, 2005) and Mark Katz, "The Breaks and The Bronx: 1973–1975," in *Groove Music: The Art and Culture of the Hip-Hop DJ* (New York: Oxford University Press, 2012), 14–42.

20. GrandWizzard Theodore, telephone interview with the author, December 19, 2006. Quoted in Katz, *Groove Music*, 147.

21. Iva Hađina, interview with the author, Zagreb, Croatia, May 11, 2017.

22. ABD (Mohammed Abdullah), interview with the author, November 14, 2014, Dhaka, Bangladesh. For a study of the relationship between South Asians (especially South Asian Americans) and hip hop, see Nitasha Tamar Sharma, *Hip Hop Desis: South Asian Americans, Blackness, and a Global Race Consciousness* (Durham, NC and London: Duke University Press, 2010).

23. "Muhammad (name)," *Wikipedia*, https://en.wikipedia.org/wiki/Muhammad_ (name).

24. Ruchi Kumar, "Afghanistan's Rap Scene is Real, Political, and Growing," *The Establishment*, August 15, 2016, https://theestablishment.co/afghanistans-rap-scene-is-real-political-and-growing-ef47f3d92b14;    Winstone    Antonio, "Jibilika Eyes Rural Communities," *NewsDay*, October 19, 2017, https://www.newsday.co.zw/2017/10/jibilika-eyes-rural-communities.

25. Steve Inskeep, "Venezuelan Hip-Hop Takes on Police Corruption," *Morning Edition*, December 11, 2013, https://www.npr.org/2013/12/11/195566691/venezuelan-hip hop-takes-on-police-corruption; "Vanuatu DJ Uses Hip Hop and Beat Box to Engage with Melanesian Youth," June 18, 2014, *Radio Australia*, http://www.radioaustralia.net.au/international/radio/onairhighlights/vanuatu-dj-uses-hip hop-and-beat-box-to-engage-with-melanesian-youth/1329082-0.

26. ABD (Mohammed Abdullah), Facebook post, November 20, 2014.

27. Khabeer, *Muslim Cool*, 7. A good study of globalization and hip hop is Halifu Osumare, *The Hiplife in Ghana: West African Indigenization of Hip-Hop* (New York: Palgrave Macmillan, 2012).

28. See United Nations Population Fund, *The Power of 1.8 Billion: Adolescents, Youth and the Transformation of the Future* (n.p.: United Nations Population Fund, 2014). Accessible at https://www.unfpa.org/sites/default/files/pub-pdf/EN-SWOP14-Report_FINAL-web.pdf.

29. Tsiry "Panda" Kely, interview with the author, Antananarivo, Madagascar, July 30, 2018.

30. Marija Bjelopetrovic, interview with the author, Belgrade, Serbia, July 26, 2014.

31. See Mark J.C. Crescenzi, *Of Friends and Foes: Reputation and Learning in International Politics* (New York: Oxford University Press, 2018).

32. "U.S.-Brazil Priorities," https://br.usembassy.gov/our-relationship/us-brazil-priorities/.

33. Ceilândia, a city outside Brasilia where we held a week of workshops, was established in the 1970s expressly to remove poor people from the capital; its name derives from the acronym CEI, which stands for *Campanha de Erradicação de Invasões*, or Squatters Eradication Campaign.

34. "U.S.-Brazil Priorities."

35. Sunshine Ison, interview with the author, Nikšić, Montenegro, September 11, 2014.

36. United States Department of State, Office of Citizen Exchanges, Cultural Programs Division, "Project Objectives, Goals, and Implementation (POGI): Creative Arts Exchange: Arts in Collaboration ECA/PE/C/CU-13-26. Accessible at https://eca.state.gov/files/bureau/2_pogi_cae_arts_in_collaboration.pdf. Emphasis mine.

37. Ngoni Tapiwa (aka Upmost), interview with the author, Harare, Zimbabwe, February 28, 2015. Emphasis mine.

38. Rami Mhazres, interview with the author, Tunis, Tunisia, February 12, 2017.

39. MC Ko-co, interview with the author, Tegucigalpa, Honduras, January 22, 2016. Original in Spanish; translated by Rapaz.

40. Nicholas Kristof, "We're Helping Deport Kids to Die," *New York Times*, July 16, 2016, http://www.nytimes.com/2016/07/17/opinion/sunday/were-helping-deport-kids-to-die.html.

41. Kuttin Kandi, Skype interview with the author, November 21, 2018.

42. Rabbi Darkside, interview with the author, Entebbe, Uganda, June 29, 2015.

43. Elijah Wald, Facebook post, January 27, 2018. Used with permission.

44. After stepping down as Next Level co-director I stayed on as an advisor, but was no longer involved in the day-to-day business of the program.

45. Jorge "Popmaster Fabel" Pabon, conversation with the author, Chapel Hill, NC, February 3, 2009.

46. DJ Cash Money, telephone interview with the author, June 23, 2008. Quoted in Katz, *Groove Music*, 12.

# CHAPTER 1

1. Dizzy Gillespie and Al Fraser, *To Be, Or Not—To Bop* (New York: Doubleday, 1979; Minneapolis, University of Minnesota Press, 2009), 498.

2. "Kenyan Tenth Anniversary Celebration," Communication from United States Embassy in Nairobi to United States Department of State, 29 August 1973. Accessible at https://wikileaks.org/plusd/cables/1973NAIROB05782b.html. See also Penny Von Eschen, *Satchmo Blows up the World: Jazz Ambassadors Play the Cold War* (Cambridge, MA and London: Harvard University Press, 2004), 235.

3. "Dizzy Gillespie and Kenyan Tenth Anniversary: Summary Report," Communication from United States Embassy in Nairobi to United States Department of State, December 18, 1973. Accessible at https://wikileaks.org/plusd/cables/1973NAIROB08567b.html. The author of the report, identified only as Lindstrom, was almost certainly Deputy Chief of Mission, Ralph E. Lindstrom.

4. For more on this party and its significance to hip hop, see Mark Katz, *Groove Music: The Art and Culture of the Hip-Hop DJ* (New York: Oxford University Press, 2012), 17–19, 22–23 and Jeff Chang, *Can't Stop, Won't Stop: A History of the Hip-Hop Generation* (New York: Picador, 2005).

5. See Von Eschen, *Satchmo Blows Up the World*, 226 and 233; Francis B. Tenny, "The Philadelphia Orchestra's 1973 Tour: A Case Study of Cultural Diplomacy During the Cultural Revolution," *American Diplomacy* (September 2012), http://www.unc.edu/depts/diplomat/item/2012/0712/fsl/tenny_orchestra.html; Adam Cathart, "Nixon, Kissinger and Musical Diplomacy in the Opening of China, 1971–1973," *Yonsei Journal of International Studies* 4 (2012): 131–39.

6. Felix Belair, "United States has Secret Sonic Weapon—Jazz," *New York Times*, 6 November 1955, 1, 42.

7. Cordell Hull, quoted in Carol A. Hess, "Copland in Argentina: Pan Americanist Politics, Folklore, and the Crisis in Modern Music," *Journal of the American Musicological Society* 66 (Spring 2013): 207–8.

8. For more on the Nazi threat in Latin America, see Max Paul Friedman, "Specter of a Nazi Threat: United States–Colombia Relations, 1939–1945," *The Americas* 56 (April 2000): 563–89.

9. The early history of the Division of Cultural Relations is chronicled in J. Manuel Espinosa, *Inter-American Beginnings of U.S. Cultural Diplomacy, 1936–1948* (Washington, DC: US Department of State, 1976), 89–107.

10. Report of the Committee of the Conference on Inter-American Relations in the Field of Music (Washington, DC: US Department of State, 1940), 2.

11. Charles Seeger, quoted in C.B. Brown, "Inter-American Exchange of Music in Formation," *Washington Post*, 29 October 1939, A5.

12. Brown, "Inter-American Exchange of Music in Formation."

13. The OIAA was originally called the Office for the Coordination of Commercial and Cultural Relations between the American Republics (OCCCRBAR).

14. For more on this subject, see Jennifer L. Campbell, "Shaping Solidarity: Music, Diplomacy, and Inter-American Relations, 1936–1946," PhD diss., University of Connecticut, 2010.

15. This is quoted from a draft of a "Handbook for the Cultural Presentations Program of the United States Government." Jennifer L. Campbell, "Creating Something Out of Nothing: The Office of Inter-American Affairs Music Committee (1940–1941) and the Inception of a Policy for Musical Diplomacy," *Diplomatic History* 36 (January 2012): 37n32.

16. Unsigned report from Santiago, Chile, to Nelson Rockefeller, July 24, 1941, quoted in Campbell, "Creating Something Out of Nothing," 37.

17. For a study of the mixed local reactions to Aaron Copland's South American tours, see Hess, "Copland in Argentina."

18. For a detailed and helpful searchable database, see Danielle Fosler-Lussier and Eric Fosler-Lussier, "Database of Cultural Presentations: Accompaniment to *Music in America's Cold War Diplomacy*," version 1.1, last modified 1 April 2015, http://musicdiplomacy.org/database.html.

19. Emily Abrams Ansari, "Shaping the Policies of Cold War Musical Diplomacy: An Epistemic Community of American Composers," *Diplomatic History* 36 (January 2012): 44.

20. Andrew H. Berding, quoted in Danielle Fosler-Lussier, *Music in America's Cold War Diplomacy* (Berkeley: University of California Press, 2015), 23.

21. Belair, "United States has Secret Sonic Weapon—Jazz," 42.

22. Quoted in Ingrid Monson, *Freedom Sounds: Civil Rights Call Out to Jazz and Africa* (New York: Oxford University Press, 2007), 113.

23. The State Department did not refer to "Jazz Ambassadors" in any official way at the time. It was not until 1997 that the Department's Bureau of Educational and Cultural Affairs designated certain touring groups as "Jazz Ambassadors." Outside of the State Department, the United States Army supports a big band known as the Jazz Ambassadors.

24. See Conover's obituary, Robert McG. Thomas, Jr., "Willis Conover, 75, Voice of America Disc Jockey," *New York Times*, 19 May 1996, p. 35. For an assessment of the complex influence of Conover's program, see Rüdiger Ritter, "Broadcasting Jazz into the Eastern Bloc—Cold War Weapon or Cultural Exchange? The Example of Willis Conover," *Jazz Perspectives* 7 (2013): 111–31.

25. Quoted in Von Eschen, *Satchmo Blows up the World*, 33.

26. Von Eschen, *Satchmo Blows up the World*, 187 ff.

27. Dave Brubeck, quoted in Stephen A. Crist, "Jazz as Democracy? Dave Brubeck and Cold War Politics," *Journal of Musicology* 26 (Spring 2009): 137.

28. Dave Brubeck and Iola Brubeck, "Cultural Exchange," from *The Real Ambassadors*, CBS LP 467140 2, 1961.

29. Von Eschen, *Satchmo Blows up the World*, 4.

30. Jazz scholar Marshall Stearns, who accompanied the tour, reported that Gillespie's performances had a pacifying effect on the student demonstrators, whereas reports from the US Embassy in Athens suggested otherwise. See Darren Mueller, "The Ambassadorial LPs of Dizzy Gillespie: *World Statesman* and *Dizzy in Greece*," *Journal of the Society for American Music* 10 (August 2016): 239–69 and Andrea Georgina Marina Franzius, "Soul Call: Music, Race and the Creation of American Cultural Policy," PhD diss., Duke University, 2006, 435–37.

31. Toni Blackman, quoted in Alex Dwyer, "Samsonite Man: A Look at Hip Hop's Diplomatic Affairs," *HipHopDX*, January 27, 2012, http://hiphopdx.com/editorials/id.1845/title.samsonite-man-a-look-at-hip hops-diplomatic-affairs.

32. See Jacqueline Trescott, "The Artist Lovingly Known as EJ," *IRAA+*, http://iraaa.museum.hamptonu.edu/page/The-Artist-Lovingly-Known-As-EJ.

33. Toni Blackman, Skype interview with the author, July 18, 2016.

34. Advisory Committee on Cultural Diplomacy, *Cultural Diplomacy: The Linchpin of Public Diplomacy* (Washington, DC: US Department of State, 2005), 4.

35. Cynthia P. Schneider, *Culture Communicates: US Diplomacy that Works* (n.p.: Netherlands Institute of International Relations, 2004), 3.

36. *Newsweek* poll, September 30, 2000. Results from Polling the Nations, http://www.orspub.com/.

37. National Urban League, Inc. poll, 2001. Results from Polling the Nations, http://www.orspub.com/.

38. Blackman, Skype interview with the author.

39. Jeff Hoodock, "Toni Blackman at Dance Place," *Washington Post*, 15 February 1999, p. C5; Eric Brace, "The Circuit," *Washington Post*, October 16, 1998, p. 7.

40. A good deal has been written about the role of women, and gender more broadly, in hip hop. See, for example, Tricia Rose, "Bad Sistas: Black Women Rappers and Sexual Politics in rap Music," in *Black Noise: Rap Music and Black Culture in Contemporary America* (Hanover, NH and London: Wesleyan University Press, 1994), 146–82; Joan Morgan, *When Chickenheads Come Home to Roost: A Hip-Hop feminist Breaks it Down* (New York: Simon & Schuster, 1999); Imani Perry, *Prophets of the Hood: Politics and Poetics in Hip Hop* (Durham, NC and London: Duke University Press, 2004); and Bettina L. Love, *Hip Hop's Li'l Sistas Speak: Negotiating Hip Hop Identities and Politics in the New South* (New York: Peter Lang, 2012).

41. The State Department's organizational structure is explained on its website at http://www.state.gov/r/pa/ei/rls/dos/436.htm. An organizational chart may be found at http://www.state.gov/r/pa/ei/rls/dos/99494.htm. State is actually one of the smaller federal executive departments, both in terms of the number of employees and its budget.

42. Blackman, Skype interview with the author. Unless otherwise noted, subsequent quotes from Blackman in this chapter come from this interview.

43. Toni Blackman, quoted in "Hip-Hop Takes on Diplomatic Role with State Department," *NPR*, January 24, 2007, http://www.npr.org/templates/transcript/transcript.php?storyId=6997064.

44. Blackman, quoted in "Hip-Hop Takes on Diplomatic Role with State Department." For more on Blackman's experience in Senegal, see Nicole Hodges Persley, "West African Remix: Tracks of Change in Dakar," *American Theatre* 31 (May–June 2014): 30–33.

45. I'm grateful to Rod Murray, one of the program's primary hosts, for information on "Hip Hop Connection." Rod Murray, Skype interview with the author, October 31, 2017.

46. Joseph S. Nye, Jr., *Soft Power: The Means to Success in World Politics* (New York: Public Affairs, 2004), 5.

47. E. Huseynzade, "Baku Jazz Festival кошмарно провалился [has Failed Badly]," *News Day* April 11, 2004, http://news.day.az/showbiz/6367.html.

48. John Ferguson, Skype interview with the author, September 23, 2016.

49. "Youth Extravaganza Kicks Off 10th Anniversary of US-Vietnam Normalization of Relations," communication from United States Embassy in Hanoi to United

States Department of State, April 21, 2005. Accessible at http://wikileaks.org/plusd/cables/05HANOI924_a.html.

50. "Youth Extravaganza Kicks Off 10th Anniversary of US-Vietnam Normalization of Relations."

51. Itineraries for these artists are reproduced in Joseph Jones, "Hegemonic Rhythms: The Role of Hip-Hop Music in 21st Century American Public Diplomacy, " PhD diss., Clark Atlanta University, 2009, 98–99.

52. Karen Hughes, "'Waging Peace': A New Paradigm for Public Diplomacy," *Mediterranean Quarterly* 18 (Spring 2007): 18–36.

53. Ozomatli, "Coming War" on *Ozomatli*, Almo Sounds compact disc, AMSD-80020, 1998.

54. See http://centerstageus.org/artists/jogja_hip_hop_foundation.

55. The rappers were Alesh (Congo, 2012), Paul Pissety Sagna (Senegal, 2012), Toussa Senerap (Senegal, 2013), and Ahmed Rock (Egypt, 2013). See http://1beat.org/projects/ for a list of OneBeat artists through the years.

56. My reporting of the events leading to the creation of the program that became Next Level are based on informal, unrecorded conversations with Jill Staggs and Michele Peregrin between 2013 and 2018 in the course of working with them as the program officers who oversaw Next Level.

57. See https://www.gpo.gov/fdsys/pkg/STATUTE-75/pdf/STATUTE-75-Pg527.pdf or http://www2.ed.gov/about/offices/list/ope/iegps/fulbrighthaysact.pdf.

58. The original State Department press release, dated February 12, 2013, reads in part: "The US Department of State's Bureau of Educational and Cultural Affairs is pleased to announce that San Francisco-based hip hop group Audiopharmacy will tour Southeast Asia and the Pacific as part of the American Music Abroad program. [ . . . ] The American Music Abroad program, a partnership with American Voices, sends American musical groups overseas to engage with audiences and communities, especially underserved youth. American Music Abroad is part of the Department of State's cultural diplomacy efforts, which support people-to-people connections and foster mutual understanding through the arts." Accessible at http://www.state.gov/r/pa/prs/ps/2013/02/204522.htm.

59. Daniel Halper, "State Dept. Announces 'Hip Hop Group Audiopharmacy to Tour,'" *Weekly Standard*, February 13, 2013, http://www.weeklystandard.com/state-dept.-announces-hip     hop-group-audiopharmacy-to-tour/article/701181; Cheryl K. Chumley, "Taxpayers Pick Up Asian Hip-Hop Tour Promoted by U.S. State Department," *Washington Times*, February 13, 2013, http://m.washingtontimes.com/news/2013/feb/13/state-department-announces-asian-hip hop-tour-taxp/.

60. Paul Rockower, email message to the author, August 3, 2016.

61. United States Department of State, Office of Citizen Exchanges, Cultural Programs Division, "Project Objectives, Goals, and Implementation (POGI): Creative Arts Exchange: Arts in Collaboration ECA/PE/C/CU-13-26. Accessible at https://eca.state.gov/files/bureau/2_pogi_cae_arts_in_collaboration.pdf.

62. United States Department of State, Office of Citizen Exchanges, Cultural Programs Division, "Project Objectives, Goals, and Implementation (POGI)."

63. Plot Mhako, interview with author, Harare, Zimbabwe, March 1, 2015. Fortunately, the program—Next Level—defied his expectations. "But ultimately when the program started I started to see it differently. And also from the sentiments that the instructors said that they thought they were going to bridge a gap, but they realized the hip hop scene in Zimbabwe is very much alive, and we are not really lagging behind. There's a lot that we need to learn, but still they also say they are learning a lot from us. So I think the program helped a lot in terms of connecting the two countries through culture and also in terms of imparting young people that are involved in the hip hop scene—dance music, beatmaking, and so forth—and I foresee a lot of positive results coming forth in the next few years from the seed that was planted by Next Level in Zimbabwe."

64. United States Department of State, Office of Citizen Exchanges, Cultural Programs Division, "Project Objectives, Goals, and Implementation (POGI)."

65. Pierce Freelon, email message to the author, April 15, 2013.

66. See http://www.beatmakinglab.com/.

67. Mark Katz, email message to Jill Staggs, October 9, 2013.

68. Kane Smego, quoted in Pierce Freelon, email message to the author, October 21, 2013.

69. Jorge "Fabel" Pabon, email message to the author, May 1, 2014. This statement, and those by Amirah Sackett and Diamond D following, were in response to a message sent to the first group of Next Level artists asking them to explain what the phrase "next level" meant to them.

70. Amirah Sackett, email message to the author, May 2, 2014.

71. Diamond D, email message to the author, May 2, 2014.

72. Shirlette Ammons, application to Next Level program, January 3, 2014. Used with permission.

73. See David K. Johnson, *The Lavender Scare: The Cold War Persecution of Gays and Lesbians in the Federal Government* (Chicago: University of Chicago Press, 2004).

74. Stacy White, remarks to Next Level artists, April 28, 2014, United States Department of State, Washington, DC.

75. See remarks by Anthony Colon and BOM5 in Joseph G. Schloss, *Foundation: B-Boys, B-Girls and Hip-Hop Culture in New York* (New York: Oxford University Press, 2009), 85.

## CHAPTER 2

1. Boom bap also refers to a style of beats that evokes early 1990s hip hop, with its emphasis on hard-hitting drum samples.

2. The jam session took place on February 18, 2016 at Suratthani Rajabhat University in Surat Thani, Thailand.

3. Benjamin Brinner, *Knowing Music, Making Music: Javanese Gamelan and the Theory of Musical Competence and Interaction* (Chicago and London: University of Chicago Press, 1995), 285–86.

4. Musicians and scholars often idealize or romanticize musical collaboration, especially improvisation, and its ability to model or affect social relationships. For a thoughtful discussion of common claims about improvisation, see Jeff R.

Warren, *Music and Ethical Responsibility* (Cambridge: Cambridge University Press, 2014).

5. For more on the theory and practice of cyphers, see Imani Kai Johnson, "Dark Matter in B-Boying Cyphers: Race and Global Connection in Hip Hop," PhD diss., University of Southern California, 2009; Joseph G. Schloss, *Foundation: B-boys, B-girls and Hip-Hop Culture in New York* (New York: Oxford University Press, 2009), 94–106; and Paul J. Kuttner and Mariama White-Hammond, "(Re) building the Cypher: Fulfilling the Promise of Hip Hop for Liberation," in *The Organic Globalizer: Hip Hop, Political Development, and Movement Culture*, ed. Christopher Malone and George Martinez, Jr. (New York: Bloomsbury, 2015), 43–57.

6. Trac 2, quoted in Schloss, *Foundation*, 85.

7. Frankie Perez, telephone interview with the author, September 13, 2016.

8. T.R.U.T.H, interview with the author, Azerbaijan, Baku, October 23, 2017.

9. Randy Weston, *African Rhythms: The Autobiography of Randy Weston* (Durham, NC and London: Duke University Press, 2010), 176.

10. For a scholarly introduction to *gnawa* music, see Maisie Sum, "Staging the Sacred: Musical Structure and Processes of the Gnawa *Lila* in Morocco," *Ethnomusicology* 55 (Winter 2011): 77–111.

11. All quotes from Klevah come from Klevah and Zephyr Ann Doles, interview with the author, Meknes, Morocco, September 13, 2017.

12. Konshens the MC, telephone interview with the author, December 10, 2017. All subsequent quotations from Koshens in this section come from this interview.

13. M'allem Abdenbi El Fakir, aka El Meknassi, email message to the author, January 28, 2018. Original in French; translations by the author. All subsequent quotations from El Meknassi in this section come from this source.

14. One remark by El Meknassi nicely captures the success of the public concert, resonating—probably unintentionally—with the languages of both diplomacy and hip hop. As he wrote to me, "Les musiciens sont totalement en accord et bien déchaîner avec la musique gnawa." In saying that the musicians were completely together, the French word *accord* evokes the term for a diplomatic treaty or agreement—a peace accord, for example. In the phrase, "bien déchaîner avec la musique gnawa," *déchaîner* literally means to remove a chain, as if unleashing an aggressive dog. The raucous concert was definitely, to translate El Meknassi's French into hip hop slang, "off the chain."

15. See Dee Reynolds and Matthew Reason, eds., *Kinesthetic Empathy in Creative and Cultural Practices* (Bristol, UK and Chicago: Intellect, 2012).

16. Andjelko Pavlovic, conversation with the author, Belgrade, Serbia, April 18, 2014. For a study of hip hop as a means to bridge ethnic divides in the Balkans, see Alexandria Balandina, "Rap Music as a Cultural Mediator in Postconflict Yugoslavia," in Milosz Miszczynski and Adriana Helbig, eds., *Hip Hop at Europe's Edge: Music, Agency, and Social Change* (Bloomington and Indianapolis: Indiana University Press, 2017), 63–81.

17. Daniel Fischlin, Ajay Heble, and George Lipsitz, *The Fierce Urgency of Now: Improvisation, Rights, and the Ethics of Cocreation* (Durham, NC and London: Duke University Press, 2013), xii.

18. United States Department of State, Office of Citizen Exchanges, Cultural Programs Division, "Project Objectives, Goals, and Implementation (POGI): Creative Arts Exchange: Arts in Collaboration ECA/PE/C/CU-13-26," https://eca.state.gov/files/bureau/2_pogi_cae_arts_in_collaboration.pdf.

19. D.S.Sense interview with the author, Cartagena, Colombia, August 19, 2016.

20. Perez, telephone interview with the author. Judith Lynne Hanna discusses dance as self-mastery in *To Dance is Human: A Theory of Nonverbal Communication* (Austin and London: University of Texas Press, 1979), 132–33.

21. T.R.U.T.H, interview with the author.

22. Konshens the MC, telephone interview with the author, December 10, 2017. All subsequent quotations from Koshens in this section come from this interview.

23. Hanna, *To Dance is Human*, 146.

24. Elliott Gann, quoted in Joseph G. Schloss, "Roots & Branches: Dr. Elliot Gann, aka Phillipdrummond, *Next Level Blog*, December 10, 2017, https://www.nextlevel-usa.org/blog/roots-branches-dr-elliot-gann-aka-phillipdummond. The text has been condensed slightly.

25. As Lugaflow rapper MC Sypda explained to me, the term "Lugaflow" is derived from the Swahili word *lugha*, or language. As he tells it, the term originated when some Ugandan MCs were performing in Kenya, and the local MCs questioned why they didn't rap in their own language, or *lugha*. Spyda said that the term Lugaflow is sometimes mistakenly understood to mean Lugandan-language rap. It simply means rapping in one's first native language, whether Luganda, Lusago (which Spyda started rhyming in), or any of Uganda's forty indigenous languages. Spyda, interview with the author, Kampala, Uganda, June 27, 2015.

26. Deison Luis Dimas Hoyos, "Panorama de las amenazas con panfletos en el Caribe Colombiano," *CEPSCA*, May 6, 2016, http://cepsca.org/index.php/8-inicio/244-informe-panorama-de-las-amenazas-con-panfletos-en-el-caribe-colombiano.

27. Spyda, interview with the author.

28. For more on Rumah Cemara, see its website at http://rumahcemara.or.id/.

29. Ginandjar Koesmayadi, interview with the author, Bandung, Indonesia, November 30, 2016.

30. Haleem "Stringz" Rasul, interview with the author, Bandung, Indonesia, December 1, 2016.

31. Wanda, interview with the author, Bandung, Indonesia, November 30, 2016.

32. See Tom Boellstorff, "The Emergence of Political Homophobia in Indonesia: Masculinity and National Belonging," *Ethnos: Journal of Anthropology* 69 (December 2004): 465–86.

33. Junious Brickhouse, email message to the author, December 24, 2018.

34. A video of this segment is accessible at https://www.youtube.com/watch?v=x9kNxc4ZDx8.

35. For a brief piece on jit, one that cites Stringz' role in the dance form, see Alistair Macaulay, "Fast-Stepped Fury, Rooted in Detroit: Detroit Jit, a '70s Street Dance Reborn and Revved Up," *New York Times*, August 10, 2014, https://www.nytimes.com/2014/08/11/arts/dance/detroit-jit-a-70s-street-dance-reborn-and-revved-up.html.

36. As ethnomusicologist Peter Manuel has written, "The rise of *jaipongan* social dancing has, indeed, led to the flowering of innumerable private dance instruction schools where middle-class teenagers may attend classes in *jaipongan* much as would Westerners amuse themselves learning the foxtrot and the *chachachá* at an Arthur Murray dance studio." Peter Manuel, *Popular Musics of the Non-Western World: An Introductory Survey* (New York: Oxford University Press, 1988), 214.

37. Stringz, interview with the author.

38. Supria "Iya" Budiman, interview with the author, Bandung, Indonesia, December 1, 2016.

39. Wanda, interview with the author. Based on appearance, my assumption was that Wanda was male, but our interpreter—Lufthi "Uphie" Abdurrahman, a locally employed staff member from the US Embassy in Jakarta—did not refer to Wanda as "he" or "she." As he explained, the Indonesian language does not use gender-specific pronouns, and he didn't want to make any assumptions in Wanda's case.

40. Clare Croft, "Introduction," in *Queer Dance: Meanings & Makings*, ed. Clare Croft (New York: Oxford University Press, 2017), 1.

41. Croft, "Introduction," in *Queer Dance*, 2.

42. Anti-LBGTQ activity in Indonesia was on the rise in the years after this performance in late 2016. See Gisela Swaragita, "State Sponsored Homophobia Forces LGBT Community to Lay Low," *Jakarta Post*, May 17, 2018, http://www.thejakartapost.com/news/2018/05/16/state-sponsored-homophobia-forces-lgbt-community-to-lay-low.html.

43. All the quotations from Budiman in this paragraph come from Supria "Iya" Budiman, email message to the author, January 4, 2018.

44. Sukarno, quoted in Richard Wright, *The Color Curtain: A Report on the Bandung Conference* (New York: World Publishing, 1956), 139.

45. Adam Clayton Powell, Jr., *Adam by Adam: The Autobiography of Adam Clayton Powell, Jr.* (New York: Dial Press, 1971), 103.

46. Adam Clayton Powell, Jr., quoted in Aidi, "The Grand (Hip-Hop) Chessboard: Race, Rap, and Raison d'Etat," *Middle East Report*, no. 260 (Fall 2011): 26.

## CHAPTER 3

1. Robert Muggah, "It's Official: San Salvador is the Murder Capital of the World," *Los Angeles Times*, March 2, 2016, http://www.latimes.com/opinion/op-ed/la-oe-0302-muggah-el-salvador-crime-20160302-story.html.

2. Houston recorded 297 homicides in 2015. St. John Barned-Smith, "Variety of Factors Cited in Rise in Houston Murders in 2015," *Houston Chronicle*, December 31, 2015, http://www.chron.com/news/houston-texas/houston/article/Variety-of-factors-cited-in-rise-in-Houston-6730937.php.

3. Mari Carmen Aponte, quoted in "Jóvenes bailan 'hip hop' para alejarse de la violencia," *El Mundo*, December 15, 2015, http://elmundo.sv/jovenes-bailan-hip hop-para-alejarse-de-la-violencia/. The full quotation is as follows: "Es un placer saber que todo este esfuerzo es para prevenir la violencia en El Salvador y eso

es lo que me llena de felicidad,' dijo la embajadora de los Estados Unidos, Mari Carmen Aponte, tras presenciar una muestra del baile que fue organizada por los jóvenes. 'La situación de seguridad es una situación difícil, lo he dicho antes. Hay que trabajar con el gobierno, con la sociedad civil, va a necesitar de todos, de la empresa privada. El flagelo es tan fuerte que no hay un solo segmento del pueblo que pueda manejarlo, tenemos que unirnos todos,' argumentó la embajadora estadounidense."

4. Muggah, "It's Official."

5. Raymond Bonner, "Time for a US Apology to El Salvador," *The Nation*, April 15, 2016, https://www.thenation.com/article/time-for-a-us-apology-to-el-salvador/.

6. These deportations increased significantly with the passage of the Illegal Immigration Reform and Immigrant Responsibility Act (IIRIRA) in 1995. The Act established that illegal immigrants serving a prison sentence of more than one year were subject to deportation after completing their terms. It would be wrong to say that the gang scourge in El Salvador is wholly or even mostly due to actions by the United States; still, there is no question that the United States' role both in the civil war and in its response to Salvadoran criminals in the country intensified the problem.

7. I am grateful to Professor Frauke Berndt of the University of Zurich for introducing me to the concept of the zone of ambiguity.

8. See Frances Stonor Saunders, *The Cultural Cold War: The CIA and the World of Arts and Letters* (New York: New Press, 2000).

9. Desmond Butler, Michael Weissenstein, Laura Wides-Muñoz, and Andrea Rodriguez, "USAID Op Undermines Cuba's Hip-Hop Protest Scene," *Associated Press*, December 11, 2014, https://apnews.com/7c275c134f1b4a0ca3428929fcece 82d.

10. See "Executive Order 13288: Blocking Property of Persons Undermining Democratic Processes or Institutions in Zimbabwe," *Federal Register*, March 10, 2003, https://www.gpo.gov/fdsys/pkg/FR-2003-03-10/pdf/03-5848.pdf. More limited sanctions were enforced starting in 2001. See also "U.S. Sanctions Policy: Facts and Myths," March 14, 2016, https://harare.usembassy.gov/sanctions_facts_ myths.html.

11. "About the Embassy," https://harare.usembassy.gov/about_the_embassy.html.

12. Roberta Levitow, quoted in Daniel Banks, "The Question of Cultural Diplomacy: Acting Ethically," *Theatre Topics* 21 (September 2011): 111.

13. Joan Channick, "The Artist as Cultural Diplomat," *American Theatre* 22 (May–June 2005): 4.

14. Advisory Committee on Cultural Diplomacy, *Cultural Diplomacy: The Linchpin of Public Diplomacy* (Washington, DC: US Department of State, 2005), 1.

15. Richard T. Arndt, *The First Resort of Kings: American Cultural Diplomacy in the Twentieth Century* (Washington, DC: Potomac Books, 2005), x.

16. "History and Mission of ECA," https://eca.state.gov/about-bureau/history-and-mission-eca.

17. Stacy White, remarks during Next Level orientation, Washington, DC, April 28, 2014.

18. For an appreciation of locally employed staff (then acronymically referred to as FSNs, for Foreign Service Nationals), see Paul Rockower, "Keepers of the PD Flame: An Appreciation of Embassy Local Staff," *CPD Blog*, August 6, 2013, http://uscpublicdiplomacy.org/blog/keepers-pd-flame-appreciation-embassy-local-staff.

19. See "Preserving India," https://www.youtube.com/watch?v=JdUZvzOZkkE, June 20, 2014. See also "Girls Be Brave," https://www.youtube.com/watch?v=c_hH3HcCeX8, June 20, 2014 and "Use Your Rights," https://www.youtube.com/watch?v=baTV2a74f-g, June 20, 2014.

20. Quoted in Chérie Rivers Ndaliko, *Necessary Noise: Music, Film, and Charitable Imperialism in the East of Congo* (New York: Oxford University Press, 2016), 153–54; 155.

21. Kendra Salois, "The US Department of State's 'Hip-Hop Diplomacy' in Morocco," in *Music and Diplomacy from the Early Modern Era to the Present*, ed. Rebekah Ahrendt, Mark Ferraguto, and Damien Mahiet (New York: Palgrave Macmillan, 2014), 242.

22. Hillary Clinton, interview with Rita Braver, *CBS Morning News*, July 4, 2010. Accessible at https://archive.org/details/WUSA_20100704_130000_CBS_News_Sunday_Morning#start/960/end/1020.

23. Aidi, "The Grand (Hip-Hop) Chessboard: Race, Rap, and Raison d'Etat," *Middle East Report*, no. 260 (Fall 2011): 39.

24. Maxi Krezy (Amadou Aw), conversation with the author, Dakar, Senegal, October 13, 2014.

25. "U.S. Embassy Builds the Capacities of Hip Hoppers with Maxi Krezy and the Fifth Element," undated press release, Embassy of the United States, Dakar, Senegal, https://dakar.usembassy.gov/fifth_element2.html. The official launch of the project took place on June 8, 2014.

26. "Ambassador Helps Inaugurate Hip Hop Akademy," undated press release, Embassy of the United States, Dakar, Senegal, https://dakar.usembassy.gov/hip hop-akademy2.html. The event took place on January 19, 2012.

27. Katherine Otto warns of the burdens that foreigners create for those they intend to help in *Everyday Ambassador: Make A Difference by Connecting in a Disconnected World* (New York: Atria, 2015), xi.

28. Aminata Samb, interview with the author, January 16, 2015, Dakar, Senegal.

29. Fatou Cisse, "Senegal," in *Remittance Markets in Africa*, ed. Sanket Mohapatra and Dilip Ratha (Washington, DC: World Bank, 2011), 221–41. Accessible at http://documents.worldbank.org/curated/en/248331468193493657/pdf/613100PUB0mark158344B09780821384756.pdf.

30. My thanks to Ali Colleen Neff, an anthropologist who has lived in and studied music scenes in Senegal, for bringing the issue of remittances and visas to my attention.

31. Chimamanda Ngozi Adichie, "The American Embassy," in *The Thing Around Your Neck* (New York: Anchor, 2009), 128–41.

32. Next Level invites one workshop participant from each country to participate in a two-week artistic and professional development residency in the United States, and assists them in obtaining their visas. Just one out of twenty visas for this

residency was denied between 2015 and 2018. Cue Bass, a DJ from El Salvador who attended the US residency, recalled how his family warned him that he might well be denied. His experienced surprised him. "The day I went for the interview, the consul [consular services officer], he asked me two, three questions and that's it. I expected it to be a very hard interview, so I was prepared. Let me tell you, I was a little nervous, but he was very polite, very friendly with me. He approved the visa and I was like, 'Yes!'" Given how difficult it typically is to obtain visas to travel to the United States, this makes the visa-granting power of US cultural diplomacy programs that much more valuable. Cue Bass (Carlos Alfredo Godínez Garcia), interview with the author, Carrboro, NC, April 6, 2016.

33. Petna Ndaliko Katondolo, conversation with the author, Tunis, Tunisia, February 11, 2017.

34. Toni Blackman, remarks at Next Level orientation, Washington, DC, April 29, 2014.

35. Junious Brickhouse, interview with the author, Dakar, Senegal, January 16, 2015.

36. Michele Peregrin, telephone interview with the author, February 28, 2018.

37. This was in response to a question from Meli Kimathi during Peregrin's Skype discussion with students in my Hip Hop Diplomacy seminar at the University of North Carolina at Chapel Hill, April 11, 2018.

38. Bruce Armstrong, remarks during Next Level orientation, Washington, DC June 10, 2015. Kendra Salois quotes US Foreign Service Officer Sam Werberg making a similar remark: "The best thing we can do at the Embassy is connect people and step out of the way." Kendra Salois, "Connection and Complicity in the Global South: Hip Hop Musicians and US Cultural Diplomacy," *Journal of Popular Music Studies* 27 (2015): 413.

39. Suzy Hansen, *Notes on a Foreign Country: An American Abroad in a Post-American World* (New York: Farrar, Straus and Giroux, 2017), 10–11, 22–23. US citizens widely accept the notion of American exceptionalism. See Laura Thorsett and Jocelyn Kiley, "U.S. is among World's Greatest Countries, Say Most Americans," Pew Research Center, June 30, 2017, http://www.pewresearch.org/fact-tank/2017/06/30/most-americans-say-the-u-s-is-among-the-greatest-countries-in-the-world/.

40. Banks, "The Question of Cultural Diplomacy: Acting Ethically," 119.

## CHAPTER 4

1. "Complicit," March 12, 2017, https://www.youtube.com/watch?v=F7o4oMKbStE.

2. "Ivanka Trump interview: 'If being complicit is wanting to be a force for good . . . then I'm complicit,'" *CBS News*, April 4, 2017, https://www.cbsnews.com/news/ivanka-trump-interview-what-it-means-to-be-complicit/.

3. Jeff Flake, "Flake Announces Senate Future," October 24, 2017, https://www.flake.senate.gov/public/index.cfm/press-releases?ID=5BA26227-82BA-406A-B5F3-3683A7619086.

4. "Word of the Year 2017," http://www.dictionary.com/e/word-of-the-year-2017/.

5. Nerisha Penrose, "'The Storm': 17 Rappers Who Have Dropped Anti-Trump Songs," *Billboard*, October 11, 2017, https://www.billboard.com/articles/columns/hip hop/7997503/rappers-dis-trump-eminem-the-storm-freestyle.

6. Maxwell Strachan, "The Definitive History of 'George Bush Doesn't Care About Black People,'" *Huffington Post*, August 28, 2015, https://www.huffingtonpost.com/entry/kanye-west-george-bush-black-people_us_55d67c12e4b020c386de2f5e. In 2016, West called Donald Trump's campaign "genius" and later met with the president-elect; he continued to praise Trump into his presidency. See Philip Bump, "The Symbiotic Trump-Kanye West Relationship," *Washington Post*, October 1, 2018, https://www.washingtonpost.com/politics/2018/10/01/symbiotic-trump-kanye-west-relationship/.

7. See Michael P. Jeffries, "Is Obama Really the Hip-Hop President?" *Atlantic*, January 26, 2011, https://www.theatlantic.com/entertainment/archive/2011/01/is-obama-really-the-hip hop-president/70061/; Travis L. Gosa and Erick Nielson, eds., *The Hip Hop & Obama Reader* (New York: Oxford University Press, 2015).

8. MC Solaar and Guru, "Le Bien, Le Mal," from *Jazzmatazz*, vol. 1, Chrysalis CD 0946 3 21998 2 9, 1993.

9. There is an extensive literature on hip hop as a form of resistance. Examples include Adam Haupt, *Stealing Empire: P2P, Intellectual Property, and Hip-Hop Subversion* (Cape Town: HSRC Press, 2008); Msia Kibona Clark, "Hip Hop as Social Commentary in Accra and Dar es Salaam," *Africa Studies Quarterly* 13 (Summer 2012): 23–46; Damon Chandru Sajnani, "Deepening Democracy Galsen Style: Y'en a Marre, HipHop and Politics in Senegal," PhD diss., Northwestern University, 2015; and Meghan Drury, "Counterorienting the War on Terror: Arab Hip Hop and Diasporic Resistance," *Journal of Popular Music Studies* 29 (June 2017): n.p.

10. Cristina Moreno Almeida, *Rap Beyond Resistance: Staging Power in Contemporary Morocco* (Cham, Switzerland: Palgrave Macmillan, 2017), 14.

11. Rayya El Zein, "Performing el Rap el 'Arabi 2005–2015: Feeling Politics amid Neoliberal Incursions in Ramallah, Amman, and Beirut," PhD diss., City University of New York, 2016, 25. My thanks to Chris Nickell for alerting me to El Zein's work.

12. Public Enemy, "Black Steel in the Hour of Chaos," *It Takes a Nation of Millions to Hold Us Back*, Def Jam Recordings CD, CK 44303, 1988.

13. Zephyr Ann Doles, telephone interview with Erica Fedor, March 23, 2018. Used with permission.

14. Asheru, interview with the author. Asheru quotes the 1975 song, "Rat Race," by Bob Marley and the Wailers.

15. Gomez, interview with the author.

16. Jaci Caprice and Kane Smego, interview with the author, Harare, Zimbabwe, February 28, 2015; Junious Brickhouse, interview with the author, Dakar, Senegal, January 14, 2015; Def-i, interview with the author, Washington, DC, June 5, 2018; DJ 2-Tone Jones, interview with the author, Kolkata, India, June 4, 2014; CHINO BYI, interview with the author, Brooklyn, NY, December 18, 2018.

17. Kareem Gwinn, email message to the author, December 15, 2018. His original remark, "I've never been a part of something as hip hop as this," was made in Villa Neuva, Guatemala, December 8, 2015.

18. Diamond D, interview with the author, Belgrade, Serbia, July 28, 2014.

19. Doles, telephone interview with Erica Fedor.

20. Suzi Analogue, interview with the author, Entebbe, Uganda, June 29, 2015.

21. Gang Starr, "Code of the Streets," *Hard to Earn*, Chrysalis CD 7243 8 28435 2 8, 1994.

22. Gabriel "Asheru" Benn, interview with the author, Dhaka, Bangladesh, November 14, 2014.

23. Toni Blackman, telephone interview with the author, March 18, 2015.

24. Medusa the Gangsta Goddess, interview with the author, San Salvador, El Salvador, December 7, 2015.

25. Audre Lorde, "A Burst of Light: Living with Cancer," in *A Burst of Light: Essays by Audre Lorde* (Ithaca, NY: Firebrand, 1988), 131.

26. J-Live, interview with the author, Zagreb, Croatia, May 11, 2017.

27. For documents related to this trip, see Francis Johnson: Music Master of Early Philadelphia, https://www.library.upenn.edu/exhibits/music/fjohnson/ case6.html.

28. Javier Garcia and Rocc Williams, Skype interview with the author August 11, 2016.

29. Akim Funk Buddha, interview with the author, Baku, Azerbaijan, October 22, 2017.

30. Mahogany Jones, interview with the author, Sarajevo, Bosnia, September 14, 2014.

31. Marc Bayangos, interview with the author, Sarajevo, Bosnia, September 14, 2014.

32. Akim Funk Buddha, interview with the author.

33. Cue Bass (Carlos Alfredo Godínez Garcia), interview with the author, Carrboro, NC, April 6, 2016.

34. Kiche Legend (Amani Msangi), interview with the author, Carrboro, NC, April 6, 2016.

35. Charles Burchell, interview with the author, San Salvador, El Salvador, December 7, 2015.

36. See S. Craig Watkins, *Representing: Hip Hop Culture and the Production of Black Cinema* (Chicago: University of Chicago Press, 1998).

37. Diamond D, interview with the author.

38. Brickhouse, interview with the author.

39. Louis Armstrong, "Remember Who You Are," *The Real Ambassadors*, CBS LP 467140 2, 1961.

40. Baba Israel, interview with the author, Zagreb, Croatia, May 11, 2017.

41. Toki Wright, telephone interview with Aldwyn Hogg Jr., March 11, 2018. Used with permission.

42. Pinqy Ring, interview with the author, Durham, NC, May 19, 2018.

43. Toni Blackman, telephone interview with the author.

44. Kendra Salois, "Connection and Complicity in the Global South: Hip Hop Musicians and US Cultural Diplomacy," *Journal of Popular Music Studies* 27 (2015): 408–23.

45. G Yamazawa, featuring Joshua Gunn and Kane Smego, "North Cack," May 7, 2017, https://www.youtube.com/watch?v=lqWxGE7zSPA.

46. *Family Affair Mixtape* was released by Ammons's label, SugarQube Records, and distributed at no cost to Next Level participants and the public.

47. Juan Gomez, interview with the author, Harare, Zimbabwe, February 28, 2015.

48. Su'Ad Abdul Khabeer, *Muslim Cool: Race, Religion, and Hip Hop in the United States* (New York: New York University Press, 2016), 202.

49. Harry Allen, telephone interview with the author, April 13, 2018.

50. Ramón Grosfoguel, "The Divorce of Nationalist Discourses from the Puerto Rican People: A Sociohistorical Perspective," in *Puerto Rican Jam: Rethinking Colonialism and Nationalism*, ed. Frances Negrón-Mutaner and Ramón Grosfoguel (Minneapolis and London: University of Minnesota Press, 1997), 68.

51. Jaci Caprice and Kane Smego, interview with the author.

52. Cruz Medina, "(Who Discovered) America: Ozomatli and the Mestiz@ Rhetoric of Hip Hop," *alter/nativas latin american cultural studies journal*, no. 2 (2014): 10.

53. Alicia, "Interview: Ozomatli Sits Down with Killahbeez," *killahbeez*, April 20, 2009, http://www.killahbeez.com/2009/04/20/interview-ozomatli-sits-down-with-killahbeez/.

54. Pinqy Ring, "Revolución," https://soundcloud.com/pinqyring/revolucion.

55. Pinqy Ring, email message to the author, June 11, 2018.

56. Rebecca Ballhaus, "Trump Defends West Wing Turnover: 'I Like Conflict,'" *Wall Street* Journal, March 8, 2018, https://www.wsj.com/articles/trump-defends-west-wing-turnover-i-like-conflict-1520375738. The language of conflict resolution with respect to Next Level can be found in United States Department of State, Office of Citizen Exchanges, Cultural Programs Division, "Project Objectives, Goals, and Implementation (POGI): Creative Arts Exchange: Arts in Collaboration ECA/PE/C/CU-13-26, https://eca.state.gov/files/bureau/2_pogi_cae_arts_in_collaboration.pdf.

57. Def-i (Christopher Mike-Bidtah), Facebook post, November 2, 2018. Used with permission.

58. Dionne Searcy and Emmanuel Akinwotu, "Nigerian Army Uses Trump's Words to Justify Fatal Shooting of Rock-Throwing Protesters," *New York Times*, November 3, 2018, https://www.nytimes.com/2018/11/02/world/africa/nigeria-trump-rocks.html.

59. "Our Mission, Values, and History," November 15, 2016, https://www.state.gov/s/d/rm/rls/perfrpt/2016/html/265067.htm.

60. "What is the Mission of the U.S. Department of State?" https://www.state.gov/discoverdiplomacy/diplomacy101/issues/170606.htm.

61. For criticism of the 2017 statement from both Democrats and Republicans, see Josh Rogin, "State Department Considers Scrubbing Democracy Promotion from its Mission," *Washington Post*, August 1, 2017, https://www.washingtonpost.com/news/josh-rogin/wp/2017/08/01/state-department-considers-scrubbing-democracy-promotion-from-its-mission/.

62. Kuttin Kandi, Skype interview with the author, November 21, 2018.

63. Will Power, telephone interview with the author, August 12, 2016.

## CHAPTER 5

1. Pape Mamadou Camara, interview with author, Guédiawaye, Senegal, January 17, 2015.

2. The question of whether music is *haram* (prohibited) or *halal* (permitted) under Islam is an ancient one. The case for music's prohibition often appeals to the prophet Muhammad's statement, "There will be among my Ummah [the collective Muslim community] people who will regard as permissible adultery, silk, alcohol, and musical instruments." However, some scholars interpret this to refer to specific musical practices as *haram* and point to other sources that suggest the permissibility of music. The debate also turns on various definitions of music. In particular, unaccompanied singing is often excluded from the definition of music, so that Qur'anic chant is *halal* because it is not considered a form of music. For a scholarly discussion of the matter see Lois Ibsen al Faruqi, "Music, Musicians, and Muslim Law," *Asian Music* 17 (Autumn–Winter 1985): 3–36.

3. Algerian beatmakers, discussion with the author, February 15, 2017, Algiers, Algeria.

4. In her dissertation on Moroccan hip hop, ethnomusicologist (and non-Muslim) Kendra Salois offers this useful caution: "In order to demonstrate my good faith as a researcher—as someone interested in musical practice rather than the fetishized Muslim status of the musickers themselves—I consistently deferred initiating conversations about faith until the third or fourth encounter." Kendra Salois, "The Networked Self: Hip Hop Musicking and Muslim Identities in Neoliberal Morocco," PhD diss., University of California, Berkeley, 2013, 22.

5. A Pew Research Center Study estimated that there were 1.8 billion Muslims in the world as of 2015, representing about 24 percent of the population. See Michael Lipka, "Muslims and Islam: Key Findings in the U.S. and Around the World," Pew Research Center, August 9, 2017, http://www.pewresearch.org/fact-tank/2017/08/09/muslims-and-islam-key-findings-in-the-u-s-and-around-the-world/.

6. *Arts and Minds: Cultural Diplomacy Amid Global Tensions* (New York: National Arts Journalism Program, 2003), 49. Accessible at https://www.americansforthearts.org/sites/default/files/ArtsMinds_0.pdf.

7. Zareena Grewal, "The 'Muslim World' Does Not Exist," *Atlantic*, May 21, 2017, https://www.theatlantic.com/international/archive/2017/05/the-muslim-world-is-a-place-that-does-not-exist/527550/.

8. Cemil Aydin, *The Idea of the Muslim World: A Global Intellectual History* (Cambridge, MA and London: Harvard University Press, 2017), 6.

9. There are, however, over 20 million Christian Arabs and a smaller number of Hindu Arabs. See "Demographics of the Arab League," https://en.wikipedia.org/wiki/Demographics_of_the_Arab_League.

10. "Islam by Country," https://en.wikipedia.org/wiki/Islam_by_country.

11. Cynthia P. Schneider and Kristina Nelson, *Mightier than the Sword: Arts and Culture in the U.S.-Muslim World Relationship.* (Washington, DC: Brookings Institution, 2008), 15, 48.

12. Hillary Clinton, interview with Rita Braver, *CBS Morning News*, July 4, 2010. Accessible at https://archive.org/details/WUSA_20100704_130000_CBS_News_Sunday_Morning#start/960/end/1020. I discuss Clinton's remarks more fully in Chapter 3.

13. Advisory Committee on Cultural Diplomacy, *Cultural Diplomacy: The Linchpin of Public Diplomacy* (Washington, DC: US Department of State, 2005), 3.

14. Ronan Farrow, *War on Peace: The End of Diplomacy and the Decline of American Influence* (New York: W.W. Norton, 2018), xxiii.

15. Advisory Group on Public Diplomacy for the Arab and Muslim World, *Changing Minds, Winning Peace: A New Strategic Direction for U.S. Public Diplomacy in the Arab & Muslim World* (Washington, DC: Advisory Group on Public Diplomacy for the Arab and Muslim World, 2003), 13.

16. *U.S. Public Diplomacy: State Department Expands Efforts but Faces Significant Challenges*, (Washington, DC: United States Government Accounting Office, 2003), 3. Accessible at https://www.gao.gov/new.items/d03951.pdf.

17. Patrick Lee Plaisance, "The Propaganda War on Terrorism: An Analysis of the United States' "Shared Values" Public-Diplomacy Campaign After September 11, 2001," *Journal of Mass Media Ethics* 20 (2005): 250.

18. Plaisance, "The Propaganda War on Terrorism," 250. For a sympathetic view of the initiative, see Jami Fullerton and Alice Kendrick, *Advertising's War on Terrorism: The Story of the U.S. State Department's Shared Values Initiative* (Spokane, Washington: Marquette Books, 2006).

19. *Freedom Promotion Act of 2002*, HR 3969, 107th Cong., 2nd session, Sec. 201, https://www.congress.gov/107/crpt/hrpt493/CRPT-107hrpt493.pdf.

20. *Congressional Record*, May 10, 2002, S4199–4205, https://www.congress.gov/crec/2002/05/10/CREC-2002-05-10-pt1-PgS4199-4.pdf.

21. Mohammed el-Nawawy, "US Public Diplomacy in the Arab World: The News Credibility of Radio Sawa and Television Alhurra in Five Countries," *Global Media and Communication* 2 (August 2006): 183–203.

22. Advisory Committee on Cultural Diplomacy, *Cultural Diplomacy*, 2.

23. See http://www.yesprograms.org/about/about-us.

24. Clare Croft, "Dance Returns to American Cultural Diplomacy: The U.S. State Department's 2003 Dance Residency Program and Its After Effects," *Dance Research Journal* 45 (April 2013): 23–39.

25. A study by two political scientists noted that "in and of itself, a statement that depicted the United States as a place of religious freedom and a good place to be a practicing Muslim had little effect on subsequently expressed attitudes about the United States." Edward Schatz and Renan Levine, "Framing, Public Diplomacy, and Anti-Americanism in Central Asia," *International Studies Quarterly* 54 (2010): 865.

26. "U.S. Public Diplomacy: State Department Expands Efforts but Faces Significant Challenges," 1.

27. "Ozomatli's Music and Message Attract Thousands of Jordanians to Performances throughout the Kingdom," Communication from United States Embassy in Amman to United States Department of State, August 2, 2007. Accessible at https://wikileaks.org/plusd/cables/07AMMAN3260_a.html. The cable, signed "Hale," was probably written by then-Public Affairs Officer David Hale. In 2015 Hale became the United States Ambassador to Pakistan.

28. Charlie Ahearn, "The Five Percent Solution," *Spin* 6 (February 1991): 55.

29. Other artists who have identified as Muslim include Big Daddy Kane, Busta Rhymes, Common, Digable Planets, Erykah Badu, Lupe Fiasco, Ice Cube, J-Live, Jay-Z, Mos Def (later Yasiin Bey), Nas, Q-Tip, Queen Latifah, the World Famous Supreme Team, and Wu-Tang Clan.

30. H. Samy Alim, *Roc the Mic Right: The Language of Hip Hop Culture* (New York: Routledge, 2006), 27.

31. For more on the influence of the Five Percent Nation on hip hop, see Felicia M. Miyakawa, *Five Percenter Rap: God Hop's Music, Message, and Black Muslim Mission* (Bloomington and Indianapolis: Indiana University Press, 2005) and Michael Muhammed Knight, *The Five Percenters: Islam, Hip Hop and the Gods of New York* (Oxford: Oneworld, 2007).

32. "Supreme Mathematics," *thefivepercentnation*, February 1, 2011, https://thefivepercentnation.wordpress.com/2011/02/01/supreme-mathematics/.

33. Brand Nubian, "Allah and Justice," from *In God We Trust*, Elektra compact disc 61381, 1992. For a discussion of the song's invocation of the Science of Supreme Mathematics, Miyakawa, *Five Percenter Rap*, 56–57.

34. Brand Nubian, "Dance to My Ministry," from *One For All*, Elektra compact disc 60946-2, 1990. Emphasis mine.

35. This sentiment describes his record label, Mortier Music. "Mortier" is French for mortar, a word that encompasses both building (as in bricks and mortar) and destruction (as in mortar shells). See https://mortiermusic.com/.

36. J-Live, telephone interview with the author, September 3, 2018. J-Live also pointed out that Allah (Clarence 13X) didn't have a problem working with the government if it allowed him to serve important goals; he was a Korean War veteran and later worked with New York Mayor John Lindsey to quell racial turmoil in Crown Heights. See Barry Gottehrer, *The Mayor's Man* (Garden City, NY: Doubleday, 1975).

37. See Miyakawa, *Five Percenter Rap*, esp. 47–52.

38. Camara, interview with the author.

39. "I was heavily influenced by the beliefs of [NOI leader] Elijah Mohammad and the teachings he gave Malcolm X and Muhammad Ali . . . about dealing with life, nationalities, religion, and self." "Afrika Bambaataa Interviewed (1988): The Shape of Things Hip-Hop and Political to Come?" https://www.elsewhere.co.nz/absoluteelsewhere/3603/afrika-bambaataa-interviewed-1988-the-shape-of-things-hip hop-and-political-to-come/.

40. Nesto, interview with the author, Baku, Azerbaijan, October 23, 2017.

41. El Khayal, interview with the author, Cairo, Egypt, December 16, 2017.

42. Soultana, interview with the author, Meknes, Morocco, September 14, 2017.

43. Ahmed El Hareedy, interview with the author, Alexandria, Egypt, December 13, 2017.

44. Quoted in Joseph Hill, "'Baay is the Spiritual Leader of the Rappers': Performing Islamic Reasoning in Senegalese Sufi Hip-Hop," *Contemporary Islam* 10 (May 2016): 280.

45. Oludamini Ogunnaike, "Performing Realization: The Sufi Music Videos of the Taalibe Baye of Dakar," *African Arts* 51 (Autumn 2018): 26–39.

46. Omar Offendum, interview with the author, Chapel Hill, NC, February 25, 2018.

47. El Khayal, interview with the author.

48. Mohammad Indra Gandhi, aka Dom Dom, interview with the author, Bandung, Indonesia, November 30, 2016.

49. Amirah Sackett, email message to the author, April 21, 2015.

50. Fares "Fforsan" Forsan interview with the author, Brussels, Belgium, July 28, 2017.

51. Supria "Iya" Budiman, email message to the author, January 5, 2018.

52. Out of sensitivity to the artist, I cite this statement without attribution.

53. Algerian beatmakers, discussion with the author.

54. Amine Wakrim, interview with the author, Meknes, Morocco, September 12, 2017.

55. Cordelia Hebblethwaite, "Is Hip Hop Driving the Arab Spring?" *BBC News*, July 24, 2011, https://www.bbc.com/news/world-middle-east-14146243; "Tupac Encouraged the Arab Spring," *Tell Me More*, March 20, 2013, https://www.npr.org/2013/03/20/174839318/tupac-encouraged-the-arab-spring.

56. "The Rap Songs of the Arab Spring," *Morning Edition*, June 9, 2011, https://www.npr.org/sections/therecord/2011/06/09/137067390/the-rap-songs-of-the-arab-spring.

57. Vivienne Walt, "El Général and the Rap Anthem of the Mideast Revolution," *Time*, February 15, 2011, http://content.time.com/time/world/article/0,8599,2049456,00.html.

58. Robin Wright, *Rock the Casbah: Rage and Rebellion Across the Islamic World* (New York: Simon & Schuster, 2011), 115; 116–17.

59. Artists and groups include Chen Lo, DJ Man-O-Wax and Super InLight, FEW Collective, Havikoro, LEL Brothas, Native Deen, Will Power, Remarkable Current, and Rennie Harris Puremovement.

60. Native Deen, http://nativedeen.com/band-members/.

61. Phyllis McIntosh, "Native Deen's Muslim Rap," http://usinfo.state.gov/products/pubs/muslimlife/rap.htm. The site is no longer active but can be accessed through the Internet Archive at https://web.archive.org/web/20021201100737/http://usinfo.state.gov:80/products/pubs/muslimlife/rap.htm.

62. Quoted in Mark Oppenheimer, "A Diplomatic Mission Bearing Islamic Hip-Hop," *New York Times*, July 22, 2011, https://www.nytimes.com/2011/07/23/us/23beliefs.html.

63. "Native Deen in Africa," June 17, 2009, http://deen.tv/native-deen-on-tour/native-deen-in-africa/. At 8:00 in the video.

64. "Native Deen in Ramallah, Palestine Feb 15 2011," https://www.youtube.com/watch?v=iNifanwpuxk; "Native Deen First Ever 'Live' Showcase in Malaysia!" http://nativedeen.com/2011/wp-content/uploads/2012/02/PRESS-RELEASE-ND-SHOWCASE.pdf.

65. "Remarkable Current Musician Collective, http://www.hiphopambassadors.com/hiphopambassadors/home.html. The site is no longer active but can be accessed via the Internet Archive at https://web.archive.org/web/20110208234135/http://www.hiphopambassadors.com/hiphopambassadors/home.html.

66. "Pick up the Pieces—Anas Canon, El Général & Kumasi," Remarkable Current, November 7, 2011, http://remarkablecurrent.blogspot.com/2011/11/pick-up-pieces-by-anas-canon-featuring.html.

67. Remarkable Current, "Pick up the Pieces," https://soundcloud.com/remarkablecurrent/pick-up-the-pieces-anas-canon.

68. Maytha Alhassen, "Remixing Public Diplomacy: American 'Hip Hop Jam Sessions' in Post-Revolution Tunisia," *Huffington Post*, December 17, 2011, https://www.huffingtonpost.com/maytha-alhassen/remarkable-current-tunisia_b_1151966.html.

69. Remarkable Current: tour resumé: http://www.hiphopambassadors.com/hiphopambassadors/tour_resume/tour_resume.html. The site is no longer active but can be accessed via the Internet Archive at https://web.archive.org/web/20120201222614/http://www.hiphopambassadors.com/hiphopambassadors/tour_resume/tour_resume.html.

70. Briana Younger, "Local Trio Native Deen on Making Music for Muslim Youth and Islam's Relationship to Hip-Hop," *Washington City Paper*, March 10, 2015, https://www.washingtoncitypaper.com/arts/music/blog/13081730/local-trio-native-deen-on-making-music-for-muslim-youth-and-islams-relationship-to-hip hop.

71. Bureau of Educational and Cultural Affairs, "Functional Bureau Strategy," July 23, 2018, 9. Accessible at https://www.state.gov/documents/organization/284589.pdf.

72. Anas Canon, quoted in Paul Kuttner, "Interview with a Hip Hop Ambassador," June 14, 2012, http://culturalorganizing.org/tag/anas-canon/.

73. Comments by East Tex and Reeperbahn, in response to Michael Curtis, "Rock, Rap, Hip Hop and All that U.S. Jazz Diplomacy," *American Thinker* 7 (November 2015): https://www.americanthinker.com/articles/2015/11/rock_rap_hip_hop_and_all_that_us_jazz_diplomacy_comments.html#disqus_thread.

74. Hisham Aidi, "Leveraging Hip Hop in US Foreign Policy," *Al Jazeera*, November 7, 2011, https://www.aljazeera.com/indepth/opinion/2011/10/2011103091018299924.html. See also Aidi's "The Grand (Hip-Hop) Chessboard: Race, Rap, and Raison d'Etat," *Middle East Report*, no. 260 (Fall 2011): 25–39 and *Rebel Music: Race, Empire, and the New Muslim Youth Culture* (New York: Pantheon, 2014).

75. Torie Rose DeGhett, "'Record! I Am Arab': Paranoid Arab Boys, Global Ciphers, and Hip Hop Nationalism," in *The Hip Hop and Obama Reader*, ed. Travis L. Gosa and Erik Nielson (New York: Oxford University Press, 2015), 94–106.

76. Su'Ad Abdul Khabeer, *Muslim Cool: Race, Religion, and Hip Hop in the United States* (New York: New York University Press, 2016), 180.

77. Omar El-Khairy, "'Freedom's a Lifestyle Choice: US Cultural Diplomacy, Empire's Soundtrack, and Middle Eastern 'Youth' in our Contemporary Global Infowar," *Middle East Journal of Culture and Communication* 2 (2009): 123.

78. Peter Kovach, "Out from Under the Proscenium: A Paradigm for U.S. Cultural Diplomacy," *Public Diplomacy Magazine* (Winter 2010), https://www.publicdiplomacymagazine.com/out-from-under-the-proscenium-a-paradigm-for-u-s-cultural-diplomacy/.

79. Quoted in DeGhett, "'Record! I Am Arab,'" 99. The song's lyrics can be found at the site "Revolutionary Arab Rap: The Index," http://revolutionaryarabraptheindex.blogspot.com/2011/08/el-general-and-mr-shooma-tahya-tunis.html.

80. Executive Order 13769, "Protecting the Nation from Foreign Terrorist Entry into the United States," January 27, 2017, https://www.whitehouse.gov/the-press-office/2017/01/27/executive-order-protecting-nation-foreign-terrorist-entry-united-states. For an assessment of the Executive Order as a "Muslim Ban," see Garrett Epps, "Is President Trump's Immigration Order a 'Muslim Ban'?" *Atlantic* January 30, 2017, https://www.theatlantic.com/politics/archive/2017/01/is-president-trumps-immigration-order-a-muslim-ban/514989/.

81. Rami Mhazres, interview with the author, Tunis, Tunisia, February 12, 2017.

82. Haleem "Stringz" Rasul, email message to the author, September 27, 2018.

83. One Be Lo (Nahshid Sulaiman), email message to the author, October 24, 2018.

84. Tara "Big Tara" Crichlow, email message to the author, March 4, 2019.

85. Nick Low-Beer, aka Nick Neutronz, email message to the author February 28, 2019.

86. Konshens the MC, email message to the author, November 14, 2017.

87. Crichlow, email message to the author.

88. ADUM⁷, email message to the author, March 28, 2019.

## CONCLUSION

1. Allen J. Ellender, quoted in Penny M. Von Eschen, *Satchmo Blows up the World: Jazz Ambassadors Play the Cold War* (Cambridge MA and London: Harvard University Press, 2004), 40.

2. Michael Curtis, "Rock, Rap, Hip Hop and All that U.S. Jazz Diplomacy," *American Thinker* 7 (November 2015): http://www.americanthinker.com/articles/2015/11/rock_rap_hip_hop_and_all_that_us_jazz_diplomacy.html.

3. Commenter steveintampa, in response to Curtis, "Rock, Rap, Hip Hop and All that U.S. Jazz Diplomacy," https://www.americanthinker.com/articles/2015/11/rock_rap_hip_hop_and_all_that_us_jazz_diplomacy_comments.html#disqus_thread.

4. Frank Ninkovich, in *Arts and Minds: Cultural Diplomacy Amid Global Tensions* (New York: National Arts Journalism Program, 2003), 27–28. Accessible at https://www.americansforthearts.org/sites/default/files/ArtsMinds_0.pdf.

5. Original in Portuguese. Samuel Henrique da Silviera Lima (aka B-boy Samuka), interview with the author, Ceilândia, Brazil, March 15, 2017. See "Samuel's Next Level Story," April 3, 2017, https://www.youtube.com/watch?v=QU-UccGLs9U.

6. B-girl Key (Kifuko Moureen Drichiru), interview with the author, Kampala, Uganda, June 27, 2015.

7. Soultana, interview with the author, Meknes, Morocco, September 14, 2017.

8. Soultana, interview with the author.

9. Stimpy (Edson David Rochac Ventura), Skype interview with the author, January 14, 2016. Original in Spanish; translated by Amanda Black.

10. Linda Alcoff, "The Problem of Speaking for Others," *Cultural Critique*, no. 20 (Winter 1991–92): 7, 23. My thanks to Will Cheng for pointing me to this article.

11. Blaze Uno (Luis Balthalzar Rodríguez Del Rio), interview with the author, San Salvador, El Salvador, December 5, 2015.

12. Facebook post by Fau Sto, July 2, 2018, https://www.facebook.com/photo.php?fbid=1752491491508049.

13. Calvin Hayes, interview with the author, Dhaka, Bangladesh, November 16, 2014. Used with permission.

14. A year later, he wrote in a Facebook post, "November is the month of the memories of NEXT LEVEL. And best days of Bangladesh Hip Hop Scenario. I wish I could [go] back to that time. Golden time of my life till now."

15. Black Zang, Skype interview with the author, July 24, 2016.

16. This figure was current in 2014, the most recent data available for Bangladesh as of 2018. Pew Research Center, Global Indicators Database, http://www.pewglobal.org/database/indicator/1/survey/all/.

17. K.S. Venkatachalam, "The Rise of Islamic Extremism in Bangladesh," *The Diplomat*, July 6, 2016, https://thediplomat.com/2016/07/the-rise-of-islamic-extremism-in-bangladesh/.

18. Michael Jakub, interview with the author, Carrboro, NC, January 18, 2017.

19. In addition to the $1.4 million cost per missile, it costs about $95,000 an hour to operate the bombers that carry and launch the missiles. Amanda Macias, "US Taxpayers Paid Millions of Dollars for the Airstrikes on Syria. Here's a Breakdown of Key Costs," *CNBC*, April 16, 2018, https://www.cnbc.com/2018/04/16/syria-airstrikes-cost-to-us-taxpayers.html.

20. James Mattis, testimony before the Senate's Committee on Armed Services, March 5, 2013, https://www.armed-services.senate.gov/imo/ media/doc/13-07%20-%203-5-13.pdf.

21. Geoffrey Cowan and Amelia Arsenault, "Moving from Monologue to Dialogue to Collaboration: The Three Layers of Public Diplomacy," *Annals of the American Academy of Political and Social Science* 616 (March 2008): 11, 12.

22. "The Trump Administration is Making War on Diplomacy," *New York Times*, November 18, 2017, https://www.nytimes.com/2017/11/18/opinion/sunday/the-trump-administration-is-making-war-on-diplomacy.html.

23. Nahal Toosi and Josh Dawsey, "Trump's Team Weighs Retooling State to Focus on Terror," *Politico*, January 18, 2017, http://www.politico.com/story/2017/01/trump-terror-state-department-233733.

24. Marie Royce, "Statement of Marie Royce Nominee to be Assistant Secretary of State, Educational and Cultural Affairs Senate Committee on Foreign Relations March 7, 2018," https://www.foreign.senate.gov/imo/media/doc/030718_Royce_Testimony.pdf.

25. "Next Level Team Morocco Street Session," https://www.youtube.com/watch?v=2aMLW9l80Ok. The film, created by Saleem Reshamwala, was recorded in Morocco in September 2017.

# BIBLIOGRAPHY

## INTERVIEWS AND PERSONAL COMMUNICATIONS

DJ 2-Tone Jones (Lester Wallace). Interview with the author, Kolkata, India, June 4, 2014.

Abdullah, Mohammed (ABD). Interview with the author, Dhaka, Bangladesh, November 14, 2014.

ADUM⁷. Email message to the author, March 28, 2019.

Akim Funk Buddha (Akim Ndlovu). Interview with the author, Baku, Azerbaijan, October 22, 2017.

Algerian beatmakers. Discussion with the author, Algiers, Algeria, February 15, 2017.

Allen, Harry. Telephone interview with the author, April 13, 2018.

DJ A-Minor (Andre Barden). Interview with the author, Dhaka, Bangladesh, November 15, 2014.

Analogue, Suzi (Maya Shipman). Interview with the author, Entebbe, Uganda, June 29, 2015.

Asheru (Gabriel Benn). Interview with the author, Dhaka, Bangladesh, November 14, 2014.

Azizov, Aziz. Interview with the author, Baku, Azerbaijan, October 21, 2017.

Bayangos, Marc (Mista B.). Interview with the author, Sarajevo, Bosnia, September 14, 2014.

Bjelopetrovic, Marija. Interview with the author, Belgrade, Serbia, July 26, 2014.

Black Zang (Asiful Islam Sohan). Skype interview with the author, July 24, 2016.

Blackman, Toni. Telephone interview with the author, March 18, 2015.

Blackman, Toni. Skype interview with the author, July 18, 2016.

Blaze Uno (Luis Balthalzar Rodríguez Del Rio). Interview with the author, San Salvador, El Salvador, December 5, 2015.

DJ B*Money (Christopher Behm-Meyer). Interview with the author, Belgrade, Serbia, July 28, 2014.

Brickhouse, Junious. Interview with the author, Dakar, Senegal, January 16, 2015.

Brickhouse, Junious. Email message to the author, December 24, 2018.

Budiman, Supria (Iya). Interview with the author, Bandung, Indonesia, December 1, 2016.

Budiman, Supria (Iya). Email message to the author, January 4, 2018.

Budiman, Supria (Iya). Email message to the author, January 5, 2018.

Burchell, Charles. Interview with the author, San Salvador, El Salvador, December 7, 2015.

Bwette, Daniel Gilbert. Interview with the author, Kampala, Uganda, June 27, 2015.

Camara, Pape Mamadou. Interview with author, Guédiawaye, Senegal, January 17, 2015.

Caprice, Jaci and Kane Smego. Interview with the author, Harare, Zimbabwe, February 28, 2015.

DJ Chela (Lauren Harkrader). Telephone interview with the author, January 22, 2015.

CHINO BYI (David Villorente). Interview with the author, Brooklyn, NY, December 18, 2018.

Clemente, Deena. Interview with the author, Sarajevo, Bosnia, September 15, 2014.

Crichlow, Tara. Email message to the author, March 4, 2019.

Cue Bass (Carlos Alfredo Godínez Garcia). Interview with the author, Carrboro, NC, April 6, 2016.

Def-i (Christopher Mike-Bidtah). Interview with the author, Washington, DC, June 5, 2018.

Diamond D. Email message to the author, May 2, 2014.

Diamond D. Interview with the author, Belgrade, Serbia, July 28, 2014.

D.S.Sense (Deidre Smith). Interview with the author, Cartagena, Colombia, August 19, 2016.

Dumi Right (Dumisani Ndlovu), Skype interview with the author, December 2, 2016.

El Fakir, M'allem Abdenbi. Email message to the author, January 28, 2018.

El Hareedy, Ahmed. Interview with the author, Alexandria, Egypt, December 13, 2017.

El Khayal (Mohab). Interview with the author, Cairo, Egypt, December 16, 2017.

Ferguson, John. Skype interview with the author, September 23, 2016.

Forsan, Fares (Fforsan). Interview with the author, Brussels, Belgium, July 28, 2017.

Freelon, Pierce. Email message to the author, April 15, 2013.

Gandhi, Mohammad Indra (Dom Dom). Interview with the author, Bandung, Indonesia, November 30, 2016.

Gann, Elliot. Interview with the author, Dakar, Senegal, January 14, 2015.

Garcia, Javier and Rocc Williams. Skype interview with the author, August 11, 2016.

Gomez, Juan. Interview with the author, Harare, Zimbabwe, February 28, 2015.

Hađina, Iva. Interview with the author, Zagreb, Croatia, May 11, 2017.

Hayes, Calvin. Interview with the author, Dhaka, Bangladesh, November 16, 2014.

Ison, Sunshine. Interview with the author, Nikšić, Montenegro, September 11, 2014.

Israel, Baba. Interview with the author, Zagreb, Croatia, May 11, 2017.

Jakub, Michael. Interview with the author, Carrboro, NC January 18, 2017.

J-Live (Justice Cadet). Interview with the author, Zagreb, Croatia, May 11, 2017.

J-Live (Justice Cadet). Telephone interview with the author, September 3, 2018.

Jones, Ansley "Jukeboxx." Telephone interview with the author, June 17, 2014.

Jones, Mahogany (Charyse Bailey). Interview with the author, Sarajevo, Bosnia, September 14, 2014.

Jones, Mahogany (Charyse Bailey). Interview with the author, Tashkent, Uzbekistan, June 1, 2018.

Kaweesi, Mark. Interview with the author, Chapel Hill, NC, August 9, 2016.

Kaweesi, Mark. Interview with the author, Amsterdam, the Netherlands, July 26, 2017.

Kely, Tsiry (Panda). Interview with the author, Antananarivo, Madagascar, July 30, 2018.

B-girl Key (Kifuko Moureen Drichiru). Interview with the author, Kampala, Uganda, June 27, 2015.

Kiche Legend (Amani Msangi). Interview with the author, Carrboro, NC, April 6, 2016.

Klevah (Shasta Knox) and Zephyr Ann Doles. Interview with the author, Meknes, Morocco, September 13, 2017.

MC Ko-co. Interview with the author, Tegucigalpa, Honduras, January 22, 2016.

Koesmayadi, Ginandjar. Interview with the author, Bandung, Indonesia, November 30, 2016.

Konshens the MC (Tarik Davis). Email to the author, November 14, 2017.

Konshens the MC (Tarik Davis). Telephone interview with the author, December 10, 2017.

Kuttin Kandi. Skype interview with the author, November 21, 2018.

Ljulj, Mirta. Interview with the author, Zagreb, Croatia, May 11, 2017.

Madlines (Maddy Clifford). Interview with the author, Kampala, Uganda, June 28, 2015.

Mariposa (Lilibeth Rodriguez Diaz). Cartagena, Colombia, August 19, 2016.

Maxi Krezy (Amadou Aw). Conversation with the author, Dakar, Senegal, October 13, 2014.

Maximilian, Nbaggala Lillian. Interview with the author, Kampala, Uganda, June 27, 2015.

Medusa the Gangsta Goddess (Mone Smith). Interview with the author, San Salvador, El Salvador, December 7, 2015.

Mhazres, Rami (DJ Supaflava). Interview with the author, Tunis, Tunisia, February 12, 2017.

Mhako, Plot. Interview with author, Harare, Zimbabwe, March 1, 2015.

Milic, Marko. Interview with the author, Belgrade, Serbia, July 28, 2015.

Montesinos, Ainara Calix. Interview with the author, Carrboro, NC, April 6, 2016.

Moore, Rebekah. Skype interview with the author, February 23, 2018.

Murray, Rod. Skype interview with the author, October 31, 2017.

Mystique (Citra Resmi). Interview with the author, Bandung, Indonesia, November 30, 2016.

Nash MC. Interview with the author, Dar es Salaam, August 5, 2017.

Ndaliko Katandolo, Petna. Conversation with the author, Tunis, Tunisia, February 11, 2017.

Ngulu, Chedi. Interview with the author, Dar es Salaam, Tanzania, August 5, 2015.

Nesto. Interview with the author, Baku, Azerbaijan, October 23, 2017.

Nick Low-Beer (Nick Neutronz). Email message to the author February 28, 2019.

Nyirabu, Masero. Interview with the author, Dar es Salaam, Tanzania, August 5, 2015.

Offendum, Omar. Interview with the author, Chapel Hill, NC, February 25, 2018.

One Be Lo (Nahshid Sulaiman). Email message to the author, October 24, 2018.

Pabon, Jorge (Popmaster Fabel). Conversation with the author, Chapel Hill, NC, February 3, 2009.

Pabon, Jorge (Popmaster Fabel). Email message to the author, May 1, 2014.

Paic, Nikolina. Interview with the author, Zagreb, Croatia, May 11, 2017.

Pavlovic, Andjelko (Angelo Spaghetti). Conversation with the author, Belgrade, Serbia, April 18, 2014.

Pena, Jeremy. Interview with the author, Tegucigalpa, Honduras, January 23, 2016.

Peregrin, Michele. Telephone interview with the author, February 28, 2018.

Perez, Frankie (B-Boy Frankie). Telephone interview with the author, September 13, 2016.

Pinqy Ring (Marisol Vélez). Interview with the author, Durham, NC, May 19, 2018.

Pinqy Ring (Marisol Vélez). Email message to the author, June 11, 2018.

Power, Will. Telephone interview with the author, August 12, 2016.

Rabbi Darkside (Sam Sellers). Interview with the author, Entebbe, Uganda, June 29, 2015.

Rahman, Sabreen. Interview with the author, Dhaka, Bangladesh, November 13, 2014.

Rasul, Haleem (Stringz). Interview with the author, Bandung, Indonesia, December 1, 2016.

Rasul, Haleem (Stringz). Email message to the author, September 27, 2018.

Ritika. Interview with the author, Kolkata, India, June 4, 2014.

Rockower, Paul. Interview with the author, Kigali, Rwanda, June 30, 2016.

Rockower, Paul. Email message to the author, August 3, 2016.

Rodriguez, Daniel. Interview with the author, San Salvador, El Salvador, December 7, 2015.

Romano, Arthur. Interview with the author, Carrboro, NC, August 27, 2018.

Romualdo Belo Guse, Rafaela. Email message to the author, June 19, 2017.

Sackett, Amirah. Email message to the author, May 2, 2014.

Sackett, Amirah. Email message to the author, April 21, 2015.

Samb, Aminata. Interview with the author, Dakar, Senegal, January 16, 2015.

B-boy Samuka (Samuel Henrique da Silviera Lima). Interview with the author, Ceilândia, Brazil, March 15, 2017.

Soultana. Interview with the author, Meknes, Morocco, September 14, 2017.

Spyda (Aineomugisha Alimansi Wanzu). Interview with the author, Kampala, Uganda, June 27, 2015.

Sticklor, Russell (DJ Plain View). Interview with the author, Sarajevo, Bosnia, September 14, 2014.

Stimpy (Edson David Rochac Ventura). Skype interview with the author, January 14, 2016.

T.R.U.T.H (Tierney Reed). Interview with the author, Azerbaijan, Baku, October 23, 2017.

Upmost (Ngoni Tapiwa). Interview with the author, Harare, Zimbabwe, February 28, 2015.

Wakrim, Amine. Interview with the author, Meknes, Morocco, September 12, 2017.

Wanda. Interview with the author, Bandung, Indonesia, November 30, 2016.

Ya Ya (Cherry Khaing). Interview with the author, Yangon, Myanmar, February 6, 2018.

Zarazua, Daniel. Interview with the author, San Salvador, El Salvador, December 7, 2015.

Zenasi, Adrian (Professor). Interview with the author, Harare Zimbabwe, February 28, 2015.

## BOOKS, ARTICLES, AND FILMS

Adichie, Chimamanda Ngozi. "The American Embassy," in *The Thing Around Your Neck*, 128–41. New York: Anchor, 2009.

Advisory Committee on Cultural Diplomacy. *Cultural Diplomacy: The Linchpin of Public Diplomacy*. Washington, DC: US Department of State, 2005.

Advisory Group on Public Diplomacy for the Arab and Muslim World. *Changing Minds, Winning Peace: A New Strategic Direction for U.S. Public Diplomacy in the Arab & Muslim World*. Washington, DC: Advisory Group on Public Diplomacy for the Arab and Muslim World, 2003.

"Afrika Bambaataa Interviewed (1988): The Shape of Things Hip-Hop and Political to Come?" https://www.elsewhere.co.nz/absoluteelsewhere/3603/afrika-bambaataa-interviewed-1988-the-shape-of-things-hip hop-and-political-to-come/.

Ahearn, Charlie. "The Five Percent Solution." *Spin* 6 (February 1991): 55–57, 76.

Aidi, Hisham. "The Grand (Hip-Hop) Chessboard: Race, Rap, and Raison d'Etat." *Middle East Report*, no. 260 (Fall 2011): 25–39.

Aidi, Hisham. "Leveraging Hip Hop in US Foreign Policy." *Al Jazeera*, November 7, 2011, https://www.aljazeera.com/indepth/opinion/2011/10/2011103091018299924.html.

Aidi, Hisham. *Rebel Music: Race, Empire, and the New Muslim Youth Culture*. New York: Pantheon, 2014.

Alhassen, Maytha. "Remixing Public Diplomacy: American 'Hip Hop Jam Sessions' in Post-Revolution Tunisia." *Huffington Post*, December 17, 2011, https://www.huffingtonpost.com/maytha-alhassen/remarkable-current-tunisia_b_1151966.html.

Alicia. "Interview: Ozomatli Sits Down with Killahbeez." *killahbeez*, April 20, 2009, http://www.killahbeez.com/2009/04/20/interview-ozomatli-sits-down-with-killahbeez/.

Alim, H. Samy. *Roc the Mic Right: The Language of Hip Hop Culture*. New York: Routledge, 2006.

Allbritton, Chris. "U.S. Tries 'Hip Hop' Diplomacy in Pakistan." Reuters, November 14, 2011, http://www.reuters.com/article/us-pakistan-usa-music-idUSTRE7AD1XV20111114.

Alcoff, Linda. "The Problem of Speaking for Others," *Cultural Critique*, no. 20 (Winter 1991–92): 5–32.

Allen, Harry. "Islamic Summit." *The Source*, no. 19 (March–April 1991).

Almeida, Christina Moreno. *Rap Beyond Resistance: Staging Power in Contemporary Morocco.* Cham, Switzerland: Palgrave Macmillan, 2017.

AMS Planning and Research. *Evaluation of the Jazz Ambassadors Program.* Fairfield, CT: AMS, 2006. Accessible at https://eca.state.gov/files/bureau/jazz-amb-program-vol.-i-final-report-march-2006.pdf.

Antonio, Winstone. "Jibilika Eyes Rural Communities." *NewsDay,* October 19, 2017, https://www.newsday.co.zw/2017/10/jibilika-eyes-rural-communities.

Ansari, Emily Abrams. "Shaping the Policies of Cold War Musical Diplomacy: An Epistemic Community of American Composers." *Diplomatic History* 36 (January 2012): 41–52.

Appert, Catherine M. "Modernity Remixed: Music as Memory in Rap Galsen." PhD diss., University of California Los Angeles, 2012.

Appert, Catherine M. "Locating Hip Hop Origins: Popular Music and Tradition in Senegal." *Africa* 86 (May 2016): 237–62.

Arndt, Richard T. *The First Resort of Kings: American Cultural Diplomacy in the Twentieth Century.* Washington, DC: Potomac Book, 2005.

*Arts and Minds: Cultural Diplomacy Amid Global Tensions.* Proceedings of a conference presented by the National Arts Journalism Program, Arts International, and the Center for Arts & Culture, April 14–15, 2003. New York: National Arts Journalism Program, 2003.

Aydin, Cemil. *The Idea of the Muslim World: A Global Intellectual History.* Cambridge, MA and London: Harvard University Press, 2017.

Balandina, Alexandria. "Rap Music as a Cultural Mediator in Postconflict Yugoslavia," in Milosz Miszczynski and Adriana Helbig, eds. *Hip Hop at Europe's Edge: Music, Agency, and Social Change,* 63–81. Bloomington and Indianapolis: Indiana University Press, 2017.

Ballhaus, Rebecca. "Trump Defends West Wing Turnover: 'I Like Conflict.'" *Wall Street Journal,* March 8, 2018, https://www.wsj.com/articles/trump-defends-west-wing-turnover-i-like-conflict-1520375738.

Banks, Daniel. "The Question of Cultural Diplomacy: Acting Ethically." *Theatre Topics* 21 (September 2011): 109–23.

Banks, Daniel. "How Hiplife Theatre Was Born in Ghana." *American Theatre* (November 2008): 30–31, 90–91.

Barned-Smith, St. John. "Variety of Factors Cited in Rise in Houston Murders in 2015." *Houston Chronicle,* December 31, 2015, http://www.chron.com/news/houston-texas/houston/article/Variety-of-factors-cited-in-rise-in-Houston-6730937.php.

Barnes, William. "Can Hip-Hop Stop the Jihadis?" *Yemen Times,* August 19, 2014, http://www.yementimes.com/en/1808/opinion/4219/Can-hip      hop-stop-the-Jihadis.htm.

Bureau of Educational and Cultural Affairs, "Functional Bureau Strategy," July 23, 2018. Accessible at https://www.state.gov/documents/organization/284589.pdf.

Belair, Felix. "United States has Secret Sonic Weapon—Jazz." *New York Times,* November 6, 1955, 1, 42.

Bhabha, Homi K. *The Location of Culture.* London and New York: Routledge, 1994.

Boellstorff, Tom. "The Emergence of Political Homophobia in Indonesia: Masculinity and National Belonging." *Ethnos: Journal of Anthropology* 69 (December 2004): 465–86.

Bonner, Raymond. "Time for a US Apology to El Salvador." *The Nation*, April 15, 2016, https://www.thenation.com/article/time-for-a-us-apology-to-el-salvador/.

Brace, Eric. "The Circuit." *Washington Post*, October 16, 1998, p. 7.

Brinner, Benjamin. *Knowing Music, Making Music: Javanese Gamelan and the Theory of Musical Competence and Interaction.* Chicago and London: University of Chicago Press, 1995.

Bump, Philip. "The Symbiotic Trump-Kanye West Relationship." *Washington Post*, October 1, 2018, https://www.washingtonpost.com/politics/2018/10/01/symbiotic-trump-kanye-west-relationship/.

Butler, Desmond, Michael Weissenstein, Laura Wides-Muñoz, and Andrea Rodriguez. "USAID Op Undermines Cuba's Hip-Hop Protest Scene." *Associated Press*, December 12, 2014, http://bigstory.ap.org/article/7c275c134f1b4a0ca3428929fcece82d/us-co-opted-cubas-hiphop-scene-spark-change.

"Can Cultural Diplomacy Improve America's Standing in the Islamic World?" In *Arts and Minds: Cultural Diplomacy Amid Global Tensions*. Proceedings of a conference presented by the National Arts Journalism Program, Arts International, and the Center for Arts & Culture, April 14–15, 2003. New York: National Arts Journalism Program, 2003.

Cathart, Adam. "Nixon, Kissinger and Musical Diplomacy in the Opening of China, 1971–1973." *Yonsei Journal of International Studies* 4 (2012): 131–39.

Center for Arts and Culture. *Cultural Diplomacy: Recommendations and Research.* N.p.: Center for Arts and Culture, 2004.

Chang, Jeff. *Can't Stop, Won't Stop: A History of the Hip-Hop Generation.* New York: Picador, 2005.

Chang, Jeff. "It's a Hip-Hop World." *Foreign Policy*, no. 163 (November–December 2007): 58–65.

Channick, Joan. "The Artist as Cultural Diplomat." *American Theatre* 22 (May–June 2005): 4.

Charnas, Dan. *The Big Payback: The History of the Business of Hip-Hop.* New York: New American Library, 2010.

Chumley, Cheryl K. "Taxpayers Pick Up Asian Hip-Hop Tour Promoted by U.S. State Department." *Washington Times*, February 13, 2013, http://m.washingtontimes.com/news/2013/feb/13/state-department-announces-asian-hiphop-tour-taxp/.

Cisse, Fatou. "Senegal," in *Remittance Markets in Africa*, ed. Sanket Mohapatra and Dilip Ratha, 221–41, Washington, DC: World Bank, 2011. Accessible at http://documents.worldbank.org/curated/en/248331468193493657/pdf/613100PUB0mark158344B09780821384756.pdf.

Clark, Msia Kibona. "Hip Hop as Social Commentary in Accra and Dar es Salaam." *Africa Studies Quarterly* 13 (Summer 2012): 23–46.

Clark, Msia Kibona. *Hip-Hop in Africa: Prophets of the City and Dustyfoot Philosophers.* Athens, OH: Ohio University Press, 2018.

Council on Foreign Relations. *Public Diplomacy: A Strategy for Reform.* New York: Council on Foreign Relations, 2002.

Cowan, Geoffrey and Amelia Arsenault, "Moving from Monologue to Dialogue to Collaboration: The Three Layers of Public Diplomacy." *Annals of the American Academy of Political and Social Science* 616 (March 2008): 10–30.

Crescenzi, Mark J.C. *Of Friends and Foes: Reputation and Learning in International Politics.* New York: Oxford University Press, 2018.

Crist, Stephen A. "Jazz as Democracy? Dave Brubeck and Cold War Politics." *Journal of Musicology* 26 (Spring 2009): 133–74.

Croft, Clare. "Dance Returns to American Cultural Diplomacy: The U.S. State Department's 2003 Dance Residency Program and Its After Effects." *Dance Research Journal* 45 (April 2013): 23–39.

Croft, Clare, ed. *Queer Dance: Meanings & Makings.* New York: Oxford University Press, 2017.

Curtis, Michael. "Rock, Rap, Hip Hop and All that U.S. Jazz Diplomacy." *American Thinker* 7 (November 2015), http://www.americanthinker.com/articles/2015/11/rock_rap_hip_hop_and_all_that_us_jazz_diplomacy.html.

DeGhett, Torie Rose. "'Record! I Am Arab': Paranoid Arab Boys, Global Ciphers, and Hip Hop Nationalism," in *The Hip Hop and Obama Reader*, ed. Travis L. Gosa and Erik Nielson, 94–106. New York: Oxford University Press, 2015.

"Dizzy Gillespie and Kenyan Tenth Anniversary: Summary Report." Communication from United States Embassy in Nairobi to United States Department of State, 18 December 1973. Accessible at https://wikileaks.org/plusd/cables/1973NAIROB08567b.html.

Drury, Meghan. "Counterorienting the War on Terror: Arab Hip Hop and Diasporic Resistance." *Journal of Popular Music Studies* 29 (June 2017): n.p.

Dwyer, Alex. "Samsonite Man: A Look at Hip Hop's Diplomatic Affairs." *HipHopDX*, 27 January 2012, http://hiphopdx.com/editorials/id.1845/title.samsonite-man-a-look-at-hip hops-diplomatic-affairs.

El-Khairy, Omar. "'Freedom's a Lifestyle Choice: US Cultural Diplomacy, Empire's Soundtrack, and Middle Eastern 'Youth' in our Contemporary Global Infowar." *Middle East Journal of Culture and Communication* 2 (2009): 115–35.

el-Nawawy, Mohammed. "US Public Diplomacy in the Arab World: The News Credibility of Radio Sawa and Television Alhurra in Five Countries," *Global Media and Communication* 2 (August 2006): 183–203.

El Zein, Rayya. *"Performing el Rap el 'Arabi 2005–2015: Feeling Politics amid Neoliberal Incursions in Ramallah, Amman, and Beirut."* PhD diss, City University of New York, 2016.

Epps, Garrett. "Is President Trump's Immigration Order a 'Muslim Ban'?" *Atlantic*, January 30, 2017, https://www.theatlantic.com/politics/archive/2017/01/is-president-trumps-immigration-order-a-muslim-ban/514989/.

Farrow, Ronan. *War on Peace: The End of Diplomacy and the Decline of American Influence.* New York: W.W. Norton, 2018.

Fauser, Annegret. *Sounds of War: Music in the United States During World War II.* New York: Oxford University Press, 2013.

Fischlin, Daniel, Ajay Heble, and George Lipsitz. *The Fierce Urgency of Now: Improvisation, Rights, and the Ethics of Cocreation*. Durham, NC and London: Duke University Press, 2013.

Flake, Jeff. "Flake Announces Senate Future," October 24, 2017, https://www.flake.senate.gov/public/index.cfm/press-releases?ID=5BA26227-82BA-406A-B5F3-3683A7619086.

Fosler-Lussier, Danielle. "Music Pushed, Music Pulled: Cultural Diplomacy, Globalization, and Imperialism." *Diplomatic History* 36 (January 2012): 53–64.

Fosler-Lussier, Danielle. *Music in America's Cold War Diplomacy*. Berkeley: University of California Press, 2015.

Franzius, Andrea Georgina Marina. "Soul Call: Music, Race and the Creation of American Cultural Policy." PhD diss., Duke University, 2006.

Fredericks, Rosalind. "'The Old Man is Dead': Hip Hop and the Arts of Citizenship of Senegalese Youth." *Antipode* 46 (2013): 130–48.

Friedman, Max Paul. "Specter of a Nazi Threat: United States–Colombia Relations, 1939–1945." *The Americas* 56 (April 2000): 563–89.

Fullerton, Jami and Alice Kendrick, *Advertising's War on Terrorism: The Story of the U.S. State Department's Shared Values Initiative*. Spokane, Washington: Marquette Books, 2006.

Gillespie, Dizzy and Al Fraser. *To Be, Or Not—To Bop*. New York: Doubleday, 1979; Minneapolis, University of Minnesota Press, 2009.

Gosa, Travis L. and Erick Nielson, eds. *The Hip Hop & Obama Reader*. New York: Oxford University Press, 2015.

Gottehrer, Barry. *The Mayor's Man*. Garden City, NY: Doubleday, 1975.

Grewal, Zareena. "The 'Muslim World' Does Not Exist." *Atlantic*, May 21, 2017, https://www.theatlantic.com/international/archive/2017/05/the-muslim-world-is-a-place-that-does-not-exist/527550/.

Grosfoguel, Ramón. "The Divorce of Nationalist Discourses from the Puerto Rican People: A Sociohistorical Perspective," in *Puerto Rican Jam: Rethinking Colonialism and Nationalism*, ed. Frances Negrón-Mutaner and Ramón Grosfoguel, 57–76. Minneapolis and London: University of Minnesota Press, 1997.

Grosfoguel, Ramón. "Hybridity and Mestizaje: Sincretism or Subversive Complicity? Subalternity from the Perspective of the Coloniality of Power," in *The Masters and the Slaves: Plantation Relations and Mestizaje in American Imaginaries*, ed. Alexandra Isfahani-Hammond, 115–29. New York: Palgrave Macmillan, 2005.

Halper, Daniel. "State Dept. Announces 'Hip Hop Group Audiopharmacy to Tour.'" *Weekly Standard*, February 13, 2013, http://www.weeklystandard.com/state-dept.-announces-hip hop-group-audiopharmacy-to-tour/article/701181.

Hanna, Judith Lynne. *To Dance is Human: A Theory of Nonverbal Communication*. Austin and London: University of Texas Press, 1979.

Hansen, Suzy. *Notes on a Foreign Country: An American Abroad in a Post-American World*. New York: Farrar, Straus and Giroux, 2017.

Haupt, Adam. *Stealing Empire: P2P, Intellectual Property, and Hip-Hop Subversion*. Cape Town: HSRC Press, 2008.

Hebblethwaite, Cordelia. "Is Hip Hop Driving the Arab Spring?" *BBC News*, July 24, 2011, http://www.bbc.com/news/world-middle-east-14146243.

Hess, Carol A. "Copland in Argentina: Pan Americanist Politics, Folklore, and the Crisis in Modern Music." *Journal of the American Musicological Society* 66 (Spring 2013): 191–250.

Hill, Joseph. "'Baay is the Spiritual Leader of the Rappers': Performing Islamic Reasoning in Senegalese Sufi Hip-Hop," *Contemporary Islam* 10 (May 2016): 267–87.

Hill, Joseph. "A Mystical Cosmopolitanism: Sufi Hip Hop and the Aesthetics of Islam in Dakar." *Culture and Religion* 18 (2017): 388–408.

"Hip Hop and the Arab Uprisings." Unpublished document from the Middle East Studies Center, Portland State University. Accessible at http://www.middleeastpdx.org/resources/wp-content/uploads/2013/07/Hip-Hop-and-the-Arab-Uprisings.pdf.

"Hip-Hop Takes on Diplomatic Role with State Department." *NPR*, January 24, 2007, http://www.npr.org/templates/transcript/transcript.php?storyId=6997064.

Hoodock, Jeff. "Toni Blackman at Dance Place." *Washington Post*, February 15, 1999.

Hooton, Christopher. "Hip hop is the Most Listened to Genre in the World, According to Spotify Analysis of 20 Billion Tracks." *Independent*, July 14, 2015, http://www.independent.co.uk/arts-entertainment/music/news/hip hop-is-the-most-listened-to-genre-in-the-world-according-to-spotify-analysis-of-20-billion-10388091.html.

Hopkinson, Natalie. "In Defense of Hip-Hop Diplomacy." *The Root*, January 27, 2012, http://www.theroot.com/in-defense-of-hip hop-diplomacy-1790889642.

Hoyos, Deison Luis Dimas. "Panorama de las amenazas con panfletos en el Caribe Colombiano." *CEPSCA*, May 6, 2016, http://cepsca.org/index.php/8-inicio/244-informe-panorama-de-las-amenazas-con-panfletos-en-el-caribe-colombiano.

Hughes, Karen. "'Waging Peace': A New Paradigm for Public Diplomacy." *Mediterranean Quarterly* 18 (Spring 2007): 18–36.

Huseynzade, E. "Baku Jazz Festival кошмарно провалился [has Failed Badly]." *News Day*, April 11, 2004, http://news.day.az/showbiz/6367.html.

Inskeep, Steve. "Venezuelan Hip-Hop Takes on Police Corruption." *Morning Edition*, December 11, 2013, https://www.npr.org/2013/12/11/195566691/venezuelan-hip hop-takes-on-police-corruption.

Israel, Baba. *Remixing the Ritual: Hip Hop Theatre, Aesthetic, and Practice*. N.p.: Baba Israel, 2008.

"Ivanka Trump interview: 'If being complicit is wanting to be a force for good . . . then I'm complicit.'" *CBS News*, April 4, 2017, https://www.cbsnews.com/news/ivanka-trump-interview-what-it-means-to-be-complicit/.

Jeffries, Michael P. "Is Obama Really the Hip-Hop President?" *Atlantic*, January 26, 2011, https://www.theatlantic.com/entertainment/archive/2011/01/is-obama-really-the-hip hop-president/70061/.

Johnson, Brett and Malik Russell. "Time to Build." *Source*, no. 158 (November 2002): 118–22.

Johnson, David K. *The Lavender Scare: The Cold War Persecution of Gays and Lesbians in the Federal Government*. Chicago: University of Chicago Press, 2004.

Johnson, Imani Kai. "Dark Matter in B-Boying Cyphers: Race and Global Connection in Hip Hop." PhD diss., University of Southern California, 2009.

Jones, Joseph. "Hegemonic Rhythms: The Role of Hip-Hop Music in 21st Century American Public Diplomacy." PhD diss., Clark Atlanta University, 2009.

"Jóvenes bailan 'hip hop' para alejarse de la violencia." *El Mundo*, December 15, 2015, http://elmundo.sv/jovenes-bailan-hip hop-para-alejarse-de-la-violencia/.

Julios, Brett. "Pinqy Ring has Found a New Life in Healing through Rap Music." *Chicago Tribune*, November 30, 2017, http://www.chicagotribune.com/entertainment/music/ct-ott-chicago-music-pinqy-ring-1201-story.html#.

Kanjwal, Hafsa. "American Muslims and the Use of Cultural Diplomacy." *Georgetown Journal of International Affairs* 9 (Summer/Fall 2008): 133–39.

Katz, Mark. *Groove Music: The Art and Culture of the Hip-Hop DJ*. New York: Oxford University Press, 2012.

Kennedy, Liam and Scott Lucas. "Enduring Freedom: Public Diplomacy and U.S. Foreign Policy." *American Quarterly* 57 (June 2005): 309–33.

"Kenyan Tenth Anniversary Celebration." Communication from United States Embassy in Nairobi to United States Department of State, August 29, 1973. Accessible at https://wikileaks.org/plusd/cables/1973NAIROB05782b.html.

Khabeer, Su'Ad Abdul. *Muslim Cool: Race, Religion, and Hip Hop in the United States*. New York: New York University Press, 2016.

Killoran, Moira. "Good Muslims and 'Bad Muslims,' 'Good' Women and Feminists: Negotiating Identities in Northern Cyprus (Or, the Condom Story)." *Ethos* 26 (June 1998): 183–203.

Knight, Michael Muhammed. *The Five Percenters: Islam, Hip Hop and the Gods of New York*. Oxford: Oneworld, 2007.

Knowlton, Brian. "Digital War Takes Shape on Websites Over ISIS." *New York Times*, September 26, 2014, https://www.nytimes.com/2014/09/27/world/middleeast/us-vividly-rebuts-isis-propaganda-on-arab-social-media.html.

Koltai, Steven R. "Entrepreneurship Needs to Be a Bigger Part of U.S. Foreign Aid." *Harvard Business Review*, August 15, 2016, https://hbr.org/2016/08/entrepreneurship-needs-to-be-a-bigger-part-of-us-foreign-aid.

Kovach, Pete. "Out from Under the Proscenium: A Paradigm for U.S. Cultural Diplomacy." *Public Diplomacy Magazine*, Winter 2010, https://www.publicdiplomacymagazine.com/out-from-under-the-proscenium-a-paradigm-for-u-s-cultural-diplomacy/.

Kristof, Nicholas. "We're Helping Deport Kids to Die." *New York Times*, July 16, 2016, http://www.nytimes.com/2016/07/17/opinion/sunday/were-helping-deport-kids-to-die.html.

Kumar, Ruchi. "Afghanistan's Rap Scene is Real, Political, and Growing." *The Establishment*, August 15, 2016, https://theestablishment.co/afghanistans-rap-scene-is-real-political-and-growing-ef47f3d92b14.

Kuttner, Paul. "Interview with a Hip Hop Ambassador." June 14, 2012, http://culturalorganizing.org/tag/anas-canon/.

Kuttner, Paul J. and Mariama White-Hammond. "(Re)building the Cypher: Fulfilling the Promise of Hip Hop for Liberation," in *The Organic Globalizer: Hip Hop,*

*Political Development, and Movement Culture*, ed. Christopher Malone and George Martinez, Jr., 43–57. New York: Bloomsbury, 2015.

Lawry, Martha. "The Next Level of Hip Hop in Baku." *Visions of Azerbaijan*, October 25, 2017, http://www.visions.az/en/whats_on_in_azerbaijan/965/.

Lipka, Michael. "Muslims and Islam: Key Findings in the U.S. and Around the World." Pew Research Center, August 9, 2017, http://www.pewresearch.org/fact-tank/2017/08/09/muslims-and-islam-key-findings-in-the-u-s-and-around-the-world/.

Love, Bettina L. *Hip Hop's Li'l Sistas Speak: Negotiating Hip Hop Identities and Politics in the New South*. New York: Peter Lang, 2012.

Lorde, Audre. "A Burst of Light: Living with Cancer," in *A Burst of Light: Essays by Audre Lorde*. Ithaca, NY: Firebrand, 1988.

Macaulay, Alistair. "Fast-Stepped Fury, Rooted in Detroit: Detroit Jit, a '70s Street Dance Reborn and Revved Up." *New York Times*, August 10, 2014, https://www.nytimes.com/2014/08/11/arts/dance/detroit-jit-a-70s-street-dance-reborn-and-revved-up.html.

Macias, Amanda. "US Taxpayers Paid Millions of Dollars for the Airstrikes on Syria. Here's a Breakdown of Key Costs," *CNBC*, April 16, 2018, https://www.cnbc.com/2018/04/16/syria-airstrikes-cost-to-us-taxpayers.html.

Mamdani, Mahmood. "Good Muslim, Bad Muslim: A Political Perspective on Culture and Terrorism." *American Anthropologist* 104 (2002): 766–75.

Manuel, Peter. *Popular Musics of the Non-Western World: An Introductory Survey*. New York: Oxford University Press, 1988.

Mark, Simon. "A Greater Role for Cultural Diplomacy." Antwerp: Netherlands Institute of International Relations 'Clingendael,' 2009.

Mattis, James. Testimony before the Senate's Committee on Armed Services, March 5, 2013, https://www.armed-services.senate.gov/imo/media/doc/13-07%20-%203-5-13.pdf.

Medina, Cruz. "(Who Discovered) America: Ozomatli and the Mestiz@ Rhetoric of Hip Hop," *alter/nativas latin american cultural studies journal*, no. 2 (2014): 1–24.

Melissen, Jan, ed. *The New Public Diplomacy: Soft Power in International Relations*. Basingstoke, England: Palgrave Macmillan, 2005.

Miyakawa, Felicia M. *Five Percenter Rap: God Hop's Music, Message, and Black Muslim Mission*. Bloomington and Indianapolis: Indiana University Press, 2005.

Miyakawa, Felicia M. "Hip-Hop Diplomacy." Parts 1–4. *The Avid Listener* (November 2014): 4–24 , http://www.theavidlistener.com/2014/11/.

Monson, Ingrid. *Freedom Sounds: Civil Rights Call Out to Jazz and Africa*. New York: Oxford University Press, 2007.

Morgan, Joan. *When Chickenheads Come Home to Roost: A Hip-Hop feminist Breaks it Down*. New York: Simon & Schuster, 1999.

Morgan, Marcyliena. "'The World is Yours': The Globalization of Hip-Hop Language." *Social Identities* 22 (2016): 133–49.

Mueller, Darren. "The Ambassadorial LPs of Dizzy Gillespie: *World Statesman* and *Dizzy in Greece*." *Journal of the Society for American Music* 10 (August 2016): 239–69.

Muggah, Robert. "It's Official: San Salvador is the Murder Capital of the World." *Los Angeles Times*, March 2, 2016, http://www.latimes.com/opinion/op-ed/la-oe-0302-muggah-el-salvador-crime-20160302-story.html.

Ndaliko, Chérie Rivers. *Necessary Noise: Music, Film, and Charitable Imperialism in the East of Congo*. New York: Oxford University Press, 2016.

Neff, Ali Colleen. "Roots, Routes and Rhizomes: Sounding Women's Hip Hop on the Margins of Dakar, Senegal," *Journal of Popular Music Studies* 27 (2015): 448–77.

Niang, Abdoulaye. "Hip hop, musique et Islam: Le rap prédicateur au Sénégal." *Cahiers de recherché sociologique* 49 (2010): 63–94.

Nye, Joseph S., Jr., "Soft Power and American Foreign Policy." *Political Science Quarterly* 199 (2004): 255–70.

Nye, Joseph S., Jr.. *Soft Power: The Means to Success in World* Politics. New York: Public Affairs, 2004.

Obama, Barack. "Remarks by President Obama at YSEALI Town Hall," Ho Chi Minh City, May 25, 2016. https://obamawhitehouse.archives.gov/the-press-office/2016/05/25/remarks-president-obama-yseali-town-hall.

Ogunnaike, Oludamini. "Performing Realization: The Sufi Music Videos of the Taalibe Baye of Dakar." *African Arts* 51 (Autumn 2018): 26–39.

Oppenheimer, Mark. "A Diplomatic Mission Bearing Islamic Hip-Hop." *New York Times* July 22, 2011, https://www.nytimes.com/2011/07/23/us/23beliefs.html.

Osumare, Halifu. *The Hiplife in Ghana: West African Indigenization of Hip-Hop*. New York: Palgrave Macmillan, 2012.

Otto, Katherine. *Everyday Ambassador: Make A Difference by Connecting in a Disconnected World*. New York: Atria, 2015.

"Ozomatli's Music and Message Attract Thousands of Jordanians to Performances throughout the Kingdom." Communication from United States Embassy in Amman to United States Department of State, August 2, 2007. Accessible at https://wikileaks.org/plusd/cables/07AMMAN3260_a.html.

Palma, Agatha Evangeline. "Of Laws Tattooed in Flesh: Street Poetry, Hip-Hop, and Graffiti and the Contest for Public Space in Post-Revolutionary Tunisia." MA thesis, University of California Los Angeles, 2014.

Penrose, Nerisha. "'The Storm': 17 Rappers Who Have Dropped Anti-Trump Songs." *Billboard*, October 11, 2017, https://www.billboard.com/articles/columns/hip hop/7997503/rappers-dis-trump-eminem-the-storm-freestyle.

Perry, Imani. *Prophets of the Hood: Politics and Poetics in Hip Hop*. Durham, NC: Duke University Press, 2004.

Persley, Nicole Hodges. "West African Remix: Tracks of Change in Dakar." *American Theatre* 31 (May–June 2014): 30–33.

Plaisance, Patrick Lee. "The Propaganda War on Terrorism: An Analysis of the United States' "Shared Values" Public-Diplomacy Campaign After September 11, 2001." *Journal of Mass Media Ethics* 20 (2005): 250–68.

Powell, Adam Clayton, Jr. *Adam by Adam: The Autobiography of Adam Clayton Powell, Jr.* New York: Dial Press, 1971.

Price, Greg. "Top Trump Fundraiser Helped Congressman's Wife Land State Department Job." *Newsweek*, March 29, 2018, https://www.newsweek.com/ed-royce-elliott-broidy-marie-royce-trump-administration-job-864214.

Rampton, Sheldon. "Shared Values Revisited." *PRWatch*, October 17, 2007, https://www.prwatch.org/node/6465.

"The Rap Songs of the Arab Spring." *Morning Edition*, June 9, 2011, https://www.npr.org/sections/therecord/2011/06/09/137067390/the-rap-songs-of-the-arab-spring.

Reynolds, Dee and Matthew Reason, eds. *Kinesthetic Empathy in Creative and Cultural Practices*. Bristol, UK and Chicago: Intellect, 2012.

Ritter, Rüdiger. "Broadcasting Jazz into the Eastern Bloc—Cold War Weapon or Cultural Exchange? The Example of Willis Conover." *Jazz Perspectives* 7 (2013): 111–31.

Rockower, Paul. "Keepers of the PD Flame: An Appreciation of Embassy Local Staff." *CPD Blog*, August 6, 2013, http://uscpublicdiplomacy.org/blog/keepers-pd-flame-appreciation-embassy-local-staff.

Rogin, Josh. "State Department Considers Scrubbing Democracy Promotion from its Mission." *Washington Post*, August 1, 2017, https://www.washingtonpost.com/news/josh-rogin/wp/2017/08/01/state-department-considers-scrubbing-democracy-promotion-from-its-mission/.

Rollefson, J. Griffith. *Flip the Script: European Hip Hop and Politics of Postcoloniality*. Chicago and London: University of Chicago Press, 2017.

Rose, Tricia. *Black Noise: Rap Music and Black Culture in Contemporary America*. Hanover, NH and London: Wesleyan University Press, 1994.

Royce, Marie. "Statement of Marie Royce Nominee to be Assistant Secretary of State, Educational and Cultural Affairs Senate Committee on Foreign Relations March 7, 2018." https://www.foreign.senate.gov/imo/media/doc/030718_Royce_Testimony.pdf.

Sajnani, Damon Chandru. "Deepening Democracy Galsen Style: Y'en a Marre, HipHop and Politics in Senegal." PhD diss., Northwestern University, 2015

Saunders, Frances Stonor. *The Cultural Cold War: The CIA and the World of Arts and Letters*. New York: New Press, 2000.

Salois, Kendra. "The Networked Self: Hip Hop Musicking and Muslim Identities in Neoliberal Morocco." PhD diss., University of California, Berkeley, 2013.

Salois, Kendra. "The US Department of State's 'Hip-Hop Diplomacy' in Morocco," in *Music and Diplomacy from the Early Modern Era to the Present*, ed. Rebekah Ahrendt, Mark Ferraguto, and Damien Mahiet. New York: Palgrave Macmillan, 2014.

Salois, Kendra. "Connection and Complicity in the Global South: Hip Hop Musicians and US Cultural Diplomacy." *Journal of Popular Music Studies* 27 (2015): 408–23.

Schatz, Edward and Renan Levine. "Framing, Public Diplomacy, and Anti-Americanism in Central Asia." *International Studies Quarterly* 54 (2010): 855–69.

Schneider, Cynthia P. *Culture Communicates: US Diplomacy that Works*. N.p.: Netherlands Institute of International Relations, 2004.

Schneider, Cynthia P. "The Unrealized Potential of Cultural Diplomacy: 'Best Practices' and What Could Be, If Only . . . " *Journal of Arts Management, Law, and Society* 39 (Winter 2009): 260–78.

Schneider, Cynthia P. and Kristina Nelson. *Mightier than the Sword: Arts and Culture in the U.S.–Muslim World Relationship.* Washington, DC: Brookings Institution, 2008.

Scott, Eugene. "The White House Releases a Photo of its Interns, and the Internet Asks: Why so Few People of Color?" *Washington Post*, March 31, 2018, https://www.washingtonpost.com/news/the-fix/wp/2018/03/31/the-white-house-releases-a-photo-of-its-interns-and-the-internet-asks-where-are-the-people-of-color/.

Searcy, Dionne and Emmanuel Akinwotu. "Nigerian Army Uses Trump's Words to Justify Fatal Shooting of Rock-Throwing Protesters." *New York Times*, November 3, 2018, https://www.nytimes.com/2018/11/02/world/africa/nigeria-trump-rocks.html.

Sharma, Nitasha Tamar. *Hip Hop Desis: South Asian Americans, Blackness, and a Global Race Consciousness.* Durham, NC and London: Duke University Press, 2010.

Schloss, Joseph G. *Foundation: B-boys, B-girls and Hip-Hop Culture in New York.* New York: Oxford University Press, 2009.

Schloss, Joseph G. "Roots & Branches: Dr. Elliot Gann, aka Phillipdrummond. *Next Level Blog*, December 10, 2017, https://www.nextlevel-usa.org/blog/roots-branches-dr-elliot-gann-aka-phillipdummond.

Sisson, Patrick. "The Message: Can Better Hip-Hop Diplomacy Help Fix America's Tarnished Image Abroad?" *Urb*, no. 153 (22 April 2008): 56–58.

*Slingshot Hip Hop.* Dir. Jackie Reem Salloum, Fresh Booza DVD, 2008.

Solomon, Robin. "Hip-Hop is Tops: Embassy Bishkek Uses Music for Youth Outreach." *State Magazine*, no. 580 (July/August 2013): 10–11.

Strachan, Maxwell. "The Definitive History of 'George Bush Doesn't Care About Black People.'" *Huffington Post*, August 28, 2015, https://www.huffingtonpost.com/entry/kanye-west-george-bush-black-people_us_55d67c12e4b020c386de2f5e.

Swaragita, Gisela. "State Sponsored Homophobia Forces LGBT Community to Lay Low." *Jakarta Post*, May 17, 2018, http://www.thejakartapost.com/news/2018/05/16/state-sponsored-homophobia-forces-lgbt-community-to-lay-low.html.

Swedenburg, Ted. "Hip-Hop of the Revolution (The Sharif Don't Like It)." *Middle East Research and Information Project*, January 5, 2012, http://www.merip.org/hip hop-revolution-sharif-dont-it.

Sum, Maisie. "Staging the Sacred: Musical Structure and Processes of the Gnawa *Lila* in Morocco." *Ethnomusicology* 55 (Winter 2011): 77–111.

Tenny, Francis B. "The Philadelphia Orchestra's 1973 Tour: A Case Study of Cultural Diplomacy During the Cultural Revolution." *American Diplomacy* (September 2012), http://www.unc.edu/depts/diplomat/item/2012/0712/fsl/tenny_orchestra.html.

Thomas, Robert McG, Jr., "Willis Conover, 75, Voice of America Disc Jockey." *New York Times*, May 19, 1996.

Trescott, Jacqueline. "The Artist Lovingly Known as EJ," *IRAA+*, http://iraaa.museum.hamptonu.edu/page/The-Artist-Lovingly-Known-As-EJ.

"The Trump Administration is Making War on Diplomacy." *New York Times*, November 18, 2017, https://www.nytimes.com/2017/11/18/opinion/sunday/the-trump-administration-is-making-war-on-diplomacy.html.

United Nations Population Fund. *The Power of 1.8 Billion: Adolescents, Youth and the Transformation of the Future.* N.p.: United Nations Population Fund, 2014. Accessible at https://www.unfpa.org/sites/default/files/pub-pdf/EN-SWOP14-Report_FINAL-web.pdf

United States Department of State, Office of Citizen Exchanges, Cultural Programs Division. "Project Objectives, Goals, and Implementation (POGI): Creative Arts Exchange: Arts in Collaboration ECA/PE/C/CU-13-26, https://eca.state.gov/files/bureau/2_pogi_cae_arts_in_collaboration.pdf.

United States Embassy, Rabat. "Favorable Views of U.S. Surge Upward in Arab/Muslim Morocco: What Went Right?" Unclassified Cable, September 23. 2005. http://wikileaks.org/plusd/cables/05RABAT2004_a.html.

*U.S. Public Diplomacy: State Department Expands Efforts but Faces Significant Challenges.* Washington, DC: United States Government Accounting Office, 2003. Accessible at https://www.gao.gov/new.items/d03951.pdf.

"Vanuatu DJ Uses Hip Hop and Beat Box to Engage with Melanesian Youth." *Radio Australia*, June 18, 2014, http://www.radioaustralia.net.au/international/radio/onairhighlights/vanuatu-dj-uses-hip   hop-and-beat-box-to-engage-with-melanesian-youth/1329082-0.

Varela, Miguel Escobar. "Wayang Hip Hop: Java's Oldest Performance Tradition Meets Global Youth Culture." *Asian Theatre Journal* 31 (Fall 2014): 481–504.

Venkatachalam, K.S. "The Rise of Islamic Extremism in Bangladesh." *The Diplomat*, July 6, 2016, https://thediplomat.com/2016/07/the-rise-of-islamic-extremism-in-bangladesh/.

Von Eschen, Penny M. *Satchmo Blows up the World: Jazz Ambassadors Play the Cold War* (Cambridge, MA and London: Harvard University Press, 2004).

Walt, Vivienne. "El Général and the Rap Anthem of the Mideast Revolution." *Time*, February 15, 2011, http://content.time.com/time/world/article/0,8599,2049456,00.html.

Warren, Jeff R. *Music and Ethical Responsibility.* Cambridge: Cambridge University Press, 2014.

Watkins, Craig. *Representing: Hip Hop Culture and the Production of Black Cinema.* Chicago: University of Chicago Press, 1998.

Weston, Randy. *African Rhythms: The Autobiography of Randy Weston.* Durham, NC: Duke University Press, 2010.

Wright, Richard. *The Color Curtain: A Report on the Bandung Conference.* New York: World Publishing, 1956.

Wright, Robin. *Rock the Casbah: Rage and Rebellion Across the Islamic World.* New York: Simon & Schuster, 2011.

Younger, Briana. "Local Trio Native Deen on Making Music for Muslim Youth and Islam's Relationship to Hip-Hop." *Washington City Paper*, March 10, 2015, https://www.washingtoncitypaper.com/arts/music/blog/13081730/local-trio-native-deen-on-making-music-for-muslim-youth-and-islams-relationship-to-hip hop.

# INDEX